MW00824740

The Story of the Russian Land, Volume I:
From Antiquity to the Death of Yaroslav the Wise (1054)

THE STORY OF THE RUSSIAN LAND

VOL. I

From Antiquity to the Death of Yaroslav the Wise (1054)

ALEXANDER DMITRIEVICH NECHVOLODOV

Translated by Dennis Sinclair

ANTELOPE HILL PUBLISHING

English Translation Copyright © 2023 Antelope Hill Publishing

First edition, first printing 2023.

Translated by Dennis Sinclair, 2023.

Originally published as Сказания О Русской Земле. Ч. 1. С Древнейших Времен До Расцвета Русского Могущества При Ярославе Мудром in 1909, revised with images 1913.

Cover art by Swifty.
Edited by Malta, T. Brock, and Margaret Bauer.
Editorial footnotes and layout by Margaret Bauer.

Antelope Hill Publishing | antelopehillpublishing.com

Paperback ISBN-13: 978-1-956887-95-2
EPUB ISBN-13: 978-1-956887-96-9

Dedicated to the holy memory of Ivan Yegorovich Zabelin,
by the grace of whose many years of accomplishments,
established by his deep spirit and soulful mind, each
Russian person has been given the sacred right
to be proud of his most distant ancestors
and to look upon the coming fate
of our great nation faithfully.

Alexander Dmitrievich Nechvolodov (1864–1938)

CONTENTS

MAPS

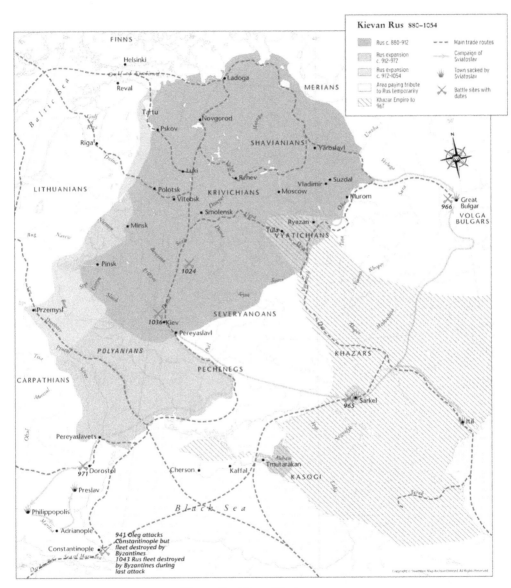

Kievan Rus' from 880 to 1054,
sourced from The Map Archive, with permission.

The Viking river road to Constantinople, also referred to in this edition as the
trade route from Scandinavia to the Byzantine Empire and as the Varangian trade
route, sourced from The Map Archive, with permission.

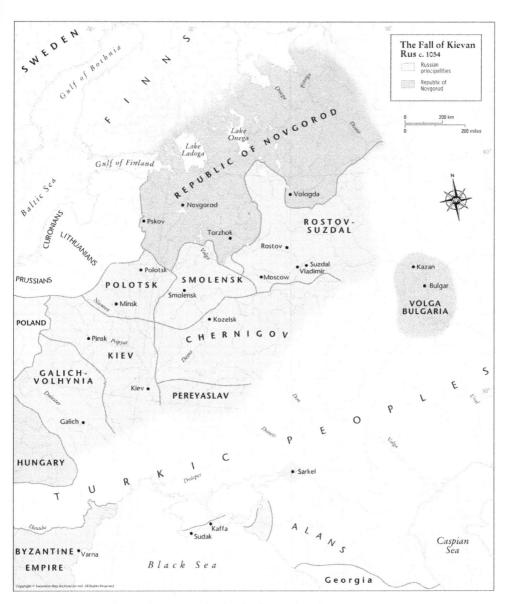

The Rus' States at the death of Yaroslav the Wise in 1054,
sourced from The Map Archive, with permission.

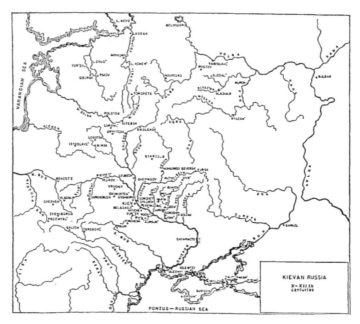

Kievan Rus' from the tenth to the twelfth centuries,
sourced from *Russian Primary Chronicle*, x.

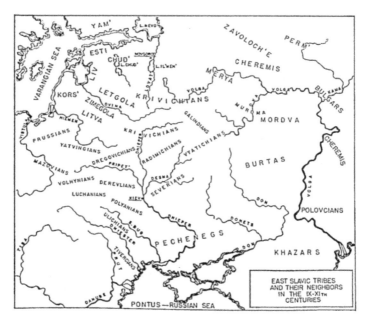

The East Slavic tribes and their neighbors in the ninth through
the eleventh centuries, sourced from *Russian Primary Chronicle*, xi.

Translator's Foreword

The Story of the Russian Land is a unique and interesting work for a number of reasons. It is not exactly presented by the author as a work of history, despite being a work of history, but instead it is called a story. Perhaps there is a reason for this, insofar as the content of the work lacks the academic depth that would stand the test of a contemporary university critic. Nevertheless, it behooves us to forgive the author for his approach to writing history. By the time of its writing, history would have come to be viewed as more of an academic pursuit than anything, and less as a living expression of organic cultural memory and tradition. For Alexander Dmitrievich Nechvolodov, the author of *The Story of the Russian Land*, the organic view of history is certainly a more accurate characterization of his pursuit.

Published at the cusp of the First World War and the Russian Revolution, before Russia had been fully given over to regicide as well as postmodern social systems and critique, *The Story* presents us with a fascinating diorama of elite Russian cultural attitudes toward politics and history prior to the Soviet regime. If it is not valuable as a work of history in the strict academic sense, it is an immeasurably valuable work of historiography and a gem of Russian reactionary nonfiction. If nothing else, Nechvolodov allows us to understand how the history of the world was *remembered* in Russian high society. While predating Lenin's seizure of power, *The Story* also postdates the nineteenth-century "golden age" of Russian literature of Pushkin, Dostoevsky, Tolstoy etc., as well as the problems following the wake of Tsar Alexander II's 1861 emancipation of the serfs. The grim thematic elements of parricide, inter-generational strife, and the advent of the hated and socially destructive "new ideas" prevalent in Dostoevsky's *Devils* and *Brothers Karamazov* as well as Turgenev's *Fathers and Sons*—all acclaimed novels which were widely read and discussed in their time—would have become more immediate and real problems in Russian society by Nechvolodov's time, and would have reinforced the convictions of reactionary circles and strengthened Russia's internal divisions.

For this reason, it is no surprise that Nechvolodov's historical account of Russia should be deeply political in nature. He makes no pretense to the contrary and admits as much in his preface. This is not a work of academic history, but it is rather an act of the "immune system" of the Russian cultural organism seeking to survive the rising tide of mass society and the chaos of the modern world. Nechvoldov is not disinterested, nor even disconnected from the subject matter; he often uses language such as *"our* history" and *"our* ancestors" throughout the work, whether referring to ancient Aryan, Scythian, or Kievan Rus people. It is rare to find such language in Western history books, even in Nechvolodov's time.

Rare also is the reference to Homer and the Bible as historical sources, of which Nechvoldov partakes. Western historical criticism had long abandoned this practice and delegated these sources (mostly) to the realm of myth and religion. Yet Nechvolodov is unafraid to claim that Achilles was not only a real person, but also a Scythian, and thus an ancestor of the Russians. He also doesn't hesitate to state with no awareness of possible controversy that Europeans descend from Noah's son Japheth. He has no fear of repercussion or criticism for freely using the term Aryan when talking about the ancient Steppe ancestors of Europe, nor of speaking ill of Jewish Khazars when discussing Russia's historic enemies. Nechvolodov's conflates Thracians with Scythians when citing Herodotus, lists Huns as direct linear ancestors of the Slavs (something no modern historian would claim), and despite providing a bibliography, often employs no in-text citations when directly quoting other sources. We can speculate that this is because there should be no need to provide citations when you are a member of the aristocratic class in a society that still has this social estate intact. Even into the early twentieth century, Russian society was still viewed as being essentially medieval by their Western contemporaries because the Tsar maintained autocratic rule of the Russian state, and power and wealth was still concentrated in the hands of the aristocracy. That Nechvolodov is a nobleman writing for other noblemen is sufficient authority for his target audience to trust his word. He also was writing for an audience that, while literate and having received a cursory exposure to the literature and history of classical antiquity and its bridge into the medieval through private gentry education, and while interested in learning more about it, may not all have had easy access to libraries or encyclopedias to research these things more deeply. A Russian perspective on classical tradition would have been more desired by a significant portion of Nechvoldov's Russian audience as well (which included Tsar Nicholas II), than a non-Russian one. After all, the Russian aristocracy believed itself to be the true inheritors of classical Rome and Greece, so it's only natural that Nechvoldov should add a Russian flair to his account of antiquity.

By today's standards, this is a wild, cavalier practice of historical writing, a long-dead system (or lack of system) of verifying information based mostly on mutual recognition that one belongs to a certain class of person. History isn't then weighed down by an obligation to constantly reference its sources, and the spirit can flow freely without being confined to the letter. This is how the history of a culture was viewed from within the culture itself, before history was domesticated by modern academic criticism. Yet admittedly, there is something fascinating and intriguing about this old-school approach, despite its fallibility and susceptibility to inaccuracy. By doing history in this way, Nechvolodov compels us to view history not as a passive, dead record of mundane events outlined in dusty old tomes kept in stuffy libraries, presided over by sickly old scatterbrained men, but as an active, living, psychic organism that permeates the blood and animates the cultural organism to reach beyond the mortal sheath. Perhaps history then becomes a part of Nikolai Fyodorovich Fyodorov's "common task" of all humanity, to which Nechvolodov makes reference in the preface to this work, and which is nothing more than literal resurrection itself: the conquering of death by the vital force of life.

History is a function of culture. History belongs to the people of culture. A disinterested academic historian may have a more accurate picture of historical events than a cultured dilettante, but the dilettante is revitalized by history and can use history to approach the inmost nature of life. An academic studies history like a medical student studies a cadaver, and both can lose sight of the fact that the corpse they are examining was once a living thing and that living bodies still walk the earth. Once we know history completely, we cease to love it and be moved by it. Even to believe that it is possible to know it completely is to commit an act of hubris, for which we are punished by the misery that arises from the foolish pride of self-delusion. The soul goes into atrophy when it falsely believes that history is completely known, and recorded adequately, requiring no active engagement nor respect, and can simply be known by rudimentary research. We hope that readers of Nechvolodov can embrace this organic view of history and allow themselves to be continually inspired by the mystery of the past.

Dennis Sinclair

PREFACE

The Story of the Russian Land is approved and recommended for distribution by the August Commander-in-Chief of the Guard and the Petersburg Military district and by the Commanders-in-Chief of the troops of all other military districts to all regiments, companies, squadrons, centesimals, battalions, and library directors; by decree of the Holy Ethical Synod for acquisition by rudimentary discipleship libraries, spiritual educational institutions, and Church libraries of the Russian empire; by decree of the Educational Council of the Holy Synod for the libraries of ecclesiastical schools and second classes, as well as for the study-libraries of parish schools; by the Ministry of National Education for teachers in all lower educational institutions of various titles, for scholars doing extracurricular reading in all secondary educational institutions, and for libraries of other sorts; by the Departmental Institution of the Empress Maria, the Ministries of Industry, Communication, and Trade Routes (respectively); by the General Directorate of Land Management and Agriculture, as well as the General Directorate of Military Educational Institutions for other sorts of subordinate student libraries; by the Chief Naval Headquarters for ship and crewmen's libraries; and by the Committee of Trustees of Moderation for libraries and readers of the nation.

We offer this book, written to give every Russian person the opportunity to learn about their ancestors' lives and acts in past times. This type of study is not only instructive but also highly necessary to show the brave, wise, and noble people from whom we descend, what great trials they were put through in the foundation of our Motherland, and how well-steeped in their blood is the whole span of the Russian Land.

Along with this, it shows us how we must go to perform our sacred duty to the Russian Land that lies before this generation—to keep intact in its entirety the sanctity of our divine ancestral legacy.

The words above are an introduction to the first part of the work here, dedicated to the memory of Ivan Zabelin and published in 1909 by the Brotherhood of the Church of Saint Nicholas of the Prague 58th Infantry Division.

That same year, the book I wrote was rewarded with the most gracious attention by His Imperial Majesty, the Tsar, who was pleased to express his wish that I continue the work I had begun.

On May 24th, 1911, I received the most gracious honor in Tsarskoye Selo, presenting to the Tsar the second volume of *The Story of the Russian Land*, whereupon my work was again delivered to what was, for me, some of the most unforgettable gestures of monarchical consideration.

On December 1st, 1911, in Livadia, the Holy Emperor was so incredibly pleased with my words that he was reading my book aloud to Her Majesty the Tsarina. After this, he expressed his wish that the book's next edition would have a more embellished layout and features such as reproductions of historical paintings by Russian artists of the time and snapshots of ancient icons, manuscripts, temple murals, old buildings, weapons, and other sorts of tools.

Given this, the current 1913 edition is published with many pictures— four parts of my labor, brought out to the election and coronation of the Tsardom of Michael Feodorovich Romanov.

During my work, I was guided by all primary sources available to me and the works of our famous historians and scholars: N. M. Karamzin, S. M. Solvev, Ivan Zabelin, V. Klyuchevsky, S. F. Platonov, A. A. Shakhmatov, N. P. Kondakov, A. I. Sobolevski, N. P. Likhachyov, and others. A detailed bibliography of the printed works and pictures I consulted, and from which I garnered more or less all my quotations, can be seen at the end of this work.

Along with this, I have endeavored to the best of my ability to keep the covenant of Ivan Zabelin, expressed by him in the following words:

It is known to all, that the ancients, especially the Greeks and Romans, were able to breed heroes. . . . This ability was made possible only by the fact that in their histories, they could portray not only the historic, but also the poetic truth of their leading figures. They were able to appreciate the merits of heroes and could discern the golden truth and divinity of these qualities from the lies and impurities of ordinary life in which each person is destined to live and by which they more or less always find themselves sullied. They were able to distinguish in these qualities not only their real and "good" essence, so to speak, but also their ideal essence, that is to say the historical idea exemplified in feats and deeds, which is necessary and which the character of the hero elevates to the point of ideal. Our Russian cultural history comes from ancients completely different from them, on the opposite side. As is well known, we only quite diligently deny and denounce our History, and we dare not to consider any such character-ideals. Of the ideal in our History, we dare not admit. All the more, the ideals we had were such "heroes" that our entire History is a dark kingdom of neglect, barbarism, gossip, slavery, and other such things. There is no other way to put it: thus do the great majority of educated Russians think. Of course, such a History would be unable to give rise to heroes, and it should view the notion of ideals as juvenile and childish and as something to be suppressed. The best role that this juvenility can play in such a History is that it would not be known to exist at all. This is how most people act toward historical ideals ... but were this not the view that the majority of educated Russians should bear, then perhaps a most just reproach, that such a view holds no ground, could be made, and Russia would not feel this negative national historical consciousness within itself, and it should find itself both mentally and morally blown by favorable winds in all directions.

Indeed, a national history serves as a firm support and unshakable ground for the national consciousness and self-knowledge.

God is not offensive to Russian History in this respect. In it, there are, or could be found common human ideas and ideals, enlightened and great-natured heroes, and creators of life. We only need to remember the truthful sayings of the writers of antiquity properly, that 'the glory of one or another nation or person in History shall not completely consist of glorious or inglorious dealings, nor of the existence of historical feats, but is derived fully from the art and skill or even simply the intention of writers to either portray gloriously or despise the affairs of the people and the deeds of historic individuals.

The preceding words of Ivan Zabelin aside, I have found for myself, in my examination of Russian history, the utmost support, confirmation, and explanation in the works of one of the most incredible and most loved contemporary Russian people—Nikolai Fyodorovich Fyodorov. In life, he was known to many as the incredibly conscientious, hard-working, and humble servant of the Rumyantsev Museum in Moscow, who had a broad and diverse range of knowledge in multiple fields and knew the contents of all the books in that enormous library resolutely. Every visitor to the library would recognize him as a dedicated employee with love for his work who could immediately refer them to the exact books they needed merely from hearing their research requirements. Naturally, then, Nikolai Fyodorov would try to be as helpful as he could, fixing himself to their research with all his heart and going above and beyond their needs, even referring the astonished visitor to two or three different books that they didn't need at all and of whose very existence they would never have even been aware and, between the contents of these unexpected books and the initial recommendations, would completely fulfill all requirements posed to him. Whenever it happened that a visitor, having gotten the attention of Nikolai Fyodorov, required certain books that were not in the Rumyantsev Museum, he would buy them with his meager funds. The people with whom he came into contact referred to him as a sage and a saint, and those closer to him said that he was one of the only few righteous men left in the world and considered him to be a true Christian soul—"a great man even among great men." After having had contact with Fyodorov, Leo Tolstoy, astonished by his personality, wrote: "Nikolai Fyodorovich Fyodorov is a saint. A closet desires no salary, for if there is no linen, there is no bed."

After the death of this remarkable Russian, in the following year, 1903, V. A. Kozhevnikov and N. P. Peterson published his extensive creative output under the title *Philosophy of the Common Task*. Still, the first release was unfortunately not put out for sale until the current time. Still, it was freely distributed to a few national libraries since the deceased stood against the sale of works that had to do with intellectual matters and considered this sacrilege.

By the most profound conviction, Fyodorov considered resurrection from the dead to be the common task of all humanity, which would follow when in all the land there comes to be a general fraternity, which in his eyes the Russian Sovereign would build. Russia shall become for all: "Dear, sweet, and cherished."

Only a few people were familiar with his views throughout his life, but such outstanding men shared these views as F. M. Dostoevsky and V. S. Solovyov; the former called his teachings "the first movement forward along the path of Christ since the appearance of Christianity."

Examining Russia's past as well as her significance among the remaining states, giving rise with his questions to a series of unique ideas and voicing predictions which have come true in his works, Nikolai Fyodorov entirely agrees with the opinion about the future of the Russian Land put forward at the start of the sixteenth century by the elder Elizerov of the Philotheou Monastery.

Since these views are also entirely accepted by me, then at the heading of every part of the present work, a few words from the elder Philotheouan shall be given about the Russian State from his messages to the clerk Misura Mukhin.

Throughout my work, I was subject to the most gracious and flattering attention from each individual from whom I sought help. Therefore, I must extend my deepest gratitude and beseech their acceptance toward His Imperial Highness, the Grand Duke Peter Nikolaevich, for his valuable insight concerning classical Russian Church architecture and two drawings of His Highness' work, sent at my request for inclusion in the publication.

I would also ask the following individuals for the acceptance of my most sincere and utmost thankfulness for their rendering assistance to my work in a broad and general way: the Eminent Vladimir, Metropolitan of Saint Petersburg and Ladozhk; Bishop George, director of the Saint Petersburg Spiritual Academy; Bishop Fyodor, director of the Moscow Spiritual Academy; the Cathedral and Viceroy of the Trinity Lavra of Saint Sergius and Her Archimandrite Toviyu; Viceroy of the Kiev Monastery of the Caves Archimandirate Ambrose; Hegumen Joseph Volokolamsky of the monastery Archmandirate Nifonta and the Hieromonk of that same cloister, Father Pafnutiya; Father Superior Feodorit, hegumen of the Kirill-Belozersky Monastery; Minister of the Imperial Court and general aide to the Count V. B. Frederisk, Chairman of Imperial Russian Society of Military History, Cavalry General D. A. Skalon; Chief of the Military Field Office of the Retinue of His Imperial Majesty, His Majesty Major General Prince V. N. Orlov; of the Retinue of His Majesty, General Major N. A. Princehevicha; Member of the State Council Senator A. A. Naryshkin; of the Academies of A. A. Shakhmatov and A. I. Sobolevsky; and the manager of the library of the Imperial Academy of Sciences V. I. Sreznevski; doctor of history and assistant director of the Imperial Public Library N. P. Likhachyov; as well as its department managers: A. I. Bychkova, V. I. Saitov, and N. D. Chechulin; director of the Saint Petersburg Archaeological Institute N. V. Pokrovsky; and also the department managers of: the Imperial Academy of Arts: Messrs. F. G. Berenshtamm, E. O. Visel, and E. A. Shultz; the State Hermitage Museum: Messrs. Y. I. Smirnov, E. M. Pridik, Baron P. F. Meyendorf, A. K. Markov, and O. F. Valdgauger; the professors of Saint Petersburg University: Baron M. A. Taube, A. I. Ivanov, and V. N. Beheshevich; member of the Imperial Archeological Commission B. V. Farmakovsky; library manager of the Saint Petersburg Spiritual Academy A. P. Krotkov; former secretary of the Russian Museum named after Emperor Alexander III in Saint Petersburg G. V. Kakhovsky and the custodian of that museum A. A. Miller; Associate to the Chairman of the Historical Museum named after Emperor Alexander III in Moscow Prince N. B. Shcherbatov and department managers of the Museums: A. V. Oreshnikov, A. I. Stankevich, V. N. Shchepkin, and I. M. Tarablin; Attorney of the Moscow Synodical Office M. P. Stepanov and the manager of the Patriarchal Library N. I. Popov; the Senior Clerk of the Moscow Chief Archive of the Ministry of Foreign Affairs S. A. Belokurov; Manager of the Moscow Synodical Printing House A. S. Orlov and Manager of the archaic printing chambers therein A. A. Pokrovsky; Managers of the Moscow Armory Messrs. S. P. Bartenev and U. V. Arsenev; managers of the library of the Imperial Rumyantzev Museum in Moscow U. V. Gote and Y. G. Kvaskov; curator of the archeological department of the Kiev City Museum of Emperor Nicholas II, V. V. Khvoyka; A. I. Kireevu, O. N. Gaken, O. A. Fribess, N. A. Butmi, E. O. Yagelsky, V. A. Kozhevnikov, S. A. Panchukizdev, G. A. Shechkov, R. R. von-Shulman, V. K. Solonin, N. V. Kirillov, D. D. Lamoniv, M. P. Tikhonov, N. C. Smirnov, and M. M. Shteinsberg; Chairman of the Novgorodian Society of Antiquarians M. V. Muravev and the curator of the Novgorodian Museum of Antiquities N. P. Volodin; member of the Yaroslavian Architectural Commission V. M. Bushuev; the venerable Polish historian F. A. Korzon; President of the Krakov Academy of Science, Mr. Ulyanovsky; Messrs. Prezhetzlavsky, Ivanovsky, Baranovsky, Semiensky, Kacheevsky, and Gembarzhevsky.

With this, I consider it my duty to mention with deep gratitude the memories of the now-deceased P. Y. Dashkov and P. I. Shschukin, who always wished me well in my work.

I ask the following people to accept my sincerest appreciation for their kind donation of pictures: Baroness O. P. Pritvitz and E. F. Rimus for the images of the Livonian castle ruins; Baroness T. I. Medem for the icon snap-shots and various other items stored in the sacristy of Pskov-Pechersky Monastery; M. P. Kaptzov for the images of Joseph Volokolamski Monastery; and K. N. Rossolimo for the pictures of the Kiev Monastery of the Caves; Envoy of the Russian Emperor in Copenhagen, Baron K. K. Bugsgevden, for supplying photographs of portraits in the Royal castle in Fredensborg, Denmark; ranks of the Imperial Russian Missions: in Madrid for snapshots of the Greek manuscript John Skylitzes, and in Stockholm for photographs of the portraits kept in the Swedish Royal Castle; the curators of the British Museum and the London National Gallery: Messrs. Camp-bell-Dogdson, Gomef, D. C. Makkol, and Messrs. Boswell and Collins-Baker; the Administrative Staff of the City Museum of Braslaw, the Com-munity Council of the Rogozhsky Old Believer Cemetery for the contribu-tion of pictures of the ancient icons of the Trinity-Sergievsky Lavra, and P. N. Puryshev for the photographs taken at the Kirillo-Belozersky Monas-tery.

I am also sincerely grateful to the masters of the Hesvizhsky castle for kindly permitting me to use their libraries and galleries; Prince M. V. Radzivill, E. G. Shvartitza, to the director of the Stallmaster Yard; His Maj-esty P. A. Demidov, Master of Vishnevetz Castle; Master of Vilyanov Castle Count K. Branitzek; Counts M. O. Zamoysky and S. S. Krasinsky; Master of Krasichin Castle in Galicia, Prince V. Sapeg; owner of the rarest collection of icons of ancient letters in Moscow, Igor Igorovich Igorov; Master of An-tiquaries in Warsaw, Mr. I. Vilder; and L. F. Vsevolozhsky, publisher of the journal *Niva* for kindly providing permission for the photographs of old drawings, constituting the exclusive property of this journal.

Valuable guidance was given to me by the artists G. P. Kondratenko and N. K. Rerikha of the journal *Old Years* as well as members of the Imperial Academy of Arts P. P. Veynera and L. K. Sabopulo and also the director of the Imperial Stroganovsky School in Moscow N. V. Globa, who provided the covers, calligraphy, and a few other illustrations by the talented teacher of that school, S. I. Yaguzhinsky—all helped this edition of my work a great deal.

Finally, I consider it my duty to provide my most sincere appreciation to the Head of the State Printing House through which the book was printed, General Major P. A. Shevelevu and his assistant, to the Stablemas-ter of His Majesty's Court, a true state councilor, G. G. Khodunov and his assistants G. L. Grentz and N. N. Shurtz; to print master M. I. Bely, typesetter P. I. Egorov and his assistant I. P. Korolev, and also to the superb lithographer of the Warsaw Military District Headquarters; N. V. Nikitin for the rendition of all plans and charts for the current edition; and B. L. Verzhbitzky, proprietor of printing establishments in Warsaw, together with his assistant artist A. Poltavsky and master zincographer Y. Endrzheevsky, under whose direct supervision all illustrations were prepared for printing.

Alexander Dmitrievich Nechvolodov

CHAPTER ONE

Our Lineage Is from Japheth's Line

Holy Scripture tells us that after the Flood, all races of people that live on Earth today came from Noah's three sons: Sham, Ham, and Japheth.

One line of Japheth's descendants settled in the upper reaches of the rivers Amu Darya and Syr Darya, which were within the borders of the Russian Empire in the province of Turkestan. This line is the origin of many tribes of Asia Minor, Persia, and India, as well as glorious and well-known races that live in Europe: Greeks, Romans, Spaniards, French, English, Germans, Swedes, Lithuanians, and others, as well as Slavic tribes: Russians, Poles, Bulgars, Serbs, and others.

The Life of Ancient Aryans

Initially, all of our ancestors that lived in the upper reaches of Amu Darya and Syr Darya bore the name Aryan. In their ancient language, Aryan meant venerated or superior. Indeed, Aryans stood out from other inhabitants of Earth of that time for their strength, height, finesse, and beauty, but especially for the nobility of their spirituality.

Although very violent customs were widespread among Aryans in those times, many thousands of years before the birth of our Savior, who preached love of your neighbor, the qualities of courage and honor, which even today are present in any man with a noble soul, were highly valued.

Our ancient ancestors came together to live in settlements and villages. They could build houses with doors and ovens made out of stone. But, like modern farmers, their primary property and wealth were domesticated animals: cows, bulls, aurochs, oxen, horses, sheep, pigs, piglets, goats, and even birds such as geese. Dogs were common by the herd and in houses, but cats were yet to be domesticated.

The Aryans' main method of obtaining food was through agriculture, but, where possible, they also bred animals and, of course, had brave hunters among them who would hunt various wild beasts.

Aryans tilled the earth with different plows; they planted barley, oats, and spelt. Rye and wheat, however, were still not known to them. Nevertheless, they could grind seeds, bake bread, eat cooked meat, and drink milk. They consumed honey as food and also as an alcoholic beverage.

Aside from bread-making and animal husbandry, Aryans knew other trades, such as weaving, wickerwork, and sewing; they also knew of polishing gold, silver, and copper and had oar-driven boats.

Our ancestors could count in tens, but when it came to more than a hundred, as in tens of tens, they could not.

The Aryans practiced marriage but came to value monogamy only later; they were not ashamed to have multiple wives for centuries.

Every family was part of a well-known clan, which always strongly supported each other. Everyone was to obey all customs determined by their lineage. In cases of harm or external aggression toward any one member of the clan, the victim would have had the fighting support of everyone in the clan. This custom was considered sacred and was referred to as the tradition of blood vengeance or family vengeance, which remained among Aryans for a long time. For this reason, there was constant killing and conflict.

Some clans who shared common lineages united into larger tribes and were led by elders and chieftains,[1] judges, executioners, and commanders. Aryans fought each other frequently, and military courage was strongly valued and diligently cultivated among our noble and brave ancestors. They fought on foot and horses, depending on the terrain; they skillfully threw spears and shot arrows from bows at their enemies, whom they would bravely strike with swords and axes when meeting them up close.

---

[1] The Russian word here is "knyaz." Initially used to denote a Slavic chieftain, the term knyaz became for the Kievan Rus' the title of the sovereign prince, the highest ruler as there was not yet a king or tsar. Likewise, "princess" is "knyaginya." Later usage of the word "prince" therefore is the same word in Russian, "knyaz," as is here translated as "chieftain." In 1547, with the reign of Ivan the Terrible as the first Russian tsar, "knyaz" became outdated and was relegated to an occasional honorific by the eighteenth century. (Unless otherwise noted as from Nechvolodov or the translator, all notes are from the editor.)

They went to death without hesitation since they believed in an afterlife where brave men who died honorable deaths in battle were rewarded.

Our ancestors also believed in God Almighty, who was called by the very same word "God," and they worshipped the heavens—divinity, sun, dawn, fire, wind, and Mother Earth.

Their Dispersal

That's how the glorious Aryans lived in their primordial motherland in the upper reaches of Amu Darya and Syr Darya. As their population grew, so did the number of clans and tribes, so they expanded their territory into other lands. Since they were agricultural peoples, Aryan expansion moved slowly; upon arrival in a new area, they would sow seeds in the fields, and only when they harvested would they move to a new place, remaining there until the next harvest.

Any time they encountered the original inhabitants of these new lands, if the natives didn't surrender voluntarily, the Aryans would wage brutal warfare against them and either exterminate them entirely or turn them into slaves and tribute-payers; that being said, they would eventually mix with the conquered natives through marriage.

In such a manner, they slowly but surely spread from their motherland as their population grew. Some Aryan tribes from the upper reaches of Amu Darya and Syr Darya continued their path to the Hindu basin and other rivers that irrigated India and founded the tribes that now populate this great country. Others went to the southwest and populated the boundaries of the later-to-be-famous kingdom of Persia. Finally, many of the Aryans drove to the west, eventually settling in Europe with their tribes.

Since written language wasn't known to ancient Aryans, they couldn't leave written accounts of their migrations, so it is impossible to determine when any specific Aryan nation came to Europe. However, the first tribes that settled in Europe came to Italy and Spain; that being said, one of such tribes had founded a solid state before the others—Rome—where everyone already lived not by the tribal customs they followed in their Aryan motherland, but by the ordinary laws of the Roman state. It was thanks to these laws that the Romans didn't have tribal and family disputes; au contraire, they were all strongly united in conflicts with other tribes and won them easily. Thus, Rome, slowly but surely, became a more vital state, which by the time of the birth of Christ in the days of Caesar Augustus' rule controlled many other nations, including Judaea, the motherland of our Savior.

After the tribes had settled in Spain and Italy, other tribes who had arrived in Europe settled in Greece, which was especially attractive to newcomers due to its mild climate, an abundance of islands with fertile lands for mooring ships, and also the words of praise for all regions of Greece, which had spread all over the beautiful sea that surrounds it. The tribes who arrived in Greece soon changed their way of life from a tribal system to an organized government, but in contrast to Rome, they didn't unite into one centralized state, instead forming a plurality of small states based in marvelous and impressive cities; these states often engaged in bitter quarrels with one another and were thus mutually weakened, which is why they were all conquered by Rome in the end.

Our Dispersal

After the Greeks came, the ancestors of the contemporary inhabitants of France arrived in Europe with the Germanic tribes behind them, from which the later Germans, as well as Anglos, Hollanders, Dutch, and Swedes, formed. The Lithuanians broke off from Germania, and in the end, Lithuania stretched out to the west and included all the numerous Slavic tribes that were considered nearest to the ancestry of the Lithuanian tribe as well as Germania, and together with this, the younger Slavic tribes and all the great families of the nation who descended from the ancient Aryans.

Before their move from the banks of Amu Darya and Syr Darya to Europe, Slavic tribes probably came by two main routes; one was their descent from the shores of Amu Darya to the southern coast of the Caspian Sea, around this sea on the south side and moving through Asia Minor toward Europe via the so-called Thracian Bosporus.[2] This is the narrow strait to Constantinople, leading from the Aegean Sea to the Black Sea, which after crossing leads to the north and the west.

Other segments of Slavic tribes were able to migrate from the place of their original homeland downstream of Syr Darya, and because of this, going around the Caspian Sea from the south to spread into our glorious southern Russian steppes and the lower reaches of our rivers, the Don, the Dnieper, the Bug, and the Dniester, up to the lower reaches of the Danube on which the Slavic tribes had settled, going into Europe via the first route

---

[2] Now called simply the Bosporus or Bosporus Strait, the descriptor Thracian differentiates it from the Crimean Bosporus, which is the modern Kerch Strait connecting the Black Sea and the Sea of Azov.

through Asia Minor.

Aside from the migration through the two aforementioned primary routes, some of the Slavic tribes were able to come to Europe via a third route, which was to follow the river Amu Darya closely upwards until the southern shore of the Caspian Sea or to go along the eastern coast of the Black Sea, to cross over the eastern Caucasus Mountains and come into the extensive and fertile plains, adjacent to the Caucasus from the north, i.e., in the lands of the present-day Kuban region.

Having settled downstream and north of the rivers Danube, Dniester, Bug, Dnieper, and Don, the Slavs didn't stop in their migrations and continued to move even further gradually.

Some of the Slavs from the middle of the Danube separated from the tribe, settling in what is now Bulgaria, Serbia, and Montenegro, up to the shores of the Adriatic. Here, they founded, under the name Veneti,[3] a famous nation of sailors, becoming well known for their intrepid seamanship all over the southern seas of Europe and their lavish nautical trade. The Veneti created the only city in the world built in the middle of the sea, Venice, with its streets as sea canals and all movement throughout the city done by boat.

Other Slavic tribes, having ascended the Danube and its upper tributaries, passed from them to the river valleys, currents to the Baltic Sea, and reaching this sea, settled firmly on its southern coast from the mouth of the river Lab to the mouth of the river Vistula and the nearby islands. All the settled Slavic tribes in this area were no less well known than the Veneti as bold sailors of the North Sea, brave warriors, and enterprising traders. The brave Varangians settled here and immediately entered a bloody war with the established western Germanic tribes.[4] From the Varangians, the Baltic Sea received the nickname "the Varangian Sea." Just then, the Veneti settled right next to them, who, aside from being great sailors, were also famous among the Germanic people—like all Slavs in general—for the exquisite

---

[3] Also known as the Adriatic Veneti.

[4] Nechvolodov credits the Varangians as an ancestor of modern Russians (see Chapter Three), but their heritage is largely considered Germanic, not Slavic, by modern scholars. The term Varangian may refer generally to the various Scandinavian peoples, or specifically to those who settled in modern Sweden and the Baltic shores, pillaging along the rivers of Eastern Europe and eventually founding the Rus' States. In the West, these Scandinavians were referred to as Vikings, though this largely refers to those who pillaged westward, but the distinction is debatable.

art of cultivating the land.[5] Many Germanic tribes learned agriculture from the Veneti, and until then, the Germanic people were called "deep and narrow trenches" by the Veneti. From their Slavic neighbors, the Germanic people took the plow. On the Baltic Sea were the Rugii people or the Ru; they gave the name to the island of Rugii or Russi,[6] on which they settled and acquired notoriety as the most famous warriors and traders. Many centuries later, their descendants—one must think—gave their name to the Russian Land.

Then there were the Slavic tribes: Bodrichi, Lyutichi, Pomeranians, and others just on the Baltic coast.

Some Slavs with the name Lyakhov or Polyakov settled on the coast of the Vistula, having settled further east along the Neman and the lower reaches of the Western Dvina (Daugava River), a tribe itself closely related to the Lithuanians.

The Czechs, Moravians, and Croats settled around the Carpathian Mountains and adjacent areas.

Finally, the eastern Slavic tribes, having dispersed into the lower reaches of rivers in the south of modern-day Russia—the Dniester, the Bug, and the Dnieper—advanced upward along these rivers to the north and the east to the upper reaches of the rivers already rushing into other seas, exactly: 1) to the upper reaches of the Neman and the Western Dvina, currents to the Baltic Sea; 2) to the upper reaches of the Shelon, Lovat, and other rivers, flowing into Lake Ilmen, and from there through Lake Ladoga and the Neva River up to the Baltic Sea; 3) to the upper reaches of the northern Danube, flowing to the White Sea and lastly; 4) to the upper reaches of the rivers Oka and Volga, which carry their waters first to the east through the entire north of Russia, and then turning sharply to the south, toward the Caspian Sea.

Occupying the upper reaches of the rivers listed above, which almost all converge closely with each other at places, and which area was called in the old days Volkovsky Woods, our ancestors acquired the ability to grad-

---

[5] These are the Vistula Veneti or the Baltic Veneti.

[6] This island is known today as Rügen, Germany. While Nechvolodov seems to make a distinction between the Rugii and the Varangians here, at the end of Chapter Two, pg. 79, he asserts that the Rugii are a tribe of Varangians, by whom the Rus' States were founded. From *The Russian Primary Chronicle*, 59: "These particular Varangians were known as Russes, just as some are called Swedes, and others Normans, English, and Gotlanders, for they were thus named."

ually move forward downstream along their currents and settle the entirety of the vast landscape of European Russia.

Here is how consecutively, over many centuries, the Slavic tribe settled in many European countries, coming to it after other Aryan nations.

Before their migration into Europe, the Slavs needed to find routes traveled by the oldest native Aryan inhabitants of the countries they were migrating to, who had already settled there.

Greek Tales of Centaurs and Amazons

We don't have accurate information about these first encounters due to the ubiquitous lack of documentation from that time. Still, we know that the ancient Greeks, who, as we have seen, came to Europe before the Slavs, preserved old myths that there were unique monsters to the north of Greece who had their backs and legs covered in fur, like animals, but the chest, heads, and hands of people. These monsters, whom the Greeks called centaurs, were characterized by their highly fierce temper and superb marksmanship, and because they were as fast as horses, they were quite elusive. According to Greek myths, there were many bloody wars between these centaurs and the Greeks.

These legendary stories of Greeks and centaurs are quite unbelievable; however, a substantial share of them are true.

The brutal battles of the ancient Greeks indeed happened with newcomers from the south, who could shoot arrows with astonishing accuracy from their bows, suddenly emerging in front of their enemy's position on fast-footed horses with whom they appeared to form one inseparable whole.

The sight of these elusive equestrian newcomers, who attacked enemies from a distance with bows before fiercely charging at full gallop, especially struck the Greeks, who, having settled in their mountainous country, had poorly grasped the art of training horses and were poor riders who fought on foot instead.

Nevertheless, despite the horror they inspired in the Greeks, these southern newcomers weren't mythical monsters but real people.

They were our exalted Slavic ancestors and precisely those tribes who founded the Great Russian nation. Moving from their far-off Aryan motherland by our open southern steppes, they had mastered the wild horse during this challenging and lengthy journey across the exalted and then-inhabited Russian steppes and made for themselves from this energetic animal the surest and most devoted friend. Much like these Aryans, our Slavic ancestors were the best horsemen and bowmen in the world and embodied the horror of all nations who tried to resist them.

The ancient Chinese also had a story that far to the west, in the vast steppes, there lived a tribe, the Ding-Long, who were master horsemen and moved with astonishing speed; because of this, the Chinese, undoubtedly, considered the Ding-Long an Aryan race, as is seen from the comparison between pictures of Aryans and people of the Ding-Long tribe here displayed from ancient Chinese drawings.

Along with the myths of centaurs, the ancient Greeks also told stories of an extraordinary race allegedly consisting only of female warriors, fearlessly fighting on fleet-footed horses and distinguished for their archery skill; the Greeks named these brave riders Amazons.

These stories of Amazons were, we must think, none other than our valiant progenitors; they, as loyal and devoted wives and daughters, supported their husbands and fathers in their dashing raids and took part in all the bloody battles, bravely fighting and unhesitatingly dying by the side of their people.

Such ancient Greek myths told of our Slavic ancestors' introduction to European life.

Slavs Near Troy

Next, we find shorter but more positive accounts about our ancestors in songs that were famous all over the ancient Greek world from the blind poet Homer, who sang of the famous siege of the Greeks against the Asia Minor city of Troy, located not far from the Thracian Bosporus. The siege of Troy was twelve hundred years before the birth of Christ and occurred because Paris, the son of the Trojan king, kidnapped the beautiful Helen, who was the wife of one of the Greek kings.

The war on Troy continued for twelve years; in those years, both well-known heroes and vast quantities of allies from other nations took part. Among these others, Homer mentions the valorous allied Slavic tribe, the Veneti.

Before we continue our narration any further, it is necessary to say that apparently, our ancestors began calling themselves Slavs, denoting by this name all the tribes who spoke to each other with a mutually intelligible language, as opposed to the Germanics, whom the Slavs called mutes because they could not speak the languages of other tribes. Therefore, the name Slavs for a long time was used only among Slavs themselves; inhabitants of other countries called them foreigners by the names of their languages. From these names, the most well-known for a very long time was the Scythians, apparently because this was what the Greeks called them; thus, this name had denoted Slavic tribes since migratory times.

One Slavic hero on the side of the Greeks during the time of the siege of Troy was King Achilles. Homer ascribes a fantastical origin to him from the marriage of the brave Greek king Peleus and a mermaid, but the later Greek chronicler Arrian firmly states that Achilles was part Scythian, having been born on the shores of the upper Sea of Azov; he was banished from his homeland for his unrestrained temper and pride and settled in Greece, where he soon became praised for his incredible bravery. Achilles' features were of Scythian origin, according to the words of Arrian—his fair hair, blue eyes, and extraordinary rage in battle, and his clothing bore Scythian-style clasps. According to this image, during the siege of Troy, the greatest Greek heroes were of Scythian-Slavic origin, native to the Sea of Azov, having their homeland in our Donetsk region, now inhabited by Cossacks.

The first written stories of Greek writers about Scythians refer to a time approximately eight hundred years before the birth of Christ. In these stories, it is told that the strong and warlike Scythians, who had appeared on the coast of the upper Sea of Azov and the mouth of the Dnieper, brought such fear to the previous inhabitants of these areas, who bore the name Cimmerian, that they completely cleared the lands they occupied hastily and without any resistance, running away through the Caucasus into Asia Minor.

These accounts demonstrate that from their first appearance in Europe, our ancestors showed themselves as brave and warlike nations who didn't hesitate to undertake a series of glorious wars and campaigns.

Military Campaigns Against Egypt and Jerusalem by Our Ancestors

The Scythians were especially revered for a massive campaign sometime around 630 BC, which was undertaken with a vast number of riders from the coasts of the Dnieper and the Don through to the Caucasus Mountains, Armenia, Persia, and Asia Minor, reaching as far as Egypt.

This campaign lasted twenty-eight years and ensured strongly-emphasized notoriety to its participants. Before this movement, the Scythians, prancing on light horses and betraying all with fire and sword, brought such horror to all whom they encountered on their way through these lands that many of them, never even entering into battle, hurried to buy out these formidable conquerors with lavish gifts. On their victorious path, the Scythians subjugated the Median king Cyaxares and forced him to pay them tribute; they then headed to Assyria, and the Assyrian king had to buy them off with the innumerable treasures of his palace. From Assyria, the Scythians returned to the west, to the prosperous city of Phoenicia, and penetrated by way of the coastline into the Philistine territory from which they marched to Egypt. Seeing this, the Egyptian pharaoh Psamtik set out toward them with lavish gifts and begged them to cease and turn back. Then, the Scythians returned north again and invaded Judaea, which they put entirely to fire and death. They nearly sacked Jerusalem, for which the Jewish nation trembled at every hour, expecting deliverance into its fate. But the young Jewish king Josiah, with his chief emissary, prevented the capital's razing with his treasure's help, with which he begged the Scythians to spare the holy city.

The prophet Jeremiah, who lived in Jerusalem at that time, foretold the invasion of the Scythians in the following grim prophecy:

Declare in Judah and proclaim in Jerusalem, and say: "Blow the trumpet in the land; Cry, 'Gather together,' and say, 'Assemble yourselves, and let us go into the fortified cities.' Set up the standard toward Zion. Take refuge! Do not delay! For I will bring disaster from the north, and great destruction." (Jer 4: 5–6)

O Jerusalem, wash your heart from wickedness, that you may be saved. How long shall your evil thoughts lodge within you? For a voice declares from Dan and proclaims affliction from Mount Ephraim: "Make mention to the nations, yes, proclaim against Jerusalem, that watchers come from a far country and raise their voice against the cities of Judah. . . ." The whole city shall flee from the noise of the horsemen and bowmen. They shall go into thickets and climb up on the rocks. Every city shall be forsaken, and not a man shall dwell in it. (Jer 4: 14–16, 29)

"Behold, I will bring a nation against you from afar, O house of Israel," says the Lord. "It is a mighty nation, it is an ancient nation, a nation whose language you do not know, nor can you understand what they say. Their quiver is like an open tomb; they are all mighty men. And they shall eat up your harvest and your bread, which your sons and daughters should eat. They shall eat up your flocks and your herds; they shall eat up your vines and your fig trees; they shall destroy your fortified cities, in which you trust, with the sword." (Jer 5: 15–17)

Thus says the Lord: "Behold, a people comes from the north country, and a great nation will be raised from the farthest parts of the earth. They will lay hold on bow and spear; they are cruel and have no mercy; their voice roars like the sea; and they ride on horses, as men of war set in array against you, O daughter of Zion." We have heard the report of it; our hands grow feeble. Anguish has taken hold of us, pain as of a woman in labor. Do not go out into the field, nor walk by the way. Because of the sword of the enemy, fear is on every side. (Jer 6: 22–25)

"The snorting of his horses was heard from Dan. The whole land trembled at the sound of the neighing of his strong ones; for they have come and devoured the land and all that is in it, the city and those who dwell in it." (Jer 8: 16)[7]

Thus prophesized Jeremiah of the invasion of the Scythians. Turning from Jerusalem to the north, the Scythians, in the prime of their glory and loaded with wealth and plunder, returned from the lands they had conquered to their vast steppes on the Don and the Dnieper.

However, very few ended up returning to their home country; most died quite unexpectedly, thanks to the pernicious Scythian affinity for wine,[8] for which they were distinguished even in those ancient times. Unfortunately, they were able to sabotage themselves and their descendants, the Russian nation.

Knowing the exorbitant avarice of the Scythians for wine and their ability to drink themselves blind, the Median king Cyaxares, whom they had conquered and forced to pay tribute, prepared for their return a rich and sumptuous feast complete with a massive supply of wine. The Scythians once again drank themselves into a stupor. When they were passing out and stumbling around from drunkenness, the insidious Cyaxares had no trouble killing many of them; only a few made it home.

A hundred years after the sad events described, in 530 BC, the Scythian's passion for fine wine again proved disastrous for them.

---

[7] Note that Nechvolodov only provided the words, not the citation of each verse, so these were added. This is using the New King James Version, which will be used throughout.

[8] Likely due to the fact that the nomadic Scythians drank primarily fermented mare's milk, which was only mildly alcoholic, and so they were not used to the higher alcohol content of wine and its effects.

Death of Cyrus

The event occurred in the following way: Cyrus, king of Persia, one of the great conquerors of the ancient world, had conquered for himself the kingdoms of Media and Assyria and all the other tribes in Asia Minor; after this, having taken the glorious city of Babylon much to the pleasure of the Jews, who had been kept there in captivity and so decided to return to Judea, Cyrus chose to attack the Scythians, who were considered undefeated, and moved toward the Scythian tribes who lived on the Amu Darya River.[9] He had previously sent a proposition of marriage to their queen Tomyris. The wise Tomyris, no longer a young girl, understood that this was only a ploy to take possession of her lands. Thus, she sent him a message declining his offer, instead ordering him to announce that they would each rule over everything in their own kingdoms and not wage war on each other, but that if Cyrus indeed wanted war, that she would accept and look forward to expanding her dominion to include his.

Cyrus, knowing the indomitable Scythian courage and skill in the art of war, as well as their irresistible passion for wine, realized that he wouldn't be able to have success against them in conventional open war, but only with the help of his cunning.

For this, having invaded Scythian lands, he gathered all his troops, weakened and weathered by the wars, which he had no problem losing, and divided them in the direction of the Scythians. At that point, he ordered this first detachment, at the break of dusk, to take a lavish supply of food and wine and wait for the arrival of the Scythians. Cyrus' strategy was executed perfectly. Soon the Scythians appeared before the first Persian detachment, with Tomyris' young son to translate for them. They attacked the Persians and killed them all easily, at which point they happened upon the strategically placed wine and foodstuffs and carelessly indulged in unbridled revelry and drunkenness. That, of course, is when Cyrus crept up. He attacked the Scythians, who were stumbling around drunkenly, killed most of them, and took many of them hostage, with Queen Tomyris' son among them. Approximately 150,000 Scythians were killed or taken captive in this exchange.

Having learned of this misfortune, Tomyris sent a message to Cyrus asking him to release her son back to her and saying that she wouldn't take

---

[9] Specifically the Massagetae.

revenge on the Persians for the treacherous attack on her warriors if they returned home. But Cyrus could not acquiesce to her request; he had only just decided to undo the shackles of the queen's young son when, out of shame and grief for having been the cause of his brave compatriots' deaths due to his weakness for wine, and knowing that he had lost his mother's trust, he took his own life. Hearing of his death, Tomyris sent all her troops, numbering around 300,000 men and 200,000 women, to attack the Persians.

What followed was one of the bloodiest battles ever to have occurred in ancient times. Both sides fought bitterly and stubbornly, and finally the Scythians won. Cyrus died in the fray. When they found his body, the Scythian queen ordered his head removed and brought to her in a leather bag filled with human blood. Upon seeing the head, she addressed it, saying, "Although I have come through battle alive and victorious, you have destroyed me by capturing my son with a trick. But I warned you that I would quench your thirst for blood, and so I shall."[10]

Darius' Campaign in Southern Russia

Twenty years after this event, in 510 BC, one of Cyrus' successors, Darius I, who, like Cyrus, was also one of the great conquerors of the ancient world, decided that he wanted to conquer the Scythians to avenge Cyrus.

To do this, he gathered a great horde in Asia Minor, led them into Europe over the Thracian Bosporus, and ordered them to the Danube. Transporting his troops across a semi-permanent bridge under the protection of the allied Greeks, Darius entered the present-day provinces of Bessarabia and Kherson, no doubt in search of a swift victory in numbers over the scattered Scythian tribes. Unfortunately, due to strife among these tribes, despite the news about the Persian invasion, the further distanced tribes didn't agree to come to aid those located in regions more directly along the Persian warpath. However, despite these disagreements among Scythians, other unexpected circumstances arose for Darius.

The Scythians, when invaded by Darius' soldiers in their home territory, moved to meet them but did not engage the army in battle before

---

[10] Herodotus, *Histories*, Book I, §214. Nechvolodov did not provide direct citations, so this and others were found by the editors and given the wording of the existing English translation. If a citation is not provided, then the translation is given by the present translator. Full citations are given in the Bibliography.

sending their children and surplus livestock to the south, constantly avoiding the Persians to the east while always keeping one day ahead on the path and burning all their pastures in retreat. The Persians, arriving at ruined fields at dusk each day, endured constant hunger for a long time. The Scythians retreated along the Dnieper and, afterward, the Don until they reached the Volga; then, bypassing the Persian army from the north, they started to move to the west, staying entirely out of reach, much to Darius' surprise.

Since this proceeded at great length and with no end to the wanderings in sight, Darius sent a rider to Idanthyrsus, king of the Scythians, retreating before him with the following statement:

> [126] . . . 'What is this extraordinary behavior? Why do you keep on running away, when you could do something different? For instance, if you think you have the ability to resist my power, then stop this aimless wandering, stay in one place and fight. But if you recognize that you are weaker than me, you can still stop running: come and discuss terms with me instead, acknowledging me as your master with gifts of earth and water.'[11]

In response, the Scythian king Idanthyrsus sent this message to Darius:

> [127] . . . 'Persian, this is how things stand with me: I have never fled from any man in fear—I never have in the past and that is not what is happening now. What I am doing now is not far removed from my usual way of life during peacetime. I'm not going to fight you, and I'll tell you why. If we had towns we might worry about the possibility of them being captured, and if we had farmland we might worry about it being laid to waste, and then we might engage you in battle quite quickly; but we don't have either. If you feel you have to get to fighting soon, there are our ancestral burial grounds. Go on, find them and try to ruin them, and then you'll see whether or not we will fight. But until then, unless it seems like a good idea, we won't join battle with you. . . . You won't be getting gifts of earth and water from me, but only what you deserve; as for this "master" business, you'll suffer for it.'[12]

---

[11] Ibid., Book IV, §126.
[12] Ibid., §127.

This was the response sent to Darius. Upon learning that Darius had spoken to one of them about an alliance to subjugate the rest of them secretly, the Scythian kings were outraged.

A group of these Scythians, who were known for their bravery and were called the Sarmatians, crossed a Danubian bridge to tell the Greeks who were guarding it to destroy that bridge, but also to leave the others in the area, for the Scythians had decided to attack the Persians each time they were to be setting out on foraging excursions.

Thus the Scythians lay in wait for when Persians would leave in search of food for the rest of their people and their horses. The Persian cavalry would always take flight and hide behind the infantry immediately upon seeing any Scythians moving toward it. The Scythians would ambush the Persian infantry and give the impression that they were standing to fight, whereupon they would hastily turn back and vanish from sight. The Scythians carried out such attacks not only by day but also by night. Keeping the Persians constantly on alert severely weakened them, thus putting Darius in a challenging position. Upon noticing this, the Scythian kings decided to send him the promised gifts.

They sent him a herald bearing a gift of birds, mice, frogs, and five arrows. The Persians asked the messenger about the significance of these gifts, but he answered that he was ordered to deliver them and quickly return; if the Persians were clever, they would be able to figure out what they symbolized for themselves.

The Persians conferred afterward to discuss this riddle. It was the opinion of Darius that the Scythians had made their offering of earth and water. He reached this conclusion on the basis that mice dwell on the land and nourish themselves on the same food as men, that frogs live in water, that birds are closer to horses in nature, and the arrows he took to mean that the Scythians were offering up their martial courage. But Gobryas, the eldest of his advisors, whose opinion Darius respected immensely, interpreted the meaning of the gifts quite differently. He said they meant precisely that:

[132] . . . 'Listen, men of Persia: if you don't become birds and fly up into the sky, or mice and burrow into the ground, or frogs and jump into the lakes, you'll never return home, because you'll be shot down by these arrows.'[13]

---

[13] Ibid., §132.

The question of how to interpret the gifts persisted without a decision for a few days until the following event:

At some point, the Scythians appeared in front of Darius' soldiers in battle formation. Darius quickly gathered his forces and prepared for a decisive battle. At this time, a hare ran by the Scythian line, and since they were passionate hunters, they very noisily tried to catch it, turning their attention away from the nearby assembled and battle-ready Persian army. When the noise and screams rang out among the Scythian troops, Darius wondered about the reason for such commotion among the enemy. Upon hearing that they were chasing a rabbit, he turned to his advisors with the following comment: "These Scythians certainly hold us in contempt. I now think that Gobryas' interpretation of their gifts was right, and what we need is a good plan for getting safely back home."[14]

The Persians decided to retreat at night, spreading giant torches across their camp to deceive the Scythians and leaving their packs of donkeys in the camp, which by their groaning, were meant to send the message to the Scythians that the Persians were not fleeing. At the same time, they hastily moved from their encampment toward the Danube, abandoning all their sick and wounded for the Scythians to find.

The Scythians followed them to the edge of the Danube, with the Persians barely reaching the bridge in time. Only with great difficulty were the Persians able to make it over the river, completing the disgraceful and unlucky journey Darius had so overconfidently begun.

The details of Darius I's excursion into Russia were recorded in the writings of the famous Greek historian Herodotus.

Herodotus' Visit to Russia and His Description of Our Country and Customs

Herodotus was born in 484 BC to wealthy aristocratic parents, who gave him an excellent education and a substantial fortune, thanks to which he could travel to all the countries known to the ancient Greeks. In 450 BC, he visited what is now southern Russia; apparently, he even traveled up the Volga, reaching the area of modern-day Saratov. Among his many writings, Herodotus left one inquisitive essay.

His stories of the Scythians quite realistically portray their subject with astonishing clarity: the weather of the country; the nature and mindset of

---

[14] Ibid., §134.

the people who lived there; their customs and daily affairs. It is as though one were truly residing there at that time among our ancient ancestors. But, unfortunately, Herodotus never had a chance to visit the north of our country and could thus only speak of it through hearsay—obscurely and in uncertain terms. He also briefly and uncertainly tells of the southern, non-Aryan tribes whom the Slavs encountered before settling; however, from the words of Herodotus, it is evident that these were all peoples of Finno-Ugric tribes, the Vepsians, the Meryans, the Muromians, the Mordvins, the Chuvash, and others, the remains of which would come together in the north and northeast of Russia.

The accounts concerning the south of Russia, which he did visit, are quite accurate and precise.

He says that the Scythians were divided by their occupation into cultivators and cattle breeders. The cultivators lived in settlements along the Dniester and Bug rivers and along the Dnieper's western coastline up to present-day Kiev. The cattle-breeding Scythians lived in the steppes, spreading out through southern Russia east of the Dnieper, up to the Donets River. A little to the northeast of the cattle breeders there lived a particular Scythian tribe: the Royal Scythians. They were considered the most famous and the oldest, and further to the east, up to the Don, lived those who were called Sarmatians; they were even more warlike and would always go to war alongside their wives. They would capture their enemies, deftly throwing a lasso around their necks at full gallop. A Sarmatian girl couldn't marry a man until she had killed an enemy. Due to the warlike nature of Sarmatian women, the Greeks believed that the Sarmatian tribe was the product of intermarriage between the Scythians and the Amazonians.

All the Scythians, along with their Aryan ancestors, lived with their clans and tribes, which were ruled by chieftains and kings. These tribes constantly feuded among themselves and would thus mutually weaken each other. Herodotus writes of one Scythian tribe that settled on an area of the Danube located in present-day Bulgaria:

> [3] ... If they were ruled by a single person or had a common purpose, they could be invincible and would be by far the most powerful nation in the world, in my opinion. This is completely impossible for them, however—this is no way that it will ever happen—and that is why they are weak.[15]

---

[15] Ibid., Book V, §3. Herodotus here is describing the Tracians, who he considers to be a distinct

By Herodotus' time, the Scythians who practiced agriculture had already begun trading their bread extensively with other countries, predominantly with the Greeks; the bread was delivered by the Scythians via the river currents flowing into the Black Sea in large ships or rowboats, much like in our time. Herodotus writes of the Dnieper with great affection and says that, after the Dunya, it is the most wonderful of rivers; her waters abound with all types of fish, and her coastline is adorned with the most excellent crops and meadows.

To oversee the purchase of bread from the Scythians as well as for all economic transactions in general, the Greeks at this time had many great cities along the northern coast of the Black Sea: Olbia, on the lower reaches of the Bug river, near its intersection with the Dnieper, about twenty-five miles to the south of modern-day Mykolaiv; Chersonesus, or Korsun, on the southern shore of the Crimean Peninsula, next to modern-day Sevastopol; Panticapaeum, on the strait between the Azov and Black Seas, where the city of Kerch now stands; and Tanais, at the mouth of the Don, which is nearby the modern-day Rostov-on-Don, a town famous for its bread trade. Of all the cities listed here, Olbia and Panticapaeum were especially revered. In Panticapaeum, the Greeks had already formed the Bosporan Kingdom, so-called for the strait between the Azov and the Black Sea, nicknamed the Cimmerian Bosporus.[16]

The ruins of these great ancient Greek cities on our Black Sea coastline still exist today, and Russian scholars have made many detailed excavations of them. It is thanks to these excavations that many artifacts have been found, including the remnants of old houses, town squares, whole cemeteries with tombs, coins of all kinds and from multiple eras, household utensils, animal bones, weapons, as well as copper and marble boards with preserved writings; from all of these items, we can picture for ourselves the sort of life that the Greeks and the Scythians who visited them to trade led in these cities.

---

people from the Scythians. Nechvolodov treats both as Scythians, perhaps because this fact may not have been clear in the edition of Herodotus that he had access to, or owing to the fact that he was more of a military man than a historian, and was engaged in a form of historical undertaking heavily influenced by reactionary Russian nationalism. According to Herodotus, Nechvolodov's agricultural Scythians are actually the Tracians and his nomadic Scythians are the true Scythians.

[16] The Bosporan Kingdom was also called the Kingdom of the Cimmerian Bosporus. Today the Cimmerian Bosporus is called the Kerch Strait.

Apart from bread, a lively trade of other Scythian-made animal products was conducted in the designated cities: furs, fish, beeswax, honey, horses, as well as male and female slaves, which is what became of all the Scythians' captured enemies. Amber was also in great demand, for it was as valuable as gold in Greece; it was mined on the Baltic coast near the mouth of the Vistula and obtained from there in the Black Sea city by long river routes with portages. Since there was a bustling trade in gold and various semi-precious stones from the Urals, as well as a trade in furs from the then completely wild Perm region and Siberia, the same enterprising Greeks ended up building another trading city on the banks of the Volga, slightly below the present-day city of Saratov, which was called Gelon.

The Scythians, in turn, would buy many things from the Greeks: thin fabrics for their clothes, fine Greek wine, pepper, walnuts, various spices, painted dishes, jewel-encrusted weapons, precious vessels, and various decorations made of gold and silver, often the highly prized works of the greatest Greek master craftsmen. They would buy such lavish things for themselves and their wives and the finest adornments for their horses, whom the Scythians always held dear to their hearts.

The most warlike were the nomadic Scythians, who lived in the wide steppes and the lower reaches of the Dnieper and the Don, and the Sarmatians, who lived on the east Don. In two places near the mouths of these rivers, precisely in two wooded areas along the eastern bank of the Dnieper—one in the so-called Olesh, where now among the floodplains and thickets stands the city of Oleshky, and the other in the lower reaches of the Don—mobs of young and adventurous Scythian warriors would always gather to make constant war raids on neighboring tribes, either on fast-moving boats or swift horses. These bands on the lower reaches of the Dnieper and Don, to which flocked all of the restless Scythian warriors, were the ancient ancestors of our Slavic Zaporozhian and Donetsk Cossacks.

Herodotus writes, speaking of these daring nomads of the steppes:

[46]...[The Scythians] have come up with the cleverest solution I know of to the single most important matter in human life. The crucial thing they have discovered is how to prevent anyone who attacks them from escaping, and how to avoid being caught unless they want to be detected. Since they have no towns or strongholds, but carry their homes around with them on wagons, since they are

all expert at using their bows from horseback, and since they de-
pend on cattle for food rather than on cultivated land, how could
they fail to be invincible and elusive? [...]

[64] Here is how they conduct themselves in war. When a
Scythian kills his first man, he drinks some of this blood. He presents the king with the heads of those he kills in battle, because his
reward for doing so is a share of the spoils they have taken in the
battle, but no head means no spoils. The way a Scythian skins a
head is as follows: he makes a circular cut around the head at the
level of the ears and then picks it up and shakes the scalp off the
skull: next he scrapes the skin with a cow's rib, and then, having
kneaded the skin with his hands, he has a kind of rag, which he
proudly fastens to the bridle of the horse he is riding. The reason
for his pride is that the more of these skin rags a man has, the
braver he is counted. Many of them make coats to wear by sewing
the scalps together into a patchwork leather garment like leather
coats. Another common practice is to skin the right arms of their
dead opponents, fingernails and all, and make covers for their
quivers out of them. Human skin, apparently, is thick and shiny-
white—shinier, in fact, than any other kind of skin. They also often
skin the whole of a corpse and stretch the skin on a wooden frame
which they then carry around on their horses.

[65] So much for these practices of theirs. As for the actual
skulls—the skulls of their enemies, that is, not all skulls—they saw
off the bottom part of the skull at the level of the eyebrows and
clean out the top bit. A poor Scythian then wraps a piece of un-
tanned cow-hide tightly around the outside of the skull and puts it
to use like that, while a rich Scythian goes further: after wrapping
it in cowhide he gilds the inside and then uses it as a cup. Also, if a
Scythian falls out with one of his relatives, they fight to the death
in the presence of their king, and the winner treats the loser's skull
in the way I have just described. When he has important visitors,
he produces these skulls and tells how they had once been his relatives, and how they made war on him, but he defeated them. This
they call courage.

[66] Once a year, each provincial governor is in charge of a ceremony that takes place in his province. He mixes a bowl of wine,
and all the Scythians who have killed an enemy that year have a
drink from it. Anyone who has not managed to do this does not

partake of the wine, but sits to one side in disgrace—which is the greatest indignity there is for them. Any of them who have killed large numbers of men are given two cups to drink together.[17]

The gods of the Scythians were the same as those of far-off Aryan tribes; they added only Ares, the god of war. To him only would they offer human sacrifices—enemies taken captive in battle; to other gods, they offered only animals. In honor of Ares, every Scythian tribe would make a massive mound of dry brushwood onto which a large antique iron sword, an *akinakes*, was hoisted. As Herodotus says:

> [62] ... The festival takes place once a year, and at it they offer this *akinakes* more domestic animals and horses as sacrificial victims than all the other gods receive. They also sacrifice prisoners of war to this *akinakes*, though the method is different from when domestic animals are the victims. One prisoner is every hundred is selected; they pour wine over the prisoner's heads, cut their throats so that the blood spills into a jar, and then carry the jars up on to the pile of sticks and pour the blood over the *akinakes*. While the jars are being taken up there, something else is happening down below, by the side of the sanctuary: they cut off the rights arms of all the slaughtered men—the whole arm, from shoulder to hand—and hurl them into the air. Then they sacrifice all the rest of the victims and leave. The arms are left lying wherever they fall, detached from the corpses.[18]

According to Herodotus, the funerals of Scythian kings and chieftains happen, in the following way:

> [71] Their kings are buried in the territory of the Gerrhians, at the point where, travelling upstream, the Borysthenes ceases to be navigable.[19] On the death of one of their kings, they dig a huge square pit in the ground there, and when this is ready they take up the wax-covered corpse (which has previously had its stomach

---

[17] Ibid, Book IV, §46, 64–6.
[18] Ibid., §62.
[19] Borysthenes is the Greek name Herodotus used to refer to the Dnieper River.

opened up, cleaned out, filled with chopped galingale, incense, celery-seeds, and aniseed, and then sewn back up again) and carry it in a wagon to another tribe. The people to whom the corpse has been brought do what the Royal Scythians have already done: they cut one of their ears, shave their heads, slash their arms, mutilate their foreheads and noses, and pierce their left hands with arrows. Then the king's corpse is taken on its wagon to another one of the tribes within the Scythian realm, with its retinue being made up of people from the tribe to which the corpse had previously been transported. Finally, after going around all the tribes with the corpse, they come to the Gerrhians, who are the most remote of the tribes within the Scythian realm, and to the tombs. Here, they lay the corpse in his grave on a pallet. Then they stick spears into the ground on both sides of the corpse and make a roof out of wooden planks covered with rush matting. There is still open space left within the grave, and in it they bury, after throttling them to death, one of the king's concubines, his wine-server, cook, groom, steward, and messenger, and some horses and a proportion of all his other possessions, including some golden cups. They do not put anything of silver or bronze in the grave. Then they cover the grave with a huge mound of earth, and they all eagerly compete with one another to make the mound as big as possible.

[72] After a year has gone by, they choose the fifty most suitable of the dead king's remaining attendants and throttle both them and his fifty finest horses to death. The king's attendants are native Scythians; there are no bought slaves in Scythia, but anyone the king orders to be his attendant complies. Once the fifty servants and the fifty horses are dead, they gut them, clean them out, fill them up with chaff, and then sew them up again. Next they halve a wheel and fix each of the two halves, cut side up, in the ground on two stakes, and repeat this process over and over again. Then they drive a thick pole through each of the horses, all the way up to their necks, and use them to mount the horses on the wheels in such a way that the front wheels support the horses' shoulders and the rear wheels support their bellies next to their thighs, and all four legs are dangling off the ground. The horses are then fitted out with bridles and bits, and the reins are pulled forward over their heads and tied to pegs. Then they mount each of the fifty young men they

have strangled to death on one of the horses by driving a pole up-
right through his body along his spine as far as his neck; and they
fix the projecting lower end of this pole into a socket bored into the
other pole, the one which goes through the horse. They set up these
horsemen in a circle around the grave, and then ride off.

[73] That is how they bury their kings.[20]

Despite their strangeness to us in modern times, Herodotus' account of
these Scythian funerary rites is quite fair and accurate, as well as frequently
confirmed by excavations of burial mounds scattered in large quantities
across the south of Russia. Many of these barrows are along the Dnieper,
near the border of the contemporary province of Yekaterinoslav.

Findings From Burial Mounds

The barrows are found in various shapes and sizes and are known by
different names throughout the country, which are given according to their
physical descriptions. Thus, one barrow site is called the *sharp* grave because it has a sharply-rounded vertex; another is called the *wide* grave for
the far-reaching slope of its sides; yet another, the *pockmarked* graves, for an
oblong visual effect is seen when two or three of them are spread out close
to another; if, however, the graves are arranged longitudinally as if they
were a rampart, the barrow is given the name *long* graves. Two barrows of
the same size, standing next to one another, are called twins.

Especially striking of all the steppe barrows are the *wide* graves. This
name, chosen by the local folk, denotes those barrows which, apart from
their considerable size, have another unique visual characteristic that dis-
tinguishes them from all the others. These are barrows with very steep
sides, which appear wide because of the vastness of their embankments. It
was discovered during excavation that the steepness of the wide graves'
sides is supported by a frame built at the foot of the mound out of large,
rough stones mined in rivers and gullies, sometimes taken from sites at a
considerable distance.

The steppe graves of small and medium size usually don't contain par-
ticularly lavish or well-endowed tombs. Still, near the wide graves, the
more ostentatious tombs of wealthier kings can be found. Although almost
all of the graves so far excavated by scholars had still, at some unknown

---

[20] Ibid., §71–3.

time, been exhumed by anonymous vandals or plundered by robbers, a few of them had enough of every type of object left to get accurate readings about the living conditions of the people buried in them. Some of the graves date to ancient times, even before the arrival of the Slavs from their Aryan homeland. Many of the graves, on the contrary, were laid down much later than the period written about by Herodotus, but large barrows and tombs can be found that are built exactly as he describes them. Upon digging out these graves in which the bones of important people were buried, we sometimes find gold and silver jewelry worn by the dead kings among their decayed clothing, weapons placed close by, and food vessels above the head; ordinarily, the king has the female corpse of a sacrificed concubine next to him, also in decayed clothing and often with golden rings, bracelets, and other jewelry on her hands. Aside from the ghoulish corpses of dead servants and horses, other artifacts such as jars and vessels of various kinds, horse harnesses, cufflinks, and various coins—gold, silver, copper, and others—can be found. All the artifacts are studied right there at the excavation—their significance, where and when each one is found, and everything else. Then, if it is at all possible to reassemble any of the broken pottery or other vessels, it is sent to special facilities, of which the main one is in Saint Petersburg, next to the Winter Palace and the State Hermitage Museum.

The objects found in the Scythian graves give us a detailed look at the characters of the buried people. Fascinating are the diverse types of jars and metallic objects on which scenes from the lives of the same Scythians are depicted in illustrations. Mostly, these illustrations were done by highly skilled Greek masters, whose fine craftsmanship is quite impressive, although some are found with rougher illustrations.

Below are some pictures of a few artifacts found in the graves with illustrations on them.[21]

Fig. 30 is a picture of a jar found near Kerch, in the grave of one Scythian king. This vessel is made from an alloy of gold and silver (with a ratio of four parts gold to one part silver). The illustrations on the jar are shown in expanded form in the same figure; one is quite curious of their significance. Furthest on the left, we see a Scythian king or chieftain with a headband; seated on a hillock, he is listening attentively to his scout, kneeling before him. They both have spears in their hands; the chief appears to have a bow

---

[21] See "Figures for Chapter One" at the end of this chapter and likewise for subsequent chapters.

on his left and his scout a leather shield. Next to the scout, a Scythian sits on one knee, forcefully stringing a bow. To the right is an illustration of two Scythians, one of which is tending to the illness or injury of the other; further to the right, there is also an injured man, whose feet are being bandaged by his comrade. All the Scythians in this image are wearing leather trousers; their belts are adorned with a metal fixture, and their boots are soft, without rebounds, as would be necessary for people who spend their whole lives riding horses. Moreover, all the Scythians have long hair and beards, as many Russian peasants now wear. A Scythian illustration on a silver pot with the same beards was found in 1910 in the Voronezhian region (fig. 31).

Fig. 32 depicts a magnificent silver jug, the most remarkable artifact in the burial mound excavations.

Its height is 28 inches. It was found in 1863 by a famous archaeologist, collector, and connoisseur of Russian antiquities, Ivan Yegorovich Zabelin, in a wide grave in the so-called Chertomlyk Barrow, located in the Yekaterinoslav region about twenty miles from the town of Nikopol.

This barrow houses a royal Scythian tomb. Unfortunately, however, it was looted by unknown grave robbers, who were caught in a landslide, and as a result of which one of their skeletons was later found in the tomb; they didn't manage to get away with much, and there was still a large number of magnificent artifacts left behind. This vessel has illustrations of the utmost value and significance among them.

While its ornamentation is quite skillfully done, this piece stands out for the series of convex gilded horses on the top rim. This rim is displayed in the expanded view in fig. 33.

Undoubtedly, this illustration depicts the most fundamental and significant undertaking in Scythian life—the training of the wild horse. The illustration goes around the whole rim and consists of two even segments—the front and the back. In the middle of the back segment, there are two horses shown, still wild and free, grazing in the steppes; on their sides, it shows Scythians catching them with lassos (the lassos on the jug were silver threads held by each Scythian in a clenched fist). The image of these Scythians and horses illustrates conflict with one another: the horses are struggling to get away while the Scythians are using all of their strength to make them stop. The middle of the front segment of the rim shows how three Scythians are trying to wrangle a wild, still untamed horse down to the ground to place a bridle on him; the other Scythians standing behind are also helping by pulling the horse to them. To the left of this horse, another horse is shown, already having been bridled, and a Scythian training him, pulling the right reins over the horse's front left leg, to leave him in this awkward position so that he will get used to the reins and follow their direction. The image on the right of the middle horse depicts a man removing a kaftan from his shoulders, and further to the right another horse, but already trained, bridled, and saddled, who is being trained by his master to keep his front legs down.

Fig. 34 shows a golden sculpture found in one of the barrows. We see two Scythians on it, embracing closely and drinking wine from a single horn together; Scythians always drank wine in this way, into which they would mix small quantities of their blood from cuts on their bodies when they were joining brotherhoods or making smaller fraternal unions among themselves.

Fig. 35 also depicts some gold work, found together with the previous figure—a mounted Scythian etched into it, using a javelin to hunt a hare lurking just in front of his horse's legs.

Finally, figs. 36 and 37 depict the ends of two golden grivnas or neck jewelry in the shape of a hoop. This grivna was in wide circulation among our ancestors, and everyone would strive to wear such a grivna around their neck. Grivnas were made from a few wires woven together, which would be—depending on status—either gold or silver, with some ornament fixed on the ends; in the images here, the parts of a few grivnas can be seen with two Scythian horsemen on the ends. These Scythians bear an astonishing resemblance to Russian peasants.

Analyzing these images of the objects found in our barrows shows that Herodotus documented Scythian character and customs remarkably well.

More than anything, these customs and temperaments of our ancient ancestors amaze and shock us with their bloodiness and brutality. Skinning the corpses of enemies, making the skulls of the relatives with whom they quarreled into wine goblets, and finally, strangling so many devoted servants to death as a sacrifice for the graves of leaders—all this cannot but amaze us.

But we must never forget the time in which our ancestors lived. We must remember that this was several centuries before the birth of Jesus Christ, who came for the exact purpose of bringing salvation to this cruel, pagan world, so mired in streams of blood and blessing it with his Gospel of love for one's neighbor.

In the time described above, nobody considered the possibility of genuine love for their neighbor; moreover, if our ancestors had been cruel to their enemies, it was only because they knew that in times of trouble, their enemies would act just the same to them, if not worse. It is essential not to forget that all warfare was conducted at that time with merciless cruelty.

Not long after Herodotus' travels to Scythia, the Greeks, the most enlightened of all cultures then living in the ancient world, entered into a massive civil war among themselves which lasted twenty-eight years, and in which they committed horrible atrocities against their fellow Greeks whom they defeated; it often happened that they would promise the inhabitants of a besieged city their lives and freedom if they surrendered, but they had no qualms with immediately breaking their word and subjecting the enemies who trusted their promises to the most ruthless slaughter of all kinds, sparing neither women nor children.

The exalted Romans also acted with even greater cruelty and mercilessness; many centuries after the writings of Herodotus' times, when Christian preachers first came to Rome, the Romans were extreme in their fanaticism toward the defenseless Christians and publicly subjected them to painful torture or gave them to be torn apart by wild beasts; it is known that the Romans would mount Christians up on high poles, coat them in oil, set fire to them, and then feast and make merry before the flames of the burning martyrs. In general, the extreme cruelty that the Romans practiced came with their fastidious luxury. Roman emperors and aristocrats spent the greater part of their time in magnificent country palaces, indulging in all sorts of excesses while mercilessly torturing their slaves.

The Scythians thus were, all in all, no crueler than others.

If they forced their young warriors to drink the blood of the first enemy they killed, this would be done, of course, only to harden the young man up into a warrior; between that, the neighbors of the Scythians—the Finnic tribes who were contemporaries to the Scythians living next to them in the south of Russia at the time of Herodotus—even had no qualms with cannibalizing the bodies of their dead parents.

On the topic of Scythian funerary customs, namely how so many people who were loyal to their kings and chieftains were sacrificed with them when they died, we must never forget that our ancestors believed deeply in the immortality of the soul. It was only by the rudeness of their pagan religion that they believed it necessary to send the dead into the next world along with their most beloved servants and horses. Only for this reason were so many killed at the burial of their leaders. More than this, we must also remember that for all the sacrificed servants, this death was considered the highest honor, and many went to it happily. This was true devotion to their lords "in living and in dying." Because of this boundless loyalty to their kings, the ancient Slavs secured many great victories and were thus considered invincible.

Herodotus considered the Scythians equal to the rest of the cultures for their spiritual nobility, reason, courage, skillful agriculture, and exceptional understanding of warfare. He called them just and fair. Moreover, he assigned the greatest merit to them, in that although they were intimate with many foreign cultures, they inherited nothing from them and closely held on to their ethnic customs and integrity.

The main criticism that Herodotus levies against them is their inclination toward conflict with each other, equally pernicious to all Scythians, as was their incontinence concerning the consumption of wine. The Scythians' unbridled drunkenness always astonished the sober Greeks, who would ordinarily only drink their wine diluted with water; the Greeks even had a common saying that if someone wanted to drink themselves to excess, they would say, "pour me some wine Scythian style" or "let's get Scythian," whereupon the cupbearer would pour the wine straight and undiluted.

Scythians were especially praised for their limitless devotion to the people closest to them, such as their kings and kinsman and those with whom they formed fraternal bonds.

Here is one of the many stories about just what friendship and brotherhood meant to the Scythians.[22]

Once, two Scythians, Dandamid and Amizok, had become blood brothers. On the fourth day after they drank each other's blood together, another Scythian tribe suddenly came into their territory—they were Sarmatians. Since nobody expected a raid, the Sarmatians killed many warriors, took many captives, and plundered the villagers to ruin. Amizok was among those taken captive. When they took him away, he shouted to his friend and reminded him of their blood pact. Upon hearing this, Dandamid galloped ahead of everyone to the enemies. The Sarmatians, brandishing spears, turned toward him intending to impale him, but he shouted, "zirin." If one were to utter this word, the Sarmatians would not kill him but accept him as coming to pay ransom for their prisoners. After greeting an enemy this way, he asked for the release of his friend; the Sarmatian looked at the ransom, saying he wouldn't release him unless he could give him more. Dandamid said, "you have plundered all that I could give, yet all that I, having

---

[22] Note that this is a folk tale as told by Nechvolodov, not a story from Herodotus.

nothing, can give as ransom, I would present willingly to you; tell me what you would have. Then, if you want, do the same to me even as you do to my friend!" The Sarmatian answered: "I need not the both of you, for you came with the word 'zirin.' Leave in place of your friend a part of your body."

Dandamid asked which part he wanted to take, to which he demanded both of his eyes, and Dandamid immediately proceeded to gouge them out. When he finished and the Sarmatians received the gruesome ransom, Dandamid, carrying Amizok, went back, relying on him to guide him; thus, they escaped. After this, the Sarmatians sang the praise of the Scythian tribe they had raided, and thus it happened that they weren't defeated, for they were not deprived of their greatest treasure—peace of mind and honor among friends.

Moreover, the Sarmatians were so taken aback by this event that they all left that night. In order not to stand out from his friend, Amizok likewise blinded himself, and they were both held in great honor according to ancient Scythian custom.

Figures for Chapter One

1. Education of the Tsar's Children. The Tsar's eldest son, seated first
in front of the teacher, has a scroll on which the words "Enlighten
me and teach me, oh Lord" can be made out. From *Tolstoy's Initial*,
one of the rarest manuscripts of the seventeenth century,
at the Russian Academy of Sciences, Saint Petersburg.

2. Prehistoric bison or aurochs hunting.

3. (Left) Depiction of an ancient hunt. Carved on a Sidonian marble tomb, which,
it has been hypothesized, houses the ashes of Alexander the Great.
4. (Right) Augustus Caesar, from the statue in the Vatican Museum in Rome.

5. Image of the ancient Capitol building in Rome.

6. An image of the ancient Acropolis in the Greek city of Athens.

7. A Battle of Greeks against centaurs. From *Alexandria*
in the State Historical Museum, Moscow.

8. Fighting between Greeks and Centaurs. On fragments of a Greek vase
from the mid-sixth century BC. The Centaurs are depicted with the
same type of beards with which the Greeks would represent
the Scythians—preserved in the British Museum, London.

9. (Left) Image of a man from the Ding-Long tribe.
From the Great Chinese collection of the Sixteenth Century.
10. (Right) Chinese Depiction of Aryans from the same source.

11. A battle between Greeks and Amazons on a Greek vase from the
mid-sixth century BC. Preserved in the British Museum, London.

12. (Left) An image of mounted and dismounted Amazonians on a vase from the fifth century BC.   13. (Right) The Amazonian queen on the march against the Greeks, from the *Illustrated Chronicle of Ivan the Terrible*[23]

---

[23] Nechvolodov's note, modified: Also called the *Illustrated Codex of Chronicles*, this is an extensive Rus' chronicle with illustrations placed on the underside of each page; these illustrations are first impressed and then painted over in watercolor. The first volumes of the *Illustrated Chronicle* center around stories of Sacred History and the Trojan War, and the following volumes give narration of the Russian Land (as an illustrated improvement on the *Nikon Chronicle*, written earlier in the reign of Ivan the Terrible), starting from the great reign of Vladimir II Monomakh. The *Illustrated Chronicle* is also known informally as the Tsar Book or the Royal Letopis, "letopis" meaning "chronicle," and was so referred to in the original version of this book. Nechvolodov wished to credit the esteemed researcher and expert of Russian antiquity N. P. Likhachyov with identifying that, by virtue of the watermark paper on which the chronicle is written, by all accounts it was very likely composed in the sixteenth century under commission by Ivan the Terrible. Later scholars have since confirmed this; thus it is now referred to as the *Illustrated Chronicle of Ivan the Terrible*. More than ten thousand pages and sixteen thousand illustrations, or miniatures, have survived, consisting of ten volumes; part of them are kept in Saint Petersburg, in the Library of the Russian Academy of Sciences and in the Russian National Library, and another part in Moscow, in the State Historical Museum. Details about this amazing collection can be found in the following places: the works of N. P. Likhachyov (*Paleographic Significance of Paper Watermarks* and *Extracts from Lectures on Diplomacy*) and also in the work of A. E. Presnyakov: *Moscow Historical Encyclopedia of the Sixteenth Century*, printed in Volume 5 of *Known Branches of the Russian Language and Literature of the Russian Imperial Academy of Science* (1900).

Studying the pictures in the *Illustrated Chronicle*, ordinarily called miniatures, with close curiosity, we see that it demonstrated the peculiar style of Russian drawings in the sixteenth century; moreover, we can recognize the same faces in a few places in the same drawing, for example: standing in front of the axe, and then right there lying with the head chopped off, etc. Sometimes also two images are presented in one illustration—higher or lower, and under or above—with the top referring to the beginning of a story about some such event, and the lower the end, or vice versa. The main significance of the miniatures is to familiarize us with the life of our ancestors; they depict the battles, the clothes, various activities, sleighs, different kinds of utensils, how temples were built, how the monks went on horseback, etc.

14. (Left) The great blind bard Homer. From an ancient Greek illustration.
15. (Right) Heroes of the Trojan War: 1. Agamemnon 2. Achilles 3. Nestor 4. Ulysses
5. Diomedes 6. Paris 7. Menelaus. Rare copper etching of images of some
Ancient Greeks by the famous Russian sculptor Nikolai Ivanovich Utkin.
Kept in the Imperial Academy of Arts, Saint Petersburg.

16. Achilles the Victor. Eighteenth-century English copper etching from a
collection of illustrations formerly belonging to the Kingdom of Poland.
Kept in the Imperial Academy of Arts, Saint Petersburg.

17. Entry of Achilles into Troy. "How Achilles entered the city of Troy"
from the *Illustrated Chronicle*.

18. An image of the ancient Assyrian kingdom in Nineveh. Layard's illustration.

19. Egypt. A view of the Sphinx and the pyramids.

20. Illustration of ancient Jerusalem, Solomon's Temple from the Mount of Olives

21. Supposed view of the Tower of Babel, according to the perspective of Henry
Rawlinson in the United States National Museum (Smithsonian), D.C.

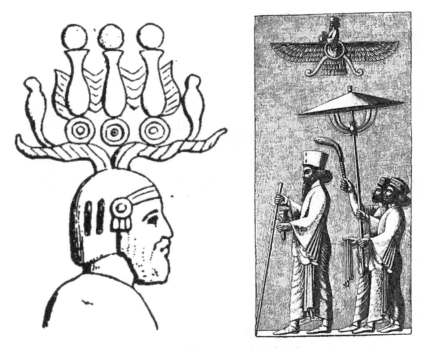

22. (Left) The Head of Cyrus from an ancient Persian monument.
23. (Right) Darius I, an Ancient Persian illustration carved in stone.

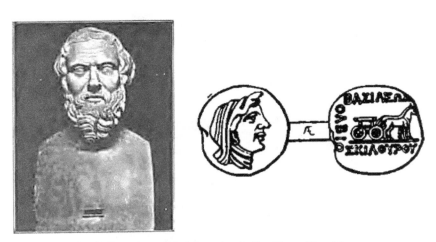

24. (Left) Herodotus Marble statue in the Neapolitan Museum.
25. (Right) Copper coin, minted in Olbia. On the face side is an image of a deity;
on the turnover side is a Scythian carriage drawn by a pair of horses.
The carriage is similar to those used now in the south of Russia.

26. (Left) View of Kerch, the location of ancient Panticapaeum.
27. (Right) Copper coin minted with the head of a bull, an ear of rye, and a mace.

28. At the burial mound of a Scythian chief. Illustration by the artist
Kandaurov in the Imperial Museum of Arts, Saint Petersburg.

29. Image of one of the burial mounds near Kerch

30. A vase found near Kerch in the so-called Kulob Mound, and a roll-out of the image depicted on the vase. Kept in the Hermitage Museum, Saint Petersburg.

31. (Left) A vase found in 1910 in Voronezh province. From the property of His Imperial Majesty Nicholas Alexandrovich's palace of Livadia. 32. (Right) A vase found by Ivan Zabelin in the Chertomlyk Barrow. Kept in Hermitage Museum.

33. Rolled-out image of the rim of a vase found by Ivan Zabelin.

34. (Left) Golden medallion with an image of two Scythians in a fraternal pact, kept in the Hermitage Museum. 35. (Right) Golden medallion with an image of a hare hunt, kept in the Hermitage Museum.

36. An image of a grivna of golden horses, kept in the Hermitage Museum.

37. Horse grivna, depicted in fig. 36, close-up view.

38. An image of an ancient Roman palace of the time of
the Empire in the locality of Bahia, near Naples.

39. A mural from the Panticapaeum tombs with an image of
Scythian warriors, excavated by V. V. Stasov in 1872.

CHAPTER TWO

Information About the Russian Land and Writers After Herodotus

Nobody wrote so comprehensively nor as realistically about the Russian Land as Herodotus,[24] right up to Saint Nestor, who is generally credited as being the first Russian chronicler.[25] Nestor was a monk of the Kiev Monastery of the Caves (Kyiv Pechersk Lavra) who lived eleven centuries after Christ, or over a millennium and a half after Herodotus.

During these one and a half thousand years, all the writers who spoke of our ancestors only knew of them through chronicles taken during war, because these were the only interactions with Slavic tribes they had had. However, because the Slavs were a militant nation, and wars were constantly happening at the various ends of the world, we can often find accounts of our ancestors from writers of other peoples.

From these sources, we can see that the Slavic tribes always, in all accounts, maintained a reputation of fearlessness, aptitude in the art of war, and were considered very honorable and sincere.

The following are some opinions of a few writers who came after Herodotus, writing about the inhabitants of the Russian Land at that time. One of these writers said:

---

[24] Nechvolodov refers to the lands held by the various Slavic tribes affectionately as the Russian Land, but note that the country of Russia would not exist for many centuries.

[25] Saint Nestor the Chronicler or Nestor the Hagiographer (c. 1056–c. 1114) is generally credited as writing the *Primary Chronicle*, also known as the *Tale of Bygone Years*, though his authorship is not certain. He also wrote the *Life of the Venerable Theodosius of the Kiev Caves* and the *Account about the Life and Martyrdom of the Blessed Passion Bearers Boris and Gleb*.

Their system of justice was written in their minds, and not in laws; theft was rare and was considered the gravest of all crimes. Gold and silver they as much despised as other souls would covet it. They are fantastic warriors because, to them, the business of war is a hard science that they study down to the last detail. The greatest honor in their eyes is to die in battle. To die of old age or some other thing—this is a shame, more humiliating than anything else that can happen. They are generally handsome and stalwart; their hair casts out in a light brown color. Their appearance is more warlike than merely ferocious.[26]

Another writes:

The Slavic tribes all have the same way of life and like the same things—they love freedom and don't tolerate slavery. They are generally brave and manly in their country and can endure all labor and hardship. They easily endure both coldness and heat as well as the nakedness of the body and all inconvenience and impediments. Exceedingly kind to foreigners, with whose safety they concern themselves more than anything, they lead them everywhere from place to place and care for them according to a sacred law which holds that a neighbor should avenge themselves and make war with them if, by their infirmities, in place of protection, the host should allow some misfortune to befall the guest.

To host guests properly, the poorest people would even be allowed to steal, although theft was considered the most serious of all crimes.

Captives of the Slavs are not held like those in other countries; they do not remain slaves forever. They are given a definite time, after which, having settled their ransom, they are liberated to return to their fatherland or to stay with their friends and be free. They will often do raids and ambushes and get up to all sorts of trickery by day and night as they go about playing soldiers.

Their greatest skill consists of their ability to hide under water. No one else can stay under water as long as they can. Often, when

---

[26] Nechvolodov does not provide the author of these quotations directly, but he does provide a list of all sources used in the Bibliography.

caught off guard by the enemy, they will lie at the bottom for a very long time and breathe, assisted by long reed tubes with the hole of one end placed in the mouth and the other above the surface of the water. In this way, they can hide inconspicuously in the murky depths. Whoever should spot these reeds, not knowing of this trick, shall consider them natural and ordinary. Those who are experienced recognize them from the holes cut into the reeds or from their position in the water and push them down into the man's mouth or move them in some way and cause the trickster to rise to the surface. The Slavs disdain any authority and harbor enmity toward one other.

In Rome, there still stands a colossal pillar, or column, carved from stone to the glory of Emperor Trajan, who lived around the end of the first and beginning of the second centuries after the birth of Christ. It was erected for his greatest feat, which was the conquest of the Slavic Dacian tribe, who lived on the Balkan Peninsula. Various episodes from the Roman conflict with the Dacians are depicted on the column and demonstrate the lionhearted valor of the Slavs and the great hardship they posed to the mighty Roman Empire and its battle-hardened soldiers in their achievement of victory against a relatively small Slavic tribe.

A few images from Trajan's column have been placed in the current chapter. In fig. 41, we see Roman soldiers defending themselves etched into the stone, standing on a fortified wall, clad in metal armor and holding shields, with Dacians attacking them fiercely, wearing only a single linen shirt each, with nothing but bows in their hands.

Fig. 42 depicts how the Dacians, going to war with the Romans, boldly swim across the river just as one of them is sinking with his horse; in the background, horse riders are seen clad in scaled armor, in the style of the Amazonians depicted in fig. 12 (Ch. 1); these riders, allied with the Dacians and rushing to their aid, are Sauromats or Sarmatians, inhabitants of the western bank of the Don.

Figs. 43 and 44 are quite remarkable. In the former, there are Slavic chieftains who, having been cornered by the Romans, have decided to poison themselves to escape the shame of captivity and are drinking chalices of poison alongside a young warrior who has already died in this way, as his weeping father hangs his head over the body. In fig. 44, we also see a few Slavic chieftains surrounded by Romans, a part of them still deliberating what course of action to take; one (furthest on the left) fiercely holds back the enemy, while another, on his knees right next to him, obviously already wounded, brandishes a knife with which to take his own life.

The greatest source of the Slavs' woes appears to have been the constant strife between themselves. Every time they have united for some general purpose, they have become formidable, undefeatable, and have easily brought those they wanted to subdue under their hand. But as soon as the Slavic internecine conflict begins, their power starts to wane. This tendency has been artfully used by their enemies, who endeavor by all means to stir up internal dissent among them.

One hundred years after Herodotus chronicled his famous travels through the Scythian lands, Alexander the Great, the greatest conqueror of all time, who in his short life (he died at thirty-one years of age) subdued all of Greece, Asia Minor, Egypt, Persia, Babylon, and some of India, was moreover especially revered for his famous battle with the mighty Darius III, marched twice against the Scythians; the first time, around 335 years before the Nativity of Christ, against the tribe who inhabited the region north of the Dunya—he also burned their main city—and the second time, in 328 BC, against the Scythian tribe who lived to the north of the Amu Darya.

The last invasion ended suddenly: Alexander, who until then had been utterly indifferent to the allure of womanly beauty, was instantly smitten by the sight of Roxana, the daughter of one of the Scythian kings, and married her instantly at that moment, solidifying a union with her father. At this time, on behalf of Alexander, one of his naval commanders surveyed the Caspian and was the first to discover that following the outflow of the Volga River, it was possible to cross over into the Baltic.

After Alexander, the Scythians no longer made war with the Macedonian kings, and 293 years before Christ, in the steppes near the Dniester, they captured one of their kings, Lysimachus, alive with all his soldiers.

Not long before the divine birth of our Lord Jesus Christ was set to take place, dominion over all the ancient world, as has already been pointed out before, fell into the hands of the illustrious Romans.

One of their most powerful enemies at that time was Mithridates the Great, king of Pontus (in Asia Minor) who lived from 121 to 64 years before the Nativity of Christ. Incidentally, he also ruled over the Bosporan Kingdom, which lay on the coast of the Sea of Azov and the Cimmerian Bosporus. This king, Mithridates, had long fought against the neighboring Scythian tribes, whom he finally defeated severely, whereupon he solidified an alliance and state of peace with all the tribes to unify their strength against the Romans, whom he despised. Aside from the well-reputed quality of the ground forces he now possessed in the united Scythian tribes, Mithridates also had the combined forces of all the coastal inhabitants of the Black Sea to bring to bear against Rome on their boats. He then formed a naval force of seafaring mercenary pirates, with which the Romans could barely compete.

Mithridates was very proud of his victory over the Scythians. He would have said, "I alone of all mortals have conquered Scythia, that Scythia, against which none before have successfully stood, nor even come close! Two kings, Darius the Persian and Philip the Macedonian, ventured not into Scythia destined to conquer it, but only to flee with great shame from that place out of which there has just now been sent a vast army against the Romans."

After Mithridates' defeat of the Scythians, the glory of the defeated warriors returned to a neighboring tribe that lived along the left bank of the Don, the Sauromats, as Herodotus called them, or the Sarmatians, as the Romans called them, and also to other Slavic tribes, who lived to the south of them, called the Roxolani. Thanks to the string of their valiant deeds, the name Sarmatian gradually became a blanket term to call all of the Slavic tribes who inhabited the Russian Land, which was at one time even given the nickname of Sarmatia.

The Sarmatians were especially distinguished for the speed and suddenness of their raids, and also for their women who played an equal role to the men in their political and military affairs. As one Greek writer narrated:

Amaga, the wife of the Sarmatian king, who lived on the coast of the Black Sea, seeing the incontinence of her husband concerning food and drink, held court herself, deployed guard detachments herself, fended off raids from enemies herself, fought in alliance with neighboring tribes, and her glory was loudly proclaimed among all the Scythians. On one occasion, one of the Scythian kings ran afoul of her because he had insulted the Khersonians, a tribe she had taken under her protection. The queen first sent an order not to touch the Khersonians. Still, when the Scythian king defied her will, taking 120 people, the strongest in spirit and body, and giving each one three horses so that they would always have two in reserve, she traversed the equivalent of two hundred miles in a single day and descended on the king's castle without warning, crashing its gates. The Scythians, taken aback by the sudden attack, thought that a great deal more attackers had come than what they could see and became confused, whereupon the queen and her troops quickly barged into the palace where the king was, killed him and all who were near, and gave all his wealth to the Khersonians.

Our nation did not remain bereft of evangelical preaching throughout the very first years after the Resurrection of Christ.

The Travels of Blessed Saint Andrew the Apostle

During his third mission, the Apostle Andrew (the First-Called), following the east coast of the Black Sea, after preaching in the Caucasus Mountains, visited the cities of Kerch, Theodosia, and Korsun, from whence he sailed up the Dnieper, and upon arriving to the then uninhabited mountains around the city of Kiev, raised a cross and said to his followers: "Look upon these mountains; from them, the grace of God shall shine, and there shall be a great city, and many churches shall be erected here for the glory of God."

The congregation of believers that Saint Andrew had established in the city of Korsun soon endured severe persecution. The Romans had made the city a destination of exile for Christians. Thus, in the first century after the Nativity of Christ, the niece of the Roman Emperors Titus and Domitian, Flavia Domitilla, a Christian, was exiled there, along with the Roman bishop Saint Clement, and sentenced to hard labor in the quarries under the reign of Emperor Trajan. Nevertheless, Saint Clement diligently planted seeds of the faith in Korsun and founded as many as seventy-five churches, due to which, under orders from Rome, he was captured, taken two miles away from the city to the sea, and thrown into the water with iron weights around his neck, so that the Christians wouldn't be able to retrieve his relics. His relics were found, however, and taken to Rome—in the second century after the Nativity of Christ—by Saint Cyril, the Philosopher; just a few of the relics remained in Korsun and were taken to Kiev by Saint Vladimir after his baptism.

Aside from Korsun, in our country, the preaching of Saint Andrew the Apostle brought no notable results; our nature was still crude and rough, and only certain individuals could perceive the divine truth of Christ's teachings.

Campaigns of Slavs Against the Roman Empire

Mithridates the Great instructed the Slavic tribes to attack the Roman borders; after the birth of Christ, both separate Slavic tribes and a few unions of tribes began often making trouble for these borders, especially since, at one time, the Roman border very nearly came to our southern Russian steppes, so far that the Roman domain, in the first century after Christ's birth, had already also captured the Greek city of Olbia, near modern Nikolaev (Ukrainian: Mykolaiv).

Subduing the Slavs was proving to be quite difficult for the Romans for the very reason that they had no central government. They lived in individual tribes and bands, each one for themselves, neither united nor in treaty with anyone; none of them answered to any other, and all of them, having waited for an opportunity and gathered their strength, acting according to their judgment and without reason, would rush into Roman territory.

Thus, the Romans recognized the necessity of buying off the Slavs, and in the year AD 69 they had already acquired the pockets of a few lesser chiefs of a few Slavic tribes who lived in Roman lands; with these simple tributes did the Romans pay these chiefs off.

Especially troublesome for the Romans were the Slavic tribes of the borderlands, for they had already united together when they started their invasions. Of these invasions, the most heinous was under the reign of Emperor Marcus Aurelius and lasted for fourteen years from AD 166 to 180. Not only did the united Slavic tribes take part in these invasions, but the Germanic nations did as well; moreover, the Romans carried out a long war with the Slavic tribes after the pacification of the Germanics. Among these Slavs, two tribes that lived in Russia were especially exalted: the Roxolani and the Iazyges.

With great bitterness was the war with these tribes carried out by the Romans, and many clans from both sides perished. Many years after the war, the Iazyges returned to Rome with a thousand Roman captives.

The Romans were unable to return such a great quantity of captives since they ordinarily treated their prisoners of war in the following inhuman ways: in Rome, there had been constructed an enormous, perfectly round building around a large open field; in this building, it was possible to house up to two thousand people at once. Roman citizens gathered here constantly to see entertainment that consisted of Christians being attacked by wild animals on the field, as well as Roman captives brought out onto the field armed with weapons they had been trained to use because they were forced to fight, either one-on-one or in groups, each group sorted according to the captives' respective countries, until they annihilated each other.

The ruins of this huge building, called the Colosseum, still stand in Rome today. There also remains an image carved into the precious rock during that time of a dying captive after a fight, made for the amusement of the depraved and bloodthirsty Roman masses. Looking at this etching, we can easily recognize our Slavic brother: the dying man has the same facial features that we often find on Russian faces, and around his neck he has draped grivnas, which our ancestors loved to wear.

In describing the fourteen-year war between Rome and the Slavs, called Sarmatians, we can say that it served as a sort of education in war for all the nations living at the border of Rome. The war taught these nations not to rise against the Roman provinces alone but as a whole union. The Slavs carried out their attacks both by land and sea; gathering on their boats at the mouths of the Dnieper and the Don, they bravely embarked out onto the sea and went not only as far as Byzantium and Asia Minor but reached even as far as Athens and Rome.

All of these excursions couldn't help but disturb powerful Rome. To stifle the constant invasions, the Roman Emperor began to use any means he could to foster quarrels among the Slavic tribes and, in this way, distract them from his major cities. This method of action is what the Romans called "divide and conquer." This inner division of enemies was especially successful for Emperor Diocletian, who took power at the start of the fourth century after the Birth of Christ and is remembered as a cruel persecutor of Christians. Nevertheless, Diocletian managed to incite the Germanic tribes, who generally took the name Goths, against the Slavs, whereupon they and the Slavs left Rome alone. As a result, they began quite fiercely to destroy each other over many years.

The Goths

This enmity between the Goths and the Slavs continued into the reign of Saint Constantine Equal-to-the-Apostles, the first of the emperors to receive holy baptism and promote the proliferation of the Christian faith along with his mother Saint Helen Equal-to-the-Apostles. Before him in 321, Slavic daredevils from the upper reaches of the Don and the coastlines of the Sea of Azov had come on ships and laid siege to a certain city, so the emperor had to rush to defend it and repel the attackers.

In 332, the Goths started attacking the Slavs living in the Russian Land excessively. The Slavs petitioned Saint Constantine with a request for his help, and the emperor subdued the Goths and ordered the two adversaries to make peace. However, this peace did not please the Slavs, and they started ravaging lands belonging to Saint Constantine—what are modern-day Serbia and Bulgaria. The emperor then subdued them and forcefully established peace.

After the end of Saint Constantine's reign, the enmity of the Goths and Slavs was renewed with even greater fervor. The Goths started to gain the upper hand, especially when they were united under the rule of their hero-conqueror Ermanaric. Ermanaric began to push against his opponents with his united forces forcefully; he passed over the Dnieper, subduing the Slavic tribes he encountered along the way, and even went as far as the Don.

But oppression by strangers soon became unbearable for our freedom-loving ancestors, and all who lived in the Russian Land at the time rose against their common enemy.

The Huns Unite the Eastern Slavs

The first to resist were the brave residents of the lower Don and Dnieper; they set out under the name Huns against Ermanaric, joining with every Slavic tribe subjugated by the Goths as they moved forward.

When news of the march of the Huns reached Ermanaric, fear gripped the Goths, and they sought council with their king about what to do. At this time, the Roxolani, who before had been subdued by the Goths, hearing of the Hunnic advance, switched over to their side; at the same time, one of the chieftains of the Roxolani, having been under Ermanaric, also had just abandoned him and left his wife, Sonilda, to rule in his place. For her husband's flight, the enraged Ermanaric ordered her to be executed; she was tied to wild horses and torn to pieces. Two of her relatives struck Ermanaric with a sword in revenge for the innocent woman's death. After this, he remained alive a little longer, but the Hunnic invasions took him by surprise. After a long battle, seeing how unsuccessful it was, in despair and fear of his inevitable death, he took his own life by diving onto his sword. He died at fifty years of age.

After Ermanaric, there came the valiant Gothic king Vinitharius. The Huns had initially defeated him, but then he captured Boz, king of the Antes, and to terrorize his enemies, crucified him along with his sons and seventy noblemen. After this, Vinitharius peacefully ruled for a whole year while the Hunnic king Balamber, busy in his own affairs, made no moves against him.

Then Vinitharius won two battles against the Huns; one cannot imagine the horrific carnage he rendered against the Hunnic army. On the third battle, the regiments converged on the Prut River. Here, Vinitharius was killed by an arrow that Balamber let fly at his head. After this, Balamber took Vinitharius' granddaughter, Vadamerca, for his wife, and the Gothic nation surrendered to the Huns without resistance.

Thus again united together under the rule of a brave and competent king, Balamber, the Slavic tribes inhabiting our land once again attained power and glory—this time, as a new community called the Huns. According to all the Germanic peoples, or rather the Gothic nations as they were then known, rumors were spreading about the appearance of an unknown, wild nation, which had either grown out of the ground or descended as a whirlwind from the high mountains. They overturned and destroyed everything that crossed their path.

Attila

The Huns became especially formidable when, in around 444, Attila became their king.

By this time, the Roman Empire, which was previously united for many centuries, had been split in two. This division happened in 395 when one of the emperors who succeeded Constantine Equal-to-the-Apostles— Theodosius the Great—died and left the Roman Empire to his two sons, who divided it into two empires: East and West. Since then, the Western emperors had resided in Rome, and the Eastern emperors in Constantinople (formerly Byzantium), which the Slavs called Tsargrad.

The division of the Roman state, which had been strong for so many centuries, soon led to internal discord between the rulers of each half to their mutual weakening. This weakening was especially impressed by Attila assuming leadership of the Huns. By request of the Western emperor, he first mobilized his forces against the Eastern, but then he fell out with the former and went to war with him.

The Goths, whom Attila decisively conquered, nicknamed him "the Scourge of God" and, in their chronicles, described him, as well as the infamous Huns, as monsters of various kinds, similar to how the ancient Greeks portrayed our ancestors—as centaurs and Amazons. These Gothic writers said that the Huns came from the coast of the Sea of Azov and the mouths of the Don and were the product of a marriage between witches and unclean spirits. The Goths said of the Huns:

> When children of the male sex are born to them, they cut their cheeks to eradicate any germ of hair. However, they all had stocky statures, strong limbs, thick necks, and massive heads. They are more like bipedal animals or stone pillars roughly hewn into the shape of people than actual people; they're awkward yet strong on their horses; it is as if they are chained and doing all sorts of things on them. At the start of a battle, they divide themselves into squadrons and, letting out a horrible cry, charge at their enemies. Then, scattered or in unison, they attack and retreat at lightning speed. But here is what especially makes them the most fearsome warriors in the world: firstly, their arrows are accurate even if shot from a distance, and secondly, when fighting one-on-one with swords at close quarters, they can, in an instant, and with extraordinary dexterity, throw a sling around their enemy and thus deprive him of any movement.
>
> They understand right and wrong no more than beasts do. They carry on conversation ambiguously and mysteriously. Their language is hardly perceivable as human.

Thus did the Goths chronicle their fierce enemies, the Huns.

If we remove all that the Gothic writer added to this passage out of spite, we would see the Huns as direct descendants of our valiant ancestors, who followed the prophet Jeremiah out of Jerusalem and banished the proud Persian king Darius from our Black Sea steppes. Moreover, it was sometimes customary for our ancestors to shave their beards and even their heads, leaving but a *chupryna* upon it, as did the glorious and well-known Zaporozhian Cossacks. Still, among the Cossacks of the Don, many shave their heads this way.

The Greeks (Byzantines) in this century wrote of the Huns completely differently than the Gothic chroniclers. From the writings of these Byzantine Greeks, it is plain to see that the Huns were direct descendants of the Scythians, Slavs, and that Attila was the wisest sovereign and leader most skilled in the art of war. He observed justice strictly and did not tolerate the oppression of the people by officers. Thus unsurprisingly, Byzantine and Roman industrialists and skilled craftsmen switched allegiances to Attila by the thousands.

We hear of one such Byzantine writer,[27] an eyewitness who himself visited the dreaded Attila the Hun, dined with him, and said how this mighty person lived. This witness, Priscus of Panium, a diplomat, was sent to Attila by the Byzantine Emperor Theodosius II in 448.

The reason for the sending of the diplomat was this: when the Huns made peace with the Byzantines after inflicting a heavy defeat on them, Attila ardently demanded that they return all their defectors; moreover, he ordered the payment of a considerable tribute and that trade on Byzantine soil between Byzantines and the Huns who came there occurred on equal footing without any danger for the Huns.

The Byzantines agreed to all of these conditions. Still, they then hesitated on the extradition of a few notable Hunnic defectors and rendition of the tribute, which was so dear that even the wealthy Byzantines put up their wives' headdresses and other possessions for sale.

Insisting on their defectors' return and honoring the tribute's payment, Attila was constantly sending ambassadors to Constantinople. Since it was the custom for ambassadors to be paid richly, he would send his favorites by whom he wanted to do well.

In 448, Attila sent another ambassador to Constantinople, Edekon, a Scythian distinguished for great military exploits.

Attila sent a message to the emperor threatening war if he did not return the deserters to him. This time, the Byzantines managed to have a secret meeting with Edekon and offered to shower him with gold if he poisoned Attila. Edekon agreed, and for this mission, the emperor sent another embassy along with him, of which Priscus was a part. All the threads of the conspiracy were in the hands of Bigilas the Byzantine, one of the members of the embassy; the Byzantine ambassador himself and Priscus, his secretary, knew nothing of the conspiracy.

The retinue, arriving on the banks of the Danube, met Attila and the

---

[27] The Byzantine Greeks referred to themselves as Romans, and to the Byzantine Empire as the Roman Empire. Likewise, the Byzantines were referred to as Romans by their contemporaries in the East, and as Greeks by those in the West, both to differentiate them from the Western Roman Empire and to associate them with the pagan Ancient Greeks. Modern scholars now refer to the people of the Byzantine Empire as Byzantine Greeks, Byzantines, or Greeks, but not Romans. While Nechvolodov more often used the term Greek for the people of the Byzantine Empire (and likewise frequently referred to the Byzantine Emperor as "the Greek Tsar" or "king of the Greeks"), this edition uses only Byzantine for consistency, reserving the term Greek for the Ancient Greeks discussed in Chapter One and for the Greek language.

Huns there during their hunting excursion. The day after their arrival, the ambassador wanted to be introduced to Attila. Attila already knew about the conspiracy against his life (most likely, the faithful Edekon warned him) and ordered the Byzantines to get out of his house immediately unless they stated the exact purpose of their embassy. Because of this, the ambassador, knowing nothing of the conspiracy, was already preparing to leave when the next day, Attila, to whom it had been explained that the ambassador knew nothing of these affairs, received their embassy.

Priscus wrote of their reception:

[41] ... And so at last we came to Attila's tent, which was guarded by a barbarian multitude arrayed in a circle.

[42] When we reached the entrance, we found Attila seated on a wooden chair. Maximinos approached, as the rest of us stood a short distance from the seat, and he greeted the barbarian. Giving him the emperor's letter, he said that the emperor prayed that he and those around him were safe. [43] Attila replied that the Romans would have what they desired for him. He turned his attention straight to Bigilas, called him a shameless beast and asked why he wanted to come to him, considering that he knew his and Anatolios' peacetime agreement that no ambassadors should come to him until all fugitives had been surrendered to the barbarians. [44] Bigilas said that there was not a single Scythian fugitive among the Romans; those who had been there had been surrendered. Growing angrier and reviling him all the more, Attila shouted that he would have crucified him and given him as food to the birds, if he did not think inflicting this penalty on his shamelessness and on the effrontery of his words would violate sacred diplomatic law.[28]

After this reception, Bigilas and the Hun Isla were sent to the Byzantine emperor under the pretense that they would collect the deserters but, in reality, to get the gold promised to Edekon.

Priscus and the ambassadors followed behind with Attila to the north, and on the way, he drove into a village where Attila married a young girl. Attila had many wives, but he wanted to marry this one per Scythian custom.

Priscus continued:

---

[28] Priscus, *Fragmentary History of Priscus*, Fragment 8, §41–4.

[83]... We crossed some rivers and arrived in a very large village, in which it was said Attila's compound was more conspicuous than everyone else's, fitted together with logs and well-polished boards and encircled with a wooden wall that contributed not to safety but to majesty.

[84] After the king's compound, Onegesios' was magnificent and also itself had an enclosing log wall. His was not equipped with towers like Attila's; rather there was a bath, not far from the enclosing wall, which Onegesios, as the preeminent man among the Scythians after Attila, built large by conveying stones from Paionia....

[87] As he entered this village, Attila was welcomed by girls who moved in lines under fine white linen sheets stretched over a great distance so that under each individual linen sheet, held up by the hands of the women on either side, seven or more girls were walking (there were many such rows of the women under the linen sheets) and singing Scythian songs. [88] As Attila approached Onegesios' compound (for the road to the palace ran through it), Onegesios' wife came out with a multitude of servants, some of whom were carrying food and others wine. This is a great honor among Scythian women. She greeted him and begged him to partake of what she was kind-heartedly offering him. Showing favor to the wife of his advisor, he ate sitting on his horse as the barbarians accompanying him raised the platter up to him. It was made of silver.[29]

Having drunk the wine brought to him by the servants, he continued riding to his house, which was higher than the others, for it was built on an elevation.

The next day at dawn, Priscus went to Onegesius with gifts to find out how the negotiations with the ambassador would be carried out.

While waiting to be received at the gate of Onegesius' house, Priscus saw a man, a Scythian judging by his clothing, who approached him and greeted him in the Greek tongue.

Priscus was greatly surprised by this, knowing that Scythians don't speak Greek, and this man was by all appearances a Scythian, richly dressed and with a head of hair cropped into a circle, asking him who he

---

[29] Ibid., §83–4, 87–8.

was in Greek. It turned out that this was a Byzantine from one of the Byzantine cities on the Danube; he was rich, but when the Huns took the city, he was captured, and his wealth went to Onegesius during the plundering because, after Attila had taken his share, wealthy people would be given to his higher commanders. According to Priscus:

> [99] He added that, after he had distinguished himself in later battles against the Romans and Akateri, he gave the barbarian ruler, according to Scythian custom, the spoils he took and so obtained his freedom. He married a barbarian woman, and now had children.
>
> As one who shared Onegesios' table, he said, he believed his present life to be better than his previous life. [100] After war Scythians spend their time at ease, with each man enjoying what is at hand and causing trouble or being troubled either not at all or only a little.[30]

After this, the Byzantine began praising the Scythian way of life above the Byzantine one.

By telling these stories, the Byzantine convinced Priscus that the Huns weren't at all the cruel and bloodthirsty monsters that the Goths had written about but were kind and honorable folk who acted as patrons toward their captives, a trait for which all the Slavs have been known from antiquity.

The day after this encounter, Priscus and the rest of the embassy were invited to the dinner table of Attila himself.

Priscus writes:

> [152] We watched for the right time and arrived at the dinner as invited guests. We and the Western Roman ambassadors stood on the threshold opposite Attila. [153] The cupbearers gave out a cup according to the local custom so that we could pray before being seated. When this was done, we sipped from the cup and moved to the chairs, where we had to dine while sitting.
>
> [154] All the chairs were placed along the walls of the house, on each side. Attila was seated on a couch in the middle.... [155] I

---

[30] Ibid., §99–100.

thought the first rank of diners was on Attila's right, and the second rank on his left, where we were, although Berichos, a well-born Scythian man, was seated ahead of us. [156] But Onegesios was seated on a chair to the right of the king's couch, and opposite Onegesios two of Attila's children were sitting on a chair. The eldest was seated on Attila's couch, not near him but at the edge, looking at the ground out of respect for his father.

[157] Once everyone was sitting in order, a cupbearer came in and gave Attila a wooden cup of wine. He took it and welcomed the man first in order. [158] After Attila so honored him, the man rose, and it was not right for him to sit until he sipped from the wooden cup or drank it down and gave it back to the cupbearer. [159] As he remained seated, everyone present honored him in the same way: receiving their cups, offering a greeting and taking a sip. For each diner, there was one cupbearer, who had to enter in a line when Attila's cupbearer departed. [160] After the second man and the rest were honored in turn, Attila greeted us in like manner according to the order of our seats. When everyone had been honored by this greeting, the cupbearers withdrew and, after Attila's, tables were set up, with three or four men or even more per table. Each man was able to partake of the dishes set out by the cook so long as he did not disrupt the order of the chairs.

[161] First Attila's servant came in carrying a platter full of meat. After him everyone's waiters placed bread and cooked food on the tables. For the other barbarians and for us lavish meals had been prepared, placed on silver trays, but for Attila there was nothing more than meat on a wooden platter. [162] He showed himself moderate in everything else too. Gold and silver goblets were given to the feasters, but his own cup was wooden. [163] His clothing too was frugal, since it cultivated no quality except cleanliness. Neither his sword, hanging beside him, nor the fastenings of his barbarian shoes nor his horse's bit, like the other Scythians', was adorned with gold or jewels or anything else that marks honor. [164] After the first course was finished, everyone rose. After we stood, no one went back to his seat until each man, in the same order as before, prayed that Attila be safe and drank the cup of wine which had been handed to him. [165] After so honoring him, we sat down and a second platter was placed on each table with other foods. [166] Once everyone partook of this too, we stood up again in the same

manner, again drank and sat down.

[167] As evening came, torches were lit. Two barbarians, taking up places opposite Attila, performed original songs, singing of his victories and his excellent military qualities, while the feasters watched them. [168] Some were enjoying the poems, others, recalling the wars, were aroused in their spirits, and still others were weeping, their bodies grown weak with the passing of time, their courage forced into repose. [169] After the songs, a certain deranged Scythians came in. He brought everyone to laughter with his meaningless and insane babbling. In the midst of all this, Zerkon the Maurousian slipped in.... [170] Exploiting the opportunity of the feast to enter just then, he put everyone in a good humor and moved everyone to unquenchable laughter with his appearance, his clothes, his voice and words that poured out indiscriminately from him (for he was jumbling up Hunnic and Gothic with Ausonian)—everyone except Attila. [171] He himself remained unmoved and unaltered in appearance, and he looked like he was not saying or doing anything resembling laughter, except that he pulled the youngest of his children closer by his cheek (his name was Ernach). He had come in and was standing nearby, and Attila looked at him with serene eyes.[31]

The next day, they started to ask about leaving. Onegesius told them that Attila also wanted to let them go. Then he held a meeting with the other dignitaries and composed a letter to be sent to Constantinople. Priscus writes:

> [178] At this time, Kreka, Attila's wife, invited us to dinner at the house of Adames, the man who oversaw her affairs. We joined him along with some of the nation's leading men, and there we found cordiality. [179] He greeted us with soothing words and prepared food. Each of those present, with Scythian generosity, arose and gave us each a full cup and then, after embracing and kissing the one who was drinking, received it back. After dinner, we went back to our tent and went to sleep.
>
> [180] On the next day, Attila summoned us again to a banquet and in the same way as before we joined him and feasted.... [187]

---

[31] Ibid., §152–71.

We left the banquet at the end of the night and, three days later, having been honored with proper gifts, we departed.[32]

During these feasts, Priscus tells us, along with wine, they were also served mead, and a special drink made from barley called kamon.

After three days had passed, the ambassadors were seen off with splendid gifts. Then, on the homeward path, they encountered Bigilas, a conspirator against Attila's life, who was now carrying the gold allotted for Edekon's bribery. But Attila, having been forewarned of this conspiracy, forced him to speak of his business, stripped him of all the gold, and ordered him to be captured and held for ransom. Then Attila sent his ambassador Eslas to Constantinople along with his loyal Roman Orestes, whom he always used for negotiations in person and written. Orestes was ordered to hang the purse around his neck in which Bigilas had carried the gold that was meant for Edekon; to appear before the emperor in this way, to show the purse to him and Chrysaphius the eunuch, the original architect of the conspiracy, and to ask them if they recognized the purse. Afterward, Eslas was to speak to the emperor in this exact way:

> [2]... While Theodosius was a child of a well-born father, Attila too, being well-born and the successor to his father Moundiouchos, carefully guarded his good breeding. Theodosius, however, had fallen away from his good breeding and so was a slave to him insofar as he had consented to the payment of tribute. [3] He was therefore not acting justly when he, like a worthless servant, secretly attacked his better and a man whom fortune had revealed to him as his master.[33]

That was Attila, the lord of the terrible Huns.

From Priscus' writings about the customs of Attila's court, we can see that they were purely Slavic and, moreover, exactly and absolutely so, as we shall see centuries later in the courts of our Muscovite tsars.

Apart from the feuds with the Byzantine emperor, Attila also had a long-standing feud with the Western Roman emperor, Valentinian III. The original cause of this feud was Valentinian's sister Honoria, who was characterized by her wild nature, for which her mother treated her very strictly

---

[32] Ibid., §178–80, 187.
[33] Ibid., Fragment 12, §2–3.

and demanded that she stay celibate. To free herself from her unhappy circumstance, she sent Attila a ring with an offer of her hand in marriage. Attila accepted this offer and demanded that her brother consent to not only the marriage but also half of the Western Roman Empire as his sister's dowry. Valentinian refused, but Attila stubbornly stood his ground, and in the end, this disagreement led to a bloody war.

Attila's campaign in this war was similar to tribal resettlement. All Germanic and Slavic tribes were forced to take part in it. Thus, they went as far as the very heart of Gaul, and here, on the Catalaunian Plains, there was a terrible battle between the nations, after which each army departed and attributed the victory to itself.

This was in 451, and Attila died two years later. He died at his own wedding, apparently from excessive wine-drinking. Given his reputation for being sober all the time, it seems most likely that he was poisoned.

After Attila, the dominion of all the tribes subject to him went to his sons. Strife arose among them almost immediately, and the power of the terrible Huns quickly disintegrated: the Germanic tribes that had been subject to them became independent; a portion of the Slavic tribes, over whom Attila's younger son held dominion, who lived on the Danube and would later become the Bulgarian people; an East Slavic tribe which migrated of their own accord toward the Dniester and Dnieper in the Russian Land and spread into the Caucasus Mountains. However, the strife between the heirs continued unabated; in light of the actions of the Goths and proto-Bulgarians, neighboring tribes did not hesitate to take advantage of the circumstances, especially the Byzantines. Attila's sons sent emissaries to Constantinople, requesting a renegotiation of terms between the Byzantines and Huns. Still, they received, regardless of the profitability of this request to the Byzantines, only refusals, an act which was surely taken to demonstrate to the sons of the formidable Attila that their requests were not worthy of attention in Constantinople.

Hostile activities between the Slavs and the Byzantines intensified, especially under the Byzantine Emperor Justinian I (who was of Slavic origin), ruling from 527 to 562.

During the time of his rule, in 558, an incalculable force of Slavic tribes crossed the Danube; a part of them headed for Greece, and the other straight to Constantinople, and the danger posed to the city was so great that not only was the entire army called to its defense, but so were the gentry and the peasants of the surrounding countryside. Only the cunning of the old Byzantine commander Belisarius could circumvent the Slavic chieftain Zabergan, who was given an immense number of slaves and a huge sum of money as ransom and returned to the Dunya.

Discord Among the Slavs

After these events, which nearly ended in the sacking of Constantinople, Justinian took every measure to ensure that such an invasion would not reoccur. To this end, he decided to cruelly sow discord among the Slavs and then send a new enemy against these weakened opponents.

This worked out extremely well for Justinian.

With a combination of lavish gifts and skillful incitement of one chieftain against another, he fought with the Slavic tribes who inhabited our southern steppes for a long time; they entered into a series of huge, bloody clashes with each other, and when they were completely exhausted, there came from the east a tribe from far-off Asia, ancestors of the modern Turks, dispatched westward by the Byzantines, called the Obri, or the Avars; the Avars crossed the Volga and the Don, and after a brutal battle, completely subdued the weakened and internally discordant southern Slavic tribes.

Invasion of the Avars

The Slavs showed the Avars the same fearless resistance everywhere they went. Still, because of their fragmentation, naturally, they were unable to gain the upper hand over the united strength of their enemy. So they ended up being enslaved, nevertheless causing great irritation in their conquerors by their stubbornness. The Avars tortured the Dulebes (Dulebians or Buzhans) who lived along the Bug River especially badly, exacting great cruelty and violence against their women. "When it so happened that an Avar needed to go somewhere, he lashed neither horses nor oxen to his cart, but rather our women in threes, fours, or fives, and thus did he go wherever he needed," says the *Radziwiłł Chronicle*.[34] (See fig. 65)

---

[34] Nechvolodov's note: Also known as the *Königsberg Chronicle*, the *Radziwiłł Chronicle* is kept in the Library of the Russian Academy of Sciences in Saint Petersburg, where it was sent from the German city of Königsberg after it was taken by our armies in 1761 during the Seven Years' War; The Königsberg library had received it as a gift from Prince Radziwiłł in the seventeenth century. The manuscript itself, representing the *Primary Chronicle* of Nestor, judging by the watermark on the paper, was written, as N. P. Likhachyov has explained, in later decades of the fifteenth century, apparently either in Moscow or in the lands of Suzdal. In 1716, the emperor Peter the Great, traveling through Koenigsberg, paid special attention to this

The power of the Avars was spread wide. However, it did not extend over all of the Slavs. To avoid the Avar yoke, a few daring bands crossed over the Dunya into Bulgaria, Serbia, and Croatia. When the Avar king, who bore the title of khagan, sent the Croats, who lived in the Carpathian Mountains, demands of submission and tribute, their king, Dobrita, answered the Avar thusly: "That man who would be able to overcome our strength has neither been born into the light nor walked under the sun. Our business is to conquer foreign lands, and we will give in captivity none of our own to anybody as long as sword and strength remain in this world." Despite the Croats having killed the Avar ambassadors after giving these magnanimous words, the king of the latter race left these brave men alone.

Having established themselves, by the invitation of the Byzantines, along the coast of the Black Sea, the Avars soon started to make war with the very same Byzantines. In 626, along with the Persians and the help of Slavs from the Russian Land, they even laid siege to Constantinople; moreover, one part of the Slavic army went by land, and the other on innumerable logboats that were set up to attack the capital by sea at a given sign. But the Byzantines, discovering this plan in time, anticipated their enemies and, going out on their boats, destroyed all the Slavic logboats, and among the dead and drowned soldiers, female corpses were also found.

The oncoming storm at that time also helped the Byzantines greatly. Somehow the surviving remnants of the Slavs made it down to the coast and gathered at the camp of the khagan, who was so angry at their failure that he ordered them all to be executed. When the Slavic land division, finding out about this affair, abandoned the khagan's army and went home, the khagan was also forced to withdraw from the city's siege.

---

manuscript, with its extremely curious drawings, smartly rendered by way of pen and water paints, and ordered exact replicas of them to be made from the manuscript.

Our famous researcher of ancient Russian art, Nikodim Pavlovich Kondakov, says that the *Radziwiłł Chronicle* is worthy of the utmost attention because it presents, by all appearances, a snapshot or a rendering of the most ancient historical records, perhaps from the end of the thirteenth century, and is extremely valuable in view of the fact that its engravings provide images of the clothing, weapons, household items, and general everyday life of the Russian people at that time.

A detailed description of the *Radziwiłł Chronicle* from our oldest academics Aleksey Aleksandrovich Shakhmatov and Nikodim Pavlovich Kondakov can be found attached to an accurate reproduction of the chronicle by the Society of Lovers of Ancient Literature. *The Story of the Russian Land* has been provided with innumerable snapshots of these highly distinctive drawings of the *Radziwiłł Chronicle* that stand out sharply from all other engravings.

The sudden storm, helping the Byzantines to destroy the Slavic log-boats, and the unreasoned anger of the khagan, as a result of which he lost his allies and had to pull back, were celebrated by the inhabitants of Constantinople as sacred and miraculous, having been caused by the interces-sion of the Theotokos,[35] since the Slavic logboats were destroyed within view of the Church of Saint Mary of Blachernae. Since this intercession oc-curred at a time of imminent doom, a special service in memory of the The-otokos was introduced: the Akathist, which means in Greek "not seated" or "not surrendered," performed by chanting a church hymn all night without sitting; since then, during all-night vigils, the hymn "To Thee, the Cham-pion Leader," in which the evil is meant to be our Slavic ancestors, is sung.[36]

This Avar campaign against the Byzantines was the last. Since that time, little by little, the name of the Avars completely disappeared and was replaced with the name Khazars because a great deal of Jews, who were the most businesslike and industrious—having dealings with foreign tribes, from the people who lived at the mouth of the Volga and along the Black Sea—had penetrated the martial environment of the Avars very quickly. At this time, as a pure warrior nation, the Avars were growing in strength and glory, ruining and conquering the Slavs, who were divided by strife. Jews quickly gained more power for themselves, getting their hands on the most valuable markets, which had belonged to our ancestors before the Avar in-vasion, for our ancestors were not only outstanding warriors but also re-spected merchants.

Russia During the Time of the Khazar Yoke

Having taken control of all the commerce in the region, Jews, due to their resourcefulness and by purely peaceful means, quickly took into their tenacious hands total power over the Avars' assets. These assets would soon come to be known under the name of the state of Khazaria, where the estate was transferred to the Jews.

The capital of Khazaria was originally on the Caspian, nicknamed the

---

[35] Theotokos is the Greek name for the Mother of God, literally God-bearer. Also known as Mary, the Blessed Virgin, the Holy Mother, and the Queen of Heaven.

[36] This hymn, known as a kontakion, is still sung in the Orthodox Church: "To thee, the Champion Leader, do I offer thanks of victory, O Theotokos, thou who hast delivered me from terror; but as thou that hast that power invincible, O Theotokos, thou alone can set me free: from all forms of danger free me and deliver me, that I may cry unto thee: 'Hail, O Bride without Bridegroom.'"

Khazar Sea, where the modern village of Tarki stands. Then it was moved to the city of Atil, just below the modern city of Astrakhan, when the Arabs pushed them into the Caucasus to the mouth of the Volga.

In principle, the Khazar state was ruled by an autocratic king—the khagan, or khakan—of Jewish origin and faith. He lived separately from his court and war retinue and rarely showed himself before his people. The power of the khagan was such that if he ordered any of the nobles: "Go die," they would invariably obey his command and kill themselves. Below the khagan was a lesser king—the viceroy of Khazaria, also a Jew. Although this king was also in charge of all affairs, he was obliged to go to the khagan barefoot, holding a matchstick of wood, which he would immediately set alight. Khazaria extended its dominion over all of the southern and central areas of modern-day Russia, and the entire population of Slavs who farmed was obliged to pay tribute to it.

The Byzantines consistently kept the closest friendship with them. Byzantine emperors even took kinship with them, daring to give their daughters away to them in marriage, even marrying Khazars themselves, if only to curb or eliminate, with marriage ties and friendship, the dangers perpetually posed to them by the Slavic bands on the lower reaches of the Dnieper and Don. Avars were called upon for this purpose, and to this end, the proud Byzantine emperors did not shy away from arranging marriages with the Khazar khagans.

In this way, there was an extended peace all along the Russian coast of the Black Sea, which was only possible, however, through the treacherous conduct of the Byzantine emperors, always inciting one of their enemies against another, and now finding their allies, the Khazars, guardians of their peace.

But of course, the magnificent successes of the Byzantine emperor's secret pursuits, more than that of any Avars or Khazars, contributed to the disenfranchisement of those Slavs whose passion for strife not only Herodotus told of but also many writers after him.

It took as long as two hundred years for our ancestors to regain their former strength and again go to work not only as traders but as warriors.

What then happened in the land of Russia during these two hundred years? The Arabian writers give us information about this, as does the *Primary Chronicle*.

The Arabs were semi-nomadic, having come from the line of Shem. They lived in separate tribes and settled along the Arabian Peninsula in Asia from antiquity.

In 571, a well-known man named Muhammad was born to the Arabs. From a young age, he stood out for his great aversion to the coarse idolatry to which his compatriots were beholden. Traveling alone on business to Syria, Muhammad met the Christian monk George, who began evangelizing to him. Muhammad did not convert to Christianity, but the studies of the One Omnipotent Christian God affected him deeply, and his aversion toward idolatry was strengthened. Having then married a rich widow whose merchant he had been, Muhammad worked as a trader and gained his fellow tribesmen's respect with honesty and righteousness. At the same time, he never stopped engaging himself in divine contemplation. In the end, he decided to found a new religion, putting his One God forward principally and announcing himself as his prophet.

At first, Muhammad's preaching was unsuccessful. He was even ridiculed, but little by little, all the Arabs, having no sympathy for idolatry, started to rally around him, all the more because Muhammad preached strict honesty, generosity, and courage, as well as permitting polygamy, and promising all who were fallen into fear of their enemies and war eternal bliss in the next world with the most beautiful women in a special heaven.

Since the Arabs are known for being the noblest of all the descendants of Shem and for their warlike nature, the teachings of Muhammad became more oriented toward the soul. As a result, many Arab tribes who were living scattered all over began to unite around him, and then, through them, his teachings were spread further by the power of the sword. Having quickly secured a few major victories, by the end of his life, Muhammad had become a terrible conqueror and ruler of almost all of Arabia; his tomb in the city of Medina is considered sacred by all Muslims in contemporary times and attracts huge numbers of pilgrims every year, as well as the ancient temple of the Kaaba in Mecca.

Muhammad's successors, called caliphs, merged into a supreme dominion as spiritual as it was warlike; under the first caliphs, the union of tribes subjugated by the Arabs and taken in by Islam happened very quickly, and soon the Arab army would conquer the former Kingdom of Persia, where they would build on the site of ancient Babylon a new and magnificent capital, Baghdad. They then expanded their domain even further, preaching Islam everywhere. Then, moving westward, the Arabs conquered Egypt and the whole northern coast of Africa and finally ferried themselves into Europe and conquered Spain for a few centuries.

In the east, they took over the entire Transcaucasian region and the coast of the Caspian Sea. Here, in the Caucasus, they clashed with the Khazars and pushed them out; as a result of which, the Khazars, as has been said before, transferred their capital from Tarki to Atil at the mouth of the Volga.

In addition to being formidable warriors, the Arabs were outstanding merchants. They quickly established trade connections with the Khazars, and a great number of them always lived in the Khazar capital of Atil. They then went up the Volga for trade and, in the middle of the ninth century, reached as far as Cuman Bulgaria, where the Cuman Bulgar tribe, of Turko-Finnic origin, lived, completely different from the Danube Bulgars. The Arabs propagated Islam among the Cuman Bulgars and, traveling up to them for furs, would encounter Russian merchants frequently. Arab coins—*dir-hams*—are still found quite frequently during archaeological excavations in many areas of the Russian Land; in addition, many purely Arabic words have survived in the Russian language: *grad*, *dyak*, *syn*, *tur*, *potok*, and others.

From the descriptions of a few Arabic trade writers of their encounters with Russians, we can get an idea of how our ancestors lived in that sorrow-ful time when a large part of the Russian Land was under Khazar rule and paying them tribute.

It turns out that despite this terrible humiliation, our ancestors were held in high esteem by the Arabs.

As one Arab writer says:

The Rus' people have a large number of cities and live in content-ment out in the open. They adore lavishness when it comes to clothing; even the men wear golden bangles on their wrists. They must care about their clothes because they are traders, and they wear large trousers, which they roll up to the knees. Some of the Rus' shave their beards, and others braid them into horse-like ma-nes and dye them blonde or black. The Rus' show honor to their guests and treat strangers well; they receive visitors often, and they allow none among them to offend, harm, or harass those people who seek their protection. If it should happen that one of them should seek to harm or oppress a visitor, they will give aid to the latter and defend them.

When a son is born to the Rus', the father of the newborn lays a naked sword before the child and says: "I will not leave you any sort of property. You will have only that which you acquire for yourself with this sword."

When one of them has business in conflict with another, they are called to trial with an overseer, before whom they present arguments; when the overseer decides the verdict, then what he says is fulfilled; if one of the involved parties is not pleased with the overseer's decision, then by his order they resolve the matter with arms; whosever sword is the sharpest prevails. The relatives of both parties involved will come to witness this fight. Then the contenders engage in their combat, and the victor can claim whatever he wants from the defeated.

When one of their kindred asks for help, everyone comes together to help as one unit, not divided into separate sections, and fight with the enemy in closed ranks until he is defeated.

The Rus' are manly and courageous. When they go to war with other people, they hold nothing back, yet they do not destroy them completely. They grow tall in stature, beautiful, and they are daring in their raids.

At the same time as this, the Arab writer Achmed al-Katib, who lived in what is now Spain, wrote of a long journey undertaken in 844 on small ships with "infidels known as Rus'" into far-off Išbīliya (modern Seville), which they had conquered.[37]

According to the accounts of the Arabs, the Rus' loved their wives very much and expended all their strength to obtain the most expensive jewelry for them. Especially valuable were necklaces with gold beads, purchased at a high price from the Arabs, and gold and silver chain necklaces. Nobody was considered wealthier than that man who could drape the greatest number of such chains around his wife's neck.

In return, wives would render the utmost fealty to their husbands, and following the example of the wives of our Scythian ancestors, often would accept death along with their husbands.

The funeral rites of the Rus' at that time consisted of burial under a mound, as in Scythian times, and cremation. In both circumstances,

---

[37] Note that these raiders of Seville were more likely Vikings from western Scandinavia, than the Varangians from eastern Scandinavia and the Baltic shores who settled in Eastern Europe, though the distinction between these groups is debatable. On page 79, Nechvolodov explains how these Varangians founded the Rus' States among the Slavs, giving them the name Rus' in 862. So, in 844, Rus' refers not to the Slavs of Eastern Europe, descendants of the Scythians, but to the Vikings/Varangians, both of whom Nechvolodov credits as ancestors of the modern Russians.

however, many fewer people were sent to the next world with the dead than in the time of Herodotus. Usually, only the wives or a few of the closest servants would be sacrificed, and certainly willingly, as well as horses and cattle.

"Their women," said a then-contemporary Arab merchant by the name of al-Masudi of the Rus', "desire to burn themselves to get into paradise alongside their husbands."

This devotion of the Slavic women to their husbands is confirmed in their records as well as by the Byzantine Emperor Maurice, who said:

> [The Slavs] observe chastity, and their women are strongly attached to their husbands, so that many of them, when they lose their husbands, seek consolation in death, and so they kill themselves, not wishing to endure the life of a widow.

If a Rus' from this time should die a bachelor, then he would ordinarily be wed posthumously, and his newlywed bride would cast herself into the fire along with the body of her deceased betrothed.

Here is how the Arab writer Ahmad ibn Fadlan described the Russian people as well as the marriage rites and cremation of their departed after death:

> [77] They disembark as soon as their boats dock. Each carries bread, meat, onions, milk, and alcohol to a large block of wood set in the ground. The piece of wood has a face on it, like the face of a man. It is surrounded by small figurines placed in front of large blocks of wood set in the ground. He prostrates himself before the large figure and says, "Lord, I have come from a distant land, with such and such a number of female slaves and such and such a number of sable pelts." He lists all his merchandise. Then he says, "And I have brought this offering." He leaves his offering in front of the piece of wood, saying, "I want you to bless me with a rich merchant with many dinars and dirhams who will buy from me whatever I wish and not haggle over any price I set." Then he leaves. . . .
>
> [80] I was told that they set fire to their chieftains when they die. Sometimes they do more, so I was very keen to verify this. Then I learned of the death of an important man. They had placed him in his grave, with a roof raised over him, for ten days while they finished cutting and sewing his garments. When the deceased is poor,

they build a small boat for him, place him inside and burn it. When he is rich, they collect his possessions and divide them into three portions. One-third goes to his household, one-third is spent on his funeral garments, and one-third is spent on the alcohol they drink the day his female slave kills herself and is cremated with her master. They are addicted to alcohol. They drink it night and day. Sometimes one of them dies cup in hand. When the chieftain dies, the members of his household ask his female and male slaves, "Who will die with him?" One answers, "I will." At this point the words become binding. There is no turning back. It is not even an option. It is usually the female slaves who offer.

[81] When the man I just mentioned died, they said to his female slaves, "Who will die with him?" One said, "I will." So they put two other female slaves in charge of her, caring for her and accompanying her wherever she went, even to the point of washing her feet with their hands. Then they attended to the chieftain, cutting his garments and setting in order what was required for him. The female slave drank alcohol every day and sang merrily and cheerfully.

[82] I arrived at the river where his boat was moored on the day the chief and the female slave were set on fire. I noticed that the boat had been beached and that it was supported by four *khadhank* props. These props were surrounded by what looked like huge structures of wood. The boat had been hauled on top of the wood. The Rūsiyyah approached, going to and fro around the boat uttering words I did not understand. The chief was still in his grave and had not been exhumed. They produced a couch and placed it on the boat, covering it with quilts and cushions made of Byzantine silk brocade. An aged woman whom they called the Angel of Death turned up. She spread the coverings on the couch. It is her responsibility to sew the chieftain's garments and prepare him properly, and it is she who kills the female slaves. I saw her myself: she was gloomy and corpulent but neither young nor old.

[83] When they arrived at his grave, they removed the soil from the wood. Then they removed the wood and exhumed him, dressed in the garment he was wearing when he died. I noticed that the coldness of the climate had turned him black. They had placed alcohol, fruit, and a *ṭanbūr* in his grave. They removed all of this. Sur-

prisingly, his corpse had not begun to stink. Only his color had de-
teriorated. They dressed him in trousers, leggings, boots, a tunic,
and a silk caftan with gold buttons. They placed a peaked silk cap
fringed with sable on his head. They carried him inside the yurt
that was on the ship and rested him on a quilt, propping him up
with the cushions. They placed the alcohol, fruit, and basil beside
him. Then they placed bread, meat, and onions in front of him.
They cut a dog in two and threw it onto the boat. They placed all his
weaponry beside him. They made two horses gallop into a sweat,
cut them into pieces with a sword, and threw the meat onto the
boat. They cut two cows into pieces and threw them on board. Then
they produced a cock and a hen, killed them, and put them on board
too.

[84] Meanwhile, the female slave who had expressed her wish
to die came and went, entering one yurt after another. The owner
of the yurt would have intercourse with her and say, "Tell your
master that I have done this out of love for you." At the time of the
Friday late afternoon prayer they brought the female slave to an
object they had built that resembled a door-frame. She stood on the
hands of the men and rose like the sun above the door-frame. She
uttered some words, and they brought her down. They lifted her up
a second time, and she did what she had done before. They lowered
her and lifted her a third time, and she did what she had done the
last two times. Then they handed her a hen. She cut off the head
and cast it aside. They picked the hen up and threw it onto the boat.
I quizzed the interpreter about her actions and he said, "The first
time they lifted her up, she said, 'Look, I see my father and mother.'
The second time she said, 'Look, I see all my dead kindred, seated.'
The third time she said, 'Look, I see my master, seated in the Garden. The Garden is beautiful and dark-green. He is with his men
and his retainers. He summons me. Go to him.'" They took her to
the boat and she removed both of her bracelets, handing them to
the woman called the Angel of Death, the one who would kill her.
She also removed two anklets she was wearing, handing them to
the two female slaves who had waited upon her, the daughters of
the woman known as the Angel of Death.

[85] They lifted her onto the boat but did not take her into the
yurt. The men approached with shields and sticks and handed her

a cup of alcohol. Before drinking it she chanted over it. The interpreter said to me, "Now she bids her female companions farewell."
She was handed another cup which she took and chanted for a long
time. The crone urged her to drink it and to enter the yurt where
her master was lying. I could see she was befuddled. She went to
enter the yurt but missed it, placing her head to one side of the yurt,
between it and the boat. The crone took hold of her head and entered the yurt with her. The men began to bang their shields with
the sticks, so that the sound of her screaming would be drowned
out. Otherwise, it would terrify the other female slaves, and they
would not seek to die with their masters.

[86] Six men entered the yurt. They all had intercourse with the
female slave and then laid her beside her master. Two held her feet,
two her hands. The crone called the Angel of Death placed a rope
around her neck with the ends crossing one another and handed it
to two of the men to pull on. She advanced with a broad-bladed
dagger and began to thrust it in between her ribs, here and there,
while the two men strangled her with the rope until she died.

[87] The deceased's nearest male relative came forward. He
picked up a piece of wood and set it alight. He was completely naked. He walked backwards, the nape of his neck towards the boat,
his face towards the people. He had the ignited piece of wood in one
hand and had his other hand on his anus. He set fire to the wooden
structures under the boat. The people came forward with sticks and
firewood. They each carried a lighted stick that they threw on top
of the wood. The wood caught fire. Then the boat, the yurt, the dead
man, the female slave, and everything else on board caught fire. A
fearsome wind picked up. The flames grew higher and higher and
blazed fiercely.

[88] One of the Rūsiyyah was standing beside me. I heard him
speaking to the interpreter who was with me. I asked him what he
had said, and he replied, "He said, 'You Arabs, you are a lot of
fools!'" "Why is that?" "Because you purposefully take your nearest and dearest and those whom you hold in the highest esteem and
put them in the ground, where they are eaten by vermin and
worms. We, on the other hand, cremate them there and then, so
that they enter the Garden on the spot." I asked about this and he
said, "My lord feels such great love for him that he has sent the
wind to take him away within an hour." In fact, it took scarcely an

hour for the boat, the firewood, the female slave, and her master to be burnt to ash and then to very fine ash.[38]

Thus did the Arabs, visiting our country as traders, write of the morals and customs of Rus' in the middle of the ninth century.

The Mission of the Slavic Principalities

From the aforementioned stories, we see that the ways of our ancestors were already a little softer than they had been in the time of the Scythians but nevertheless remained quite pagan and, just as before, were deemed to be idolatrous.

Perun, the omnipotent ancient Aryan god of thunder, was an important god depicted in idols. The next most revered god was Veles, or Volos, the god of cattle and household wealth and fortune; after him came Lado, the god of fun, love, and merriment; Yarilo, the god of fertility; Kupala, the god of the fruits of the Earth; and a few others. In addition to these principal or general gods, the Rus' also believed in lesser or household gods, boggarts, water sprites, goblins who lived in the forest, mermaids, nightmare spirits, and other evil spirits.

Our ancient pagan ancestors had no temples. Where they erected idols to their great gods were called *kapishcha*; they placed these idols on stone bases, bedrock, or logs. They also performed sacrifices here, typically offering fruit, vegetables, and cattle. Human victims at this time were rarely offered. There was no special class of clergy or a priesthood since offerings would be made by everyone for themselves or for their family or clan, but there was a great deal of *volkhvy* (magi) as well as *kudesniki* (wizards), whom people liked to consult for advice or premonitions.

In addition to the stories of the Arabs about living conditions in the Russian Land in the mid-ninth century, we also have stories of these times in the *Primary Chronicle*. It begins by telling of the resettlement of the country, coming from the line of Japheth. From this narrative, it is clear that in the middle of the ninth century, the following Slavic tribes settled in the Russian Land: along the Dnieper at Kiev and under the Khazar yoke there were the Polans; above them, further up the Dnieper, where the wide Russian plains, coming from the Black Sea, are replaced by the mighty Russian forest, lived the Drevlians, so called because they lived in the Polesia woods

---

[38] Ibn Fadlan, *Mission to the Volga*, §77, 80–8.

among the trees; south of the Drevlians, along the Pripyat River, there lived the Dregovich tribe; east of the Dregoviches, on the Sozh River, were the Radimichs; further east, along the rivers Seym and Desna, lived the Severians. On the Polota River, a tributary of the Western Dvina, and both upstream and downstream of the latter, the Polotskians. On an elevated point in the Volkovsky Forest, from whence all the Great Russian rivers first sprang, the Krivich tribe settled, so-called for the great curvature of the rivers on which they lived.

East of the Krivichs, along the Oka River, the Vyatichi people settled, and to the south of the Krivichs, around Lake Ilmen, in the contemporary region of Novgorod, were the Ilmen Slavs.

Finally, on the Western Bug, lived the Buzhanians, or Volhynians; between the Southern Bug and the Dniester, the Tivertsi; and at the mouth of the same Dniester, the Ulichs.

Thus are the names of the Slavic tribes who inhabited the Russian Land in the ninth century after the Nativity of Christ.

All these tribes, like their ancient Aryan ancestors, lived a tribal family life and retained all their everyday customs: each person would obey the elders of their clan, and the whole clan would protect every kinsman that belonged to it, and for an offense, each one was entitled to blood vengeance exacted by the whole clan.

A person with no heritage would be considered an orphan and occupy a wretched station among the people he lived with.

The majority of Slavs, as most people, occupied their time with the activities of an agrarian economy. They lived in villages; a few villages of one clan or tribe constituted an *obolost* or *volost* (modern oblast). In such regions, the power belonged to the patriarchs, the chieftains (knyazes). These patriarchs would often live in towns or cities. Warriors who were in the chieftains' bands, as well as manufacturers, artisans, and merchants, also lived in them. In a few cities that were important centers of trade, the place where many different types of people from all regions would meet with the chieftains to make decisions about common affairs was called the *vyche*; it was a meeting of elected people from the city. Towns would sometimes be cut out here and there when our ancestors were expanding into areas inhabited by indigenous tribes, mostly sections of Finnic tribes inhabiting the north and east of the Russian Land. In light of this, the towns erected fortresses where sieges would occasionally be sat out and withstood until help arrived.

The most popular cities of the ninth century were the following: La-doga, on Lake Ladoga; Izborsk, on Lake Pihkva; and soon nearby, Pskov was founded; then Novgorod on Lake Ilmen; Smolensk on the upper reaches of the Dnieper; Polotsk on the Polota River; Chernigov on the Desna River, a tributary of the Dnieper; and on the Dnieper itself, Liubech; and then Kiev, the place where the Holy Apostle Andrew the First-Called raised the cross.

Finally, the Slavs had their cities, and among the Finnic tribes in the East: Beloozero among the Vepsians; Rostov among the Meryans; and Murom, among the Muromians, Meshchera, and Mordvins.

Thus are the most important ancient cities of the Russian Land.

In general, there were many cities in the Russian Land at that time, which is why the Swedes called it Gardariki, or "land of cities."

There are two legends about the construction of the city of Kiev: accord-ing to one, it was built by three brothers—Kyi, Khoryv, and Shchek—who lived with their sister Lybid in the mountains neighboring Kiev; and the other legend states that at some point, there was a ferry there across the Dnieper and the ferryman was someone named Kyi, which is why people also would say let's take Kiev's ferry, from which the name Kiev came.

The majority of cities were, of course, located in places where one could smartly do business.

In this respect, the first place belonged to Kiev, followed by Novgorod.

Directly through these cities, there came to be the great aquatic route from Scandinavia to the Byzantine Empire (the Varangian trade route),[39] along which the majority of important trade was conducted among the tribes who lived on the Baltic shore, the Varangians, with far-off Constan-tinople. The Varangian trade route went from the Baltic Sea through to the Neva River on Lake Ladoga (or Lake Neva), along the Volkhov River into Lake Ilmen, and from there up the Lovat until her source in Volkovsky For-est; here, they would *drag* everything across the land into the upper reaches of the Dnieper and descend into the Black Sea.

Many goods passed along this route: from Scandinavia, there came cloth, linen, canvas, copper and gold crafts, tin, lead, and precious amber; in addition to this, they moved a huge amount of salted herring; as in the

---

[39] Nechvolodov refers to this trade route as from "Varangia to Greece." "Varangia" includes the various lands inhabited by the Varangians along the Baltic shore and Scandinavia, but there was no state called Varangia. Specifically, the trade route began in the Scandinavian trading centers of Birka, Hedeby, and Gotland. Regarding "to Greece," while some refer to the Byzantine Empire as Greece, the former is preferred in modern scholarship. After this occurrence, the name of the route is simplified as "the Varangian trade route."

days of Herodotus, the Russian Land traded in bread, precious furs, honey, wood, tallow, cattle, boats, and slaves. For the most part, from Constantinople there came *pavoloki,* which is what they called Byzantine silk fabric with or without gold embroidery; pavoloki were moved in large numbers, not only into the Russian Land, but also into Scandinavia, and without fail, every wealthy person would make themselves clothes from pavoloki. The Byzantines also traded in various gold and silver accessories and jewelry for both men and women: earrings, necklaces, bracelets, bangles, brooches, wedding bands, rings, pendants, and buttons; finally, from Constantinople there also came woven wrought iron lace for the trimming of clothing as well as the fruits and wines of various southern countries.

Along this Varangian trade route there also came goods from far-off Permian lands—gemstones and rare furs—as well as goods from Kapsas, carpets from Babylon, Indian fabrics with exotic patterns, beads, baubles, spices, and incense from Arabia.

In the Russian Land, money at that time was leather: snouts (marten snouts); cuts (segments), and feet (squirrel legs and ears with silver studs— the expression "half an ear" also comes from this since it's half a squirrel's ear). This leather money ended up not only in the Russian Land but also in Italy, France, and the East. In addition to leather money, both raw silver, as well as neck grivnas, were also used, each of which would be weighed by the pound.

Finally, coins of various states served as money for trade in the Russian Land at that time as well, more so in transactions with Byzantines and Arabs.

Trade on the Varangian route would begin in the spring on the thawed rivers and would cease in the autumn when the frost came. Many merchants and various people involved in trade lived along the entire route, with most of them centered in Novgorod and especially Kiev. At the same time as well, on the entire Dnieper, there was no place more pleasant and at ease than Kiev, especially for starting a business as a merchant, woodsman, fisherman, etc. It offered all types of defenses against enemy ambushes and gave every means of escaping from danger in time while simultaneously leaving itself open to every way of providing food for itself. Moreover, a caravan of ships had been exclusively set up for shipments between Constantinople; here, they were outfitted with goods consisting of items from all the various nations with which they had dealings. They also recruited fighters here as security for the ships in order not to embark into the far-off southern steppes with no defense against their predatorial inhabitants. Finally, they would also hire experienced helmsmen here to guide the ships through the dangerous rapids of the southern Dnieper. Thus, in Kiev, along with its Slavic population, there always lived many other peoples: Byzantines, Varangians, Polans, and Jews; the latter not only did business there but were also representatives of the Khazarian khagan at the previously described time, as well as bureaucrats and collectors of tribute from the local inhabitants. Because the majority of the people who lived there belonged to different groups, entire districts of the city of Kiev bore the name of the group of their inhabitants, thus: the Khazars lived in Kozar, Polans in the Lyadsky (Lach) Gates, and the Jews in Judea.

Our ancestors considered the practice of trade to be a very important business and a major affair in life. Merchants, or "guests" as they were called then, were always highly valued and honored people wherever they went. They not only had to know the conditions of life in the lands in which they did business but also had to have more than a little courage, as well as some skill in the art of combat, because it wasn't at all rare for wandering merchants to have to withstand skirmishes with bandits or wild natives. The greatest fame as sailors and respected traders was enjoyed at that time by Varangian merchants, residing predominantly among Slavic tribes situated along the southern coast of the Baltic Sea; they would, however, make daring voyages through the same far-off lands and seas without lagging behind them or other merchants native to the countryside of the Russian Land. They would also bravely embark on their logboats along the rivers of our northern and eastern lands into their very edges and would come as far as the northern Ural region and the town of Ugra, where a peculiar sort of voiceless trade would happen: when Slavic traders went into their land, they would lay out their goods in an appointed place, put notes on them, and leave; upon their leaving, locals would come and lay out their goods next to those of the Slavs, mostly furs; then the traders would come back and take what they wanted and leave their goods if they thought the item they took was of equivalent value; whoever did not consider the price suitable would take nothing until they agreed with the natives on the price.

The old custom of showing our guest traders back to their homeland so that they wouldn't be hurt shows how much we valued them; moreover, the patriarchs and chieftains not only outfitted guards for the protection of guest merchants, but would see of the merchant caravans themselves along with their bands along the Varangian trade route, when they went along the Dnieper and returned later.

This was a constant effort of the patriarchs and chieftains in the spring and summer months until the weather prevented shipping on the river routes. As soon as the rivers turned to ice in the fall and the winter, they would set out on special winter excursions that were called *poliudie* in the regions that were under their control. Here they would collect tribute, trade in boats, hunt, as well as conduct their own business of the sort that occurred in winter.

Thus did our ancestors live in the mid-ninth century, when the Khazar yoke hung over us. This yoke, as we have seen, was not especially cruel; our customs and lifestyles remained more or less the same as they had always been since the times of the ancient Slavs. Subservience to the Khazars also chiefly amounted simply to paying a tribute. But it was nevertheless a rather humiliating subservience. Given the compromised position of our ancestors in the time of the Khazars thus described, other nations also treated us with disdain. Our guest merchants were constantly ill-treated in Constantinople: robbed, insulted, ripped off, and sometimes not even allowed into the city, occasionally driven out entirely, and subjected to all sorts of hardships since people knew that nobody would ever intervene on their behalf. In the northern region of Ilmensky as well, the numerous warlike inhabitants of the Varangian (Baltic) Sea also would sometimes impose a tax on one of the various Slavic tribes who lived there.

Our lords, the Khazars, were the least powerful in these times; they strongly feared their tributaries, the Russian Slavs, and for their defense in the event of their being invaded, in 834 in the place on the Don where it comes closest to the Volga, the Khazar khagan built the stone fortress Sarkel or the Belaya Vezha (White Tower).

When the Polans living on the Dnieper once gave the Khazars as tribute a sword from each of their smelting fires, the Khazars took this new tribute to their elders, who thought about it arduously and then said to their chieftain: "Sir, the tribute is not good ... for we have weapons that are sharp on one side"—that is, sabers—"yet these weapons are sharp on both; these are swords. They shall exact tribute from us and other lands."

And, of course, to this end, it was necessary that the mighty tribes living all across the Russian Land should come together into one united and indestructible whole.

Finally, this highly significant junction in the life of our nation was realized.

In 862, the Ilmen Slavs drove away some overseas Varangians who had exacted tribute from them for three years. Then they began self-governance and recommended the custom of Slavic inner strife, rising up clan by clan, "and they began," says the *Primary Chronicle*, "to war one against an-other."[40]

This time however, they soon realized that this was no way to live, and not seeing an end to the strife, they decided to ally themselves with the foreign tribes to find a prince who would rule over them and lead them justly.

Thus, the Ilmen Slavs, the Krivichs, and the Finnic tribe they ruled—the Chuds—went to the Varangians, the Rus' people with whom they had constant dealings, and said, "Our land is great and rich, but there is no order in it. Come to rule and reign over us." (*RPC*, 59)

And three brothers set off with each of their families and tribes and settled: the eldest Rurik in Novgorod, the other Sineus in Beloozero, and the third Truvor in Izborsk. It is impossible to know exactly where the tribe that would later become our nation, the Rus', first settled. Some believe it was Sweden, others that it was among the settlers of Lithuania, but above all, there is reason to believe that our ancestors who called themselves a Slavic tribe settled on the banks of the Varangian (Baltic) Sea, maybe on the island of Rugii, or Russi, like the name of that familiar tribe of kindred spirit, custom, and language.[41]

It is supposed that this invitation of the princes was the beginning of the Rus' States.

---

[40] *Russian Primary Chronicle*, 59. Future instances of this source are abbreviated and in-text.

[41] While the term Varangian may refer to Scandinavians or Vikings generally, in this instance, Nechvolodov refers to the specific Varangian Rus'. From *RPC*, 59: "These particular Varangians were known as Russes, just as some are called Swedes, and others Normans, English, and Gotlanders, for they were thus named."

Figures for Chapter Two

40: *The Passion Road*, mural in the Kiev Monastery of the Caves.

41: (Left) Dacians attacking a Roman stronghold, from Trajan's column.
42: (Right) Dacians crossing a river.

43: (Left) The Dacian leaders choose to poison themselves.
44: (Right) The meeting of the Dacian leaders;
one of them thrusts a dagger into himself.

45: Alexander chasing Darius, from a rare Byzantine manuscript from the tenth or
eleventh century in the wooden cathedral of Saint Mark in Venice.

46: Alexander the Great bowing before the grave of Achilles, from an
eighteenth-century French copper carving. From the collection of
paintings of a former Polish king in the Imperial Academy of Arts.

47: The demise of Darious, battered by Alexander at the Battle of Arbela,
from *Of Alexander*, a Russian mural of the seventeenth century,
preserved in the Moscow State Historical Museum.

48: Illustration of Alexander the Great on a badly damaged wall
in one of the houses in the city of Pompeii, which was
destroyed by the volcanic eruption of Mt. Vesuvius in AD 79.

49: (Left) A silver coin with an illustration of Alexander the Great.
50: (Center and Right) Two coins with an illustration of Mithridates the Great.

51: Sarmatian from Trajan's Column

52: (Left) The hoisting of the cross carried to the Kievan mountains by
the Apostle Andrew, painting in the Kiev Monastery of the Caves
53: (Right) An image of the remains of a Christian church in Kherson Tavriisk
(Korsun) unearthed by the excavations of Count A. S. Uvarov.

54: (Left) Saint Clement, the Roman Bishop from Likhachyov,
Materials for a History of Russian Icon Painting.
55: (Right) *View of the Colosseum, Rome*, a painting by the artist Fedor Matveev

56: A dying slave, murdered for the enjoyment of a
Roman crowd, a stone sculpture in Rome.

57: (Left) One of our ancestor's old warships, on which they would ride to
Constantinople, Athens, and Rome.   58: (Right) Saint Equal-to-the-Apostles,
Emperor Constantine, an ancient marble sculpture.

59: (Left) Saint Equal-to-the-Apostles, Empress Helen, from a Byzantine
manuscript of Saint's Lives of the ninth century of Saint Gregory
the Nazianzen, kept in the French National Library in Paris.
60: (Right) The Erection of the Prudent Life-giving Cross of Saint Equal-to-the-
Apostles Empress Helen, a mural in the Kiev Monastery of the Caves.

61: A depiction of Goths with the inscription "Of the Goths and their cruelty"
underneath it in Old French, from Münster, *Cosmographia*, 1550.

62: (Left) A depiction of Attila in from Münster, *Cosmographia*, 1550.
63: (Right) Honoria, bride of Attila, from an ancient seal.

64: Emperor Justinian with his retinue, from an
ancient image in the city of Ravenna.

65: "When it so happened that an Avar needed to go somewhere, he lashed neither
horses nor oxen to his cart, but rather our women in threes, fours, or fives, and
thus did he go wherever he needed," from the *Radziwiłł Chronicle*.

66: An image of the Church of Saint Mary of Blachernae, with the Byzantine Emperor Theophilus riding up to it, from a priceless fourteenth-century illustration by John Skylitzes; a large part of the drawing (done in watercolor) was famously loaned from the most ancient Byzantine collection and kept in the Spanish National Library in Madrid.

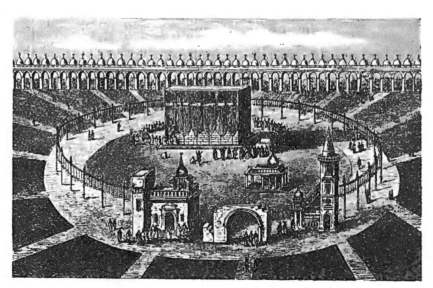

67: A highly significant Islamic holy site, the Kaaba in Mecca, as it looks now, a painting by Bukleya.

68: (Left) Illustration of a legal court procession in the city of Baghdad,
from an ancient Arabic illustration in the collection of G. M. Sheffer.
69: (Right) Preaching in a Baghdad mosque, same source

70: An Arab dirham, from the Russian treasury.

71: The old Arab quarter of the city of Seville, taken by Rus' in the year 844,
from an album of drawings belonging to the artist Meshchersky:
Travels in Spain, kept in the Imperial Academy of Arts.

72: *Funeral of a Rus' Nobleman*, a painting by Henryk Siemiradzki in the Moscow State Historical Museum.

73: *Enchantment of a Sword Before the Idols*, V. Ovsyannikov's illustration.

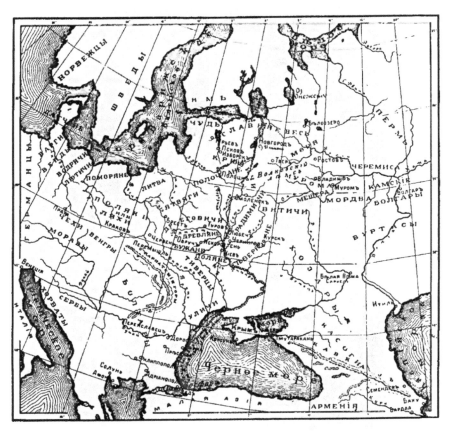

74: A map of the Russian Land in the ninth century.

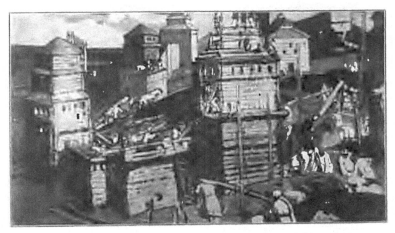

75: *The Construction of an Ancient Rus' City*, N. K. Roerich's painting.

76: Rapids of the Dnieper.

77: *The Calling of the Princes*, V. M. Vasnetsov's illustration.

78: The Destruction of Rurik's Fortress in Old Ladoga.

CHAPTER THREE

Origins of the Russian State: Cyril and Methodius, Educators of the Slavs

In the middle of the ninth century, around the approximate time when the most important event in the Russian Land occurred and initiated the transformation of life there from disjointed tribes into a Russian State, a few other significant developments took place that would subsequently have a great impact on Russian life.

One of the most important developments was the onset of Slavic literacy, thanks to the saintly brothers Equal-to-the-Apostles Cyril and Methodius, who were of Slavic origin. They were born to wealthy and aristocratic parents in the Byzantine city of Thessaloniki and, from their youth, were close with the family of the Byzantine emperors, who showed them great favor. They wanted to have Cyril marry into their family and Methodius to be appointed into a rather high office that would make him the ruler of a vast corner of the empire, but the saintly brothers voluntarily refused all honors and earthly blessings and took quite austere monastic rank, where-upon they worked hard and endured much while evangelizing to the Danube region and the Western Slavs. During the time of this service, Saint Cyril also developed Slavic literacy, which had such great significance for all the Slavic nations because they were given the ability to study Holy Scripture and establish worship in a language that was understandable to them; by the grace of a common script, all Slavs were better able to feel a brotherly connection, which united them among themselves and finally, thanks to literacy, the Slavs could chronicle the events of their lives in their native tongue, and also savor the fruits of literary illumination. Thus were the merits of Saints Cyril and Methodius. The Orthodox Church bestowed upon them the title of Equal-to-the-Apostles and celebrates their memory on April 6th, which is why Russian people continue to revere this day even into our time.

In the time of the saintly brothers' lives,[42] there happened an event of enormous significance: schism between the Catholic and Orthodox Churches.[43]

This happened because the bishops of the Roman Church—having gradually acquired immense power over their congregation, among which were the nations that had converted to Christianity: Spain, England, France, Germany, and Italy, and having also acquired significant land holdings in Russian territory—grew proud, and no longer desired to obey the synodical decrees of the entire bishopric which, as a rule, had been since the time of the Apostles. The Roman bishops, called popes, little by little became burdened by this. They began to argue that they should be supreme over all the bishopric, wherein they introduced a few unauthorized changes not only to the rites but also to the Articles of Faith, in which, contrary to the decrees of the Ecumenical Councils, they added that the Holy Spirit emanates not only from the Father but also from the Son. This all led to great disagreement within the Church, especially when Photios I, patriarch of Constantinople, appeared as a defender of apostolic tradition and sacredly guarded Orthodoxy, a man magnanimous and solid as a stone in matters of faith, and his opponent, the proud and power-hungry Roman pope Nicholas, who finally succeeded in separating from Orthodoxy and formed the self-installed Roman or Catholic Church, also called the Latin Church, because Catholics conduct worship in Latin, the language of Ancient Rome.

The schism of Catholics from Orthodoxy was a most adverse affair for all Slavs because a part of them had taken baptism under Orthodoxy, and the other under Catholicism; obviously, this strongly interfered and continues to interfere to this day in their harmonious unification, and has been the cause of many bloody wars.

Many Slavic nations had undergone the formation of states up until this time, as certain important events should indicate. The first Slavic state

---

[42] Saint Cyril lived from 826 to 869 and Saint Methodius from 815 to 885.

[43] Nechvolodov is not referring here to the Great Schism of 1054, where both Churches formally and finally excommunicated each other, but rather to an earlier schism occurring from 863 to 867, known as the Photian Schism, after which the Churches did reconcile nominally. Due to the use of Latin in the West and Greek in the East as well as largely political and cultural disagreements, discord between the Churches intensified over several centuries.

was the First Bulgarian Empire, formed around the year 650; it had subdued the neighboring Slavic tribes—the Serbs and Croats—and soon became a threat to the Byzantines. The capital of the Bulgarian Empire was
Preslav, near the fortress of Dorostopol (or Dorostolon). Oppressing the
Croats constantly, the Bulgars caused an insurrection among them, after
which, in around 750, the Croatians broke off and formed an independent
kingdom.

Next, the Czechs, after a long battle with the Arabs, who conquered
them, formed an independent government around the year 700, with Duke
Krok at the head of it. His successor was his respected daughter, Libuše,
founder of the city of Prague, who was hailed as prophetic for her wit. She
was distinguished for her extraordinary righteousness, for which, even until now, she is honored by the Czechs in the song "Libuše's Court." She chose
a simple peasant Přemysl as her husband, and from this union came the
first Czech princes.

In addition to the Czechs, the Moravians formed an independent kingdom for a short time, for it was soon destroyed by the Germanic peoples
and the Hungarians, a tribe from Asia.

Then in the year 960, the Lyashsky, or Polish tribes, also formed a state,
Poland, taking Siemowit as their king, who was also a son of a simple peasant by the name of Piast. Under the reign of Siemowit's heir, Mieszko I,[44]
the Poles took baptism from the Germans and the popes of Catholicism.

Not long before the formation of Poland, almost all the nations who
lived in the regions of France, Italy, and Germany were united into a vast
empire by Charlemagne. In the consolidation of his power, Charlemagne
started a terrible war with the mighty Slavic tribes who had settled on the
western section of the Baltic coast. These tribes unfortunately hadn't been
united into a single, solid state.

Upon his death, however, Charlemagne's empire was divided among
his three sons but, nevertheless, the business he had begun—namely, the
destruction of the Western Slavs who lived along the southern coast of the
Baltic Sea—was diligently taken up by the Germanic peoples.

In this way, we see that already by the mid-ninth century, almost no
scattered or divided tribes were living in Europe, and many consolidated
states were being formed.

---

[44] Mieszko I (c. 930–992) was the great-grandson of Siemowit (fl. 880s) according to modern
historians and is credited as the first ruler of Poland.

Rurik's Reign: Askold and Dir and Their Glorious Raid in Constantinople

During the two years after the invitation of the princes (862), Rurik's brothers, Sineus and Truvor, died. He overtook the monarchical leadership over the Novgorod Slavs, the Krivichs, and the Finnic tribes—the Vepsians, the Meryans, and the Muromians—planting in each city the stock of the old warriors who had come with him to the Russian Land.

Two men from this band who hadn't been given power in any city, Askold and Dir, beseeched Rurik to let them go seek their fortunes in Constantinople. Following the great Varangian trade route, they went along the Dnieper to Kiev.

Here, knowing that Kiev didn't have its own prince and was paying tribute to the Khazars, and having fallen in love with this lively and bountiful place, Askold and Dir decided to stay. Many Varangians had rallied around them, and they began to rule Kiev and all the land of Polesia; moreover, they freed them from their paying of tribute to Khazaria and successfully fought back bandits of the steppe and a few other neighboring tribes.

Four years later, Askold and Dir had already become so powerful that they were able to carry out the cherished desire of the Rus': to take revenge on the insidious and arrogant Byzantines for all the insults and humiliation that they had visited on our ancestors during the time of the Khazar yoke. By that time, it was considered appropriate for Byzantines in Constantinople even to kill small numbers of Rus' grain pickers for trivial reasons.

And thus, in 866, Askold and Dir decided to venture out on a daring foray into Constantinople, just as daredevils from the mouths of the Dnieper and Don would go in days of old. They gathered two hundred boats, longboats with masts and sails, outfitted each of them with forty to sixty men, and kept their passage over the Dnieper and Black Sea so secret that not even until their arrival at Constantinople did anyone suspect their attack.

Patriarch Photios I was in Constantinople and left a detailed account of the invasion.

According to his words, the Russian attack happened on the evening of one of the most beautiful summer days, by a rather calm sea. On this gorgeous summer evening, the citizens of Constantinople were admiring the beauty of their most beloved sea, not only from lofty chambers but from lowly huts as well; they admired it from their streets and squares, from innumerable gardens, and even from the walls of the city itself, which encircled it from all sides along the banks of the sea.

Emperor Michael III was absent along with his entire army because he was conducting a campaign against the Arabs, and the tranquil and carefree city expected nothing out of the ordinary when suddenly, from the Bosporus, some unrecognizable object emerged, which citizens soon discovered to be a large amount of Rus' ships. The whole city went mad with fear. Then, in a single voice, they all exclaimed: "What's this? What's this? The Rus' are floating closer and closer, casting a ferocious, wild, and deadly look on everyone; soon they shall step out onto the bank and menace the city, with their swords outstretched."

Photios says:

A gloom enveloped every trembling mind; tears and sobs spread out all over the city; the utmost despair overtook everyone; from all sides, only one message spread, one cry: "Barbarians have breached the walls! The city is overrun by the enemy!" The surprise of the disaster and inadvertence of the attack caused everyone to listen and focus on this one thing.

According to Photios' account, the Rus' attacked the city's outskirts from behind the city gates and ravaged them with fire and sword all the way to the inner citadel of Constantinople, located on a great hill that protrudes into the sea. They also decimated the marinas with fire and sword, having planned their destruction among themselves by lot.

This demonstrates that the Rus' planned the details of their attack very well; they arrived abruptly in the evening, during one of the emperor's military excursions, to strike an unsuspecting enemy and conceal their attack under cover of night to hide their small numbers; moreover, to ensure that there could be no mishaps, they determined by lot beforehand which of them would attack which parts of the city.

After the destruction of the marinas, the Rus' quickly surrounded the city walls and started to stack dirt next to them, intending to climb into the city. At this, "a cowardly shiver ran down everyone's spines and weakened even those who were disposed to such dangerous times," says Photios.

The nation, bereft of all help and defense, now thought only of prayer and crowded into the churches. Everywhere through the night, there was a vigil: with hands uplifted, they sent tearful and strenuous prayers begging for mercy. In general, misfortune makes one repent for their sins, come to their senses, and take up good deeds.

There was no hour more blessed than this for homilies and sermons about sin, repentance, and amending one's life with good deeds to be given to the people.

So Patriarch Photios began his sermon in the Hagia Sophia cathedral:

What is this? What is this grievous and heavy blow and wrath? Why has this dreadful bolt fallen on us out of the farthest north ... ? Why has this thick, sudden hail-storm of barbarians burst forth ... ? Is it not for our sins that all these things have come upon us? Are they not a condemnation and a public parading of our transgressions? Does not the terror of things present indicate the awful and inexorable judgment of the future ... ? From those who owed us small and trifling things we made relentless exaction; we chastised them. We forgot to be grateful when the benefit had gone by. Nor did we pity our neighbors because we had been pardoned ourselves.... Having been ourselves mercifully delivered from many great debts, we unmercifully enslaved others for little ones. We enjoyed ourselves, and grieved *others*; we were glorified, and dishonoured *others*; we grew strong and throve, while waxing inso-lent and foolish. We became fat, gross and thick.... Now you are weeping.... I too weep with you.... I do not see now any benefit even in the shedding of tears. For when before our eyes the enemy's swords are drenched in the blood of our fellow-countrymen, and we, as we behold this, do not take it upon ourselves to help, as we ought to, being at a loss what to do, but instead collapse in tears,— what kind of consolation is this for the victims ... ? Often have I admonished you: be on your guard, mend yourselves, convert yourselves; do not wait for the sword to be furbished: the bow is being bent (Ps. 7. 13.). Do not take *God's* long-suffering as an occa-sion for contempt; do not act wickedly in the face of His extreme gentleness....

Woe is me that I have been preserved to see these evils, that we have become a reproach to our neighbors ... that the unbelievable course of the barbarians did not give rumour time to announce it, so that some means of safety could be devised, but the sight accompanied the report, and that despite the distance, and the fact that the invaders were sundered off *from us* by so many lands and kingdoms, by navigable rivers and harbourless seas. Woe is me, that I see a fierce and savage tribe fearlessly poured round the city, ravaging the suburbs, destroying everything, ruining everything, fields, houses, herds, beasts of burden, women, children, old men, youths, thrusting their sword through everything, taking pity on nothing, sparing nothing. The destruction is universal. Like a locust ... or rather like a whirlwind, or a typhoon, or a torrent, or I know not what to say, it fell upon our land and has annihilated whole generations of inhabitants. ...

O queenly city, what a throng of evils has poured around thee. ... O city reigning over nearly the whole universe, what an uncaptained army, equipped in servile fashion, is sneering at thee as at a slave! O city adorned with the spoils of many nations, what a nation has bethought itself of despoiling thee! O thou who has erected many trophies over enemies in Europe, Asia and Libya, see how a barbarous and lowly hand has thrust its spear against thee, making bold to bear in triumph victory over thee! Everything with thee has come to such a pitch of misfortune, that thy unassailable strength has sunk to the dregs of extreme infirmity, and thy enemies, beholding thy infirmity and subjection, display the strength of their arm against thee, and try to bedeck themselves with a glorious name. O queen of queenly cities ... ! O me, holy shine of God and God's Wisdom (Hagia Sophia), sleepless eye of the universe! Wail ye virgins. ... Weep ye young men. ... Mourn ye also, mothers. Shed tears, ye babes. ... Shed tears, for our ills have been multiplied (I Macc. I. 9.), and there is none to deliver (Hos. 5. 14.), none to help.[45]

The patriarch finished his address to the people with a proclamation: "Finally, beloved ones, the time has come to have recourse to the Mother of the Word, our only hope and refuge. Imploring, let us cry out to her: save thy city, as thou knowest how, O Lady!"[46]

After this, at the confluence of the people trembling in fear, with the heated pleading for salvation, from the Church of Saint Mary of Blachernae, there was a vision of the veil of the Theotokos, which was followed in a holy procession around the walls of the city and was then immersed in the

---

[45] Photius, *Homilies*, "First Homily on the Attack of the Russians," 82–92.
[46] Ibid., 95.

water. [47]

And the Heavenly Queen heeded the prayers of her sinful yet repentant people. For the second time, just as had happened in 626 during the invasion of the Arabs and the Slavs, she bestowed her miraculous aid and sent certain destruction away from the city. [48]

The sight of an Orthodox religious procession, with the patriarchs and clergymen in full adornment, numerous banners, harmonious singing, and the miraculous veil floating in front—this extraordinary spectacle had quite the effect on the heathen Rus'; they were so frightened by it that as soon as they saw the approach of the procession, everywhere it went, they hastily abandoned the attack and ran away to their boats, after which they departed from the city.

Thus, by the intercession of the Theotokos, Constantinople was miraculously saved from total destruction. The Rus' returned home from their daring attack to Kiev with loud exaltation and rich treasures.

During the few days after the attack by the Rus', Photios again gathered his flock, and, having been blessed with holy deliverance of the city from total destruction, said, among other things:

> [T]he calamity which has just overtaken us has also burst out, revealing to our faces the censure of our sins. Nay, nor did it resemble other raids of barbarians, but the unexpectedness of the attack, its strange swiftness, the inhumanity of the barbarous tribe, the harshness of its manners and the savagery of its character proclaim the blow to have been discharged like a thunderbolt from heaven.... For the wrath of God comes upon us for our transgressions (Eph. 5. 6.), and the stuff of the perilous *drama* is the acts of the transgressors, and the exaction of punishment is *for* unrepented-of errors.... For whereas they ought to have been filled with righteous anger at the murder of fellow-countrymen by barbarians, and to have hastened to demand a requital with fair hope of *success*, they, cowering and panic-stricken, were paralysed....
>
> An obscure nation, a nation of no account, a nation ranked among slaves, unknown, but which has won a name from the

---

[47] The "garment" of the Virgin was, according to tradition, found at Capernaum, and brought to Constantinople by two patricians in the reign of Leo I (457–474). It was kept in the Church of Saint Mary of Blachernae.

[48] See Chapter Two, "Invasion of the Avars," page 62–3.

expedition against us, insignificant, but now become famous, humble and destitute, but now risen to a splendid height and immense wealth, a national dwelling somewhere far from our country, barbarous, nomadic, armed with arrogance, unwatched, unchallenged, leaderless, has so suddenly, in the twinkling of an eye, like a wave of the sea, poured over our frontiers, and as a wild boar has devoured the inhabitants of the land like grass.... One could see babes town away [and dashed against rocks]...; mothers wailing miserably, being slaughtered over their infants.... Nay, nor did the savagery stop with human beings, but over all speechless animals, oxen, horses, fowl and others, which they fell upon, did their cruelty extend.... Everything was full of dead bodies; the flow of rivers was turned into blood; some of the fountains and reservoirs it was no longer possible to distinguish, as their cavities were made level with corpses....

When, moreover, as the whole city was carrying with me her [the Mother of the Word's] raiment for the repulse of the besiegers and the protection of the besieged, we offered freely our prayers and performed the litany ... and the Lord took pity of His inheritance. Truly is this most-holy garment the raiment of God's Mother! It embraced the walls, and the foes inexplicably showed their backs; the city put it around itself, and the camp of the enemy was broken up as at a signal; the city bedecked itself with it, and the enemy were deprived of the hopes which bore them on. For immediately as the Virgin's garment went round the walls, the barbarians gave up the siege and broke camp, while we were delivered from impending capture and were granted unexpected salvation.... Unexpected was the enemy's invasion, unhoped-for appeared their departure; extreme was *God's* irritation, but His mercy inexpressible; unspeakable was the fear they inspired, but they became contemptible in fight; *God's* wrath accompanied them in the attack against us, but we have found God's compassion, routing them and checking their onset.[49]

The miraculous intercession of the Theotokos on Constantinople's behalf also strongly affected the Rus'. There had been Christians among them as well as among the Varangians before, and after the miracle from above that

---

49 Photius, *Homilies*, "Second Homily on the attack of the Russians," 96–103.

delivered the Constantinople Christians, when their doom seemed imminent, Askold and a large number of those who took part in the attack were
convinced of the undeniable superiority of the Christian religion over hea-
thenism.

They must have also been convinced of this by the occasion of the Bulgars being baptized.

In the two years after the attack, Askold sent emissaries to secure a lasting peace and agreement regarding the carrying on of trade among the Rus'
and the Byzantines so that it would be fair for both sides. Along with this,
Askold sent them to ask the Byzantines to enlighten them in the ways of the
Christian faith. The Byzantine co-emperors, Basil I and Michael III, agreed
on a lasting peace with the Rus' and generously sent a gift of gold, silver,
and silk fabrics, baptized the visitors, and the patriarch appointed a bishop
of Kiev.

Photios wrote, among other things, the following sermon for his district on this occasion:

> Not only has the Bulgarian Empire replaced their old wickedness
> with the Christian faith, but also that very nation which is said to
> exceed all others in cruelty and bloodshed: the Rus', who have en-
> slaved those who live near them as well, have been made proud by
> their victories, have raised their hands against the Byzantine Em-
> pire; and yet this nation has changed its heathen and godless doc-
> trine, to which it was previously beholden, into the pure and true
> Christian faith, and, instead of the great invasion and violence re-
> cently brought against us in hostility, with love and humility has
> entered into communion with us. And so impassioned is their love
> for the faith, that they have taken up Christian service as well as a
> bishop, a pastor, with great zeal and diligence.

According to legend, when the bishop appointed by Photios arrived in Kiev,
Askold brought him to the town hall, where the people all began to discuss
their faith and Christianity, and they asked the bishop what he wanted to
teach them. The bishop opened his Gospels and began to tell them about
our Savior and His life on earth, and also about the various miracles and
wonders of God in the Old Testament.

The Rus', listening to the sermon, said, "If we don't see anything of the
sort that took place with the three children in the fiery furnace, we won't

believe."[50]

The servant of God was unshaken; he boldly answered them, "We are insignificant before God, but tell me, what would you see?" They answered that if the Gospel were to be thrown onto the fire and come out unscathed, they would see the light of the Christian God. Then the bishop exclaimed, "O Lord, let thy name be praised before this nation," and threw the book onto the fire. The Gospel did not burn. After this, many of those who had come and were astonished by the miracle were baptized.

Oleg's Reign

Fourteen years after Askold's baptism, Rurik, living in Novgorod, died, leaving rule in the hands of his kinsman Oleg because Rurik's son Igor was still very young. This was in 882.

Three years passed, and nothing was heard of the new prince. In 885, Oleg, gathering a great host of Varangians, Novgorod Slavs, Krivichs, Chuds from Izborsk, Vesi from Beloozero, and Meryans from Rostov, went to Kiev by water.

The princely retinue was in chainmail or iron scale shirts, iron helmets, and had axes, swords, spears, and javelins. In the hands of every warrior, there was a large wooden shield covered with leather, painted with beautiful colors, and bound with iron—the warlike natives of the land, or the Voi, as they were called, dressed simpler. Few wore chainmail, and many went to some ports; they were armed with hatchets, bows, swords, and knives. Nearly all of them were on foot.

While en route to Kiev, Oleg took Smolensk and installed as its head a man from his retinue, and then he took the town of Liubech, where he also left a ruler in his stead. In this way, he took over the entire Dnieper route up to Kiev.

Approaching Kiev, Oleg concealed all his forces in the boats and told them to lie in wait, and with little Igor in his hands, disembarked onto land and sent a message to Askold and Dir that guests, Oleg and Igor the little prince, had come traveling to the Byzantine Empire and they wish to see the villagers—the Varangians. Suspecting nothing, Askold and Dir went to

---

[50] Meaning they won't believe unless they see a miracle themselves. Referring to the story in Daniel 3 whereby Nebuchadnezzar threw three devout children or young men into a fiery furnace to kill them and God protected them such that they were not harmed and sung God's praises in the midst of the flames.

the bank, but they didn't have time to say a word to Oleg when the retinue jumped out of their boats and hiding places, and Oleg said to the Kievan lords, "You are not princes nor even of princely stock, but I am of princely birth." (*RPC*, 61) Then he held the young Igor up in front of them and told them that this was the son of Rurik. After this, Askold and Dir were executed immediately, and Oleg, having avoided war with Kiev in this way, had already taken the city with no effort. Askold and Dir were solemnly buried near the city. In his memory, the Church of Saint Nicholas was built on Askold's grave; this tomb has remained buried since then, and every Orthodox person staying in Kiev goes to pray for the peaceful rest of the soul of the great knight who lies there.

The reason why Oleg acted so cruelly toward Askold and Dir is quite obvious. Wealthy Kiev lay on the great Varangian trade route, at the start of which there stood Novgorod as well, where the Rus' princes lived. Askold and Dir were their compatriots but were not of the elder ranks, thus Rurik didn't give them authority over any cities, so they asked him to seek their fortunes in Constantinople. While staying in Kiev, these knights freed it from the paying of tribute to Khazaria, subjugated the neighboring tribes, and in addition to this, carried out a great assault on Constantinople. All this added to their strength and influence and the dangers posed to the hegemony of the princes of Novgorod. Thus Oleg, planning to unite the Russian Land, to this end, gathered a large, strong army, and before doing anything, had to get control of Kiev, which is situated in the most important spot on the great Varangian trade route.

In addition to this, there is no doubt that the heathen Oleg and his heathen Novgorodian retinue found it most unpleasant that some Varangians seceded from them with Askold and Dir, who had acquired significant power and had accepted Christianity, so hated by the committed pagans.

What is also noteworthy is that Oleg had rid himself of Askold and Dir by way of trickery, which indicates that they had great strength since he did not wish to meet them in open war; it must also be said of this that the open deceit which was used against them to lure them in that way was not only *not* a malicious deed according to heathen beliefs, but on the contrary, would merit congratulation. The words "cunning" or "crafty" are considered laudable to these people who so artfully deceive their enemies.

Oleg's excursion to Kiev shows that he was actually quite prudent. Having begun his rule after Rurik, he left Askold and Dir alone in Kiev for three whole years to conceal his plan of attack from them. Remaining for these three years, it would seem, inactive in Novgorod while diligently preparing for his campaign, which between gathering a large host from all the northern tribes, arming it, and building boats to move the troops (which Novgorodians, as excellent carpenters, were masters at), he incurred great costs; yet, Oleg had kept it secret by spreading it out over three years so that the Kievan knights would never guess that a campaign was being planned against them from Novgorod by tracking goods that were being shipped along the great Varangian trade route.

Finally, coming out to Kiev with his army and boats, Oleg managed to move along the water route so secretly that he got to Kiev completely undetected and lured Askold and Dir, so skilled and experienced in war, out of the city.

Oleg's skillful preparation for the secret campaign, as well as his commitment to it, should be considered worthy of emulation, even in our time, although more than a thousand years have gone by since one ought to always be prepared to suddenly attack the enemy.

Having dispatched Askold and Dir, Oleg moved his king's table from Novgorod to Kiev. "This will be the mother city of the Rus'"—these are the first words that Oleg said of Kiev.[51] He had already installed a vassal in Novgorod. He then immediately began to build cities in key areas and install men he trusted in them.

Along with this, he decided to start the conquest of the tribes sandwiched between Kiev and Polesia. During his first summer in Kiev, he led a campaign against the Drevlians, who were constantly attacking the Polesians from their dense forest. Oleg dealt with the Drevlians sternly and "after conquering them he imposed upon them the tribute of a black marten-skin apiece." (*RPC*, 61) The next summer, he went to the northerners (Severians) and imposed a light tribute on them so that they wouldn't pay the Khazars, "on the ground that there was no reason for them to pay it as long as the Khazars were his enemies." (*RPC*, 61)

Finally, the third summer, he asked the Radimichs: "To whom do you pay tribute?"

They answered, "Khazaria."

---

[51] While this speech does not appear in the *Russian Primary Chronicle* exactly, it does appear as a narration. Nechvolodov often embellishes such narrations and paraphrases them as speech, as he is more interested in the story-telling than in the exact quotation. Often this is the case throughout Chapters Three and Four if the surrounding quotations are cited from the *Russian Primary Chronicle* (*RPC*), though some parts of the story are not included even as narrations and are from another one of the sources Nechvolodov cites in the Bibliography.

"Don't give them tribute, but give it to me." Thus did the Radimichs join him.

Having impoverished the neighboring tribes of the Polesians and owning a huge section of the path along the Varangian trade route, Oleg began to consolidate his royal authority by joining all the tribes who were under him into a united Slavic tribe; along with this, he began preparing for a huge campaign against Constantinople to reassure the Byzantines that even after Askold and Dir, Kievan Rus' would remain just as powerful and formidable to Constantinople as it had been during the time of these knights.

To this end, the industry of the land turned to preparations for an invasion of Constantinople for twenty-three years. During these twenty-three years, the *Primary Chronicle* recalls two important events in the Russian Land.

In 897, a horde of an Asiatic nomadic tribe called the Ugrians or Vengrians came past Kiev, crossing the Dnieper and moving further west. The Vengrians had no clashes with the Rus'; of course, the Rus' were so formidable that the Vengrians didn't think to attack them and asked only for permission to move through their lands to get further south to the unoccupied territory where they could settle.

Moving through the Carpathian Mountains, the Vengrians displaced a few of the inhabitants and Western Slavic tribes further to the south and settled in the wide plains of the mid-Danube to the southwest of the Carpathians.

At the instigation of the Byzantine emperors, the Vengrians immediately began fighting with their neighboring Slavic tribes here, especially the Moravians. In general, the arrival of the Ugrians, or Vengrians, into Europe and their location on the middle Danube was completely unfavorable for all of Slavdom because, with their appearance on the Danube, the South Slavic tribes were cut off from their Northern, Eastern, and Western brothers by a tribe that was completely foreign to them, and this severance persists to this day.[52]

In addition to the migration of the Vengrians, the chronicles also tell of how Prince Igor, having come of age and begun to aid Oleg in affairs of state, married a native girl from the village of Vybuta on the outskirts of the Rus' territory, about eight miles from Pskov. She was called "the beautiful one" for her radiant beauty and deeply spiritual nature. After the marriage, she took the name Olga, in honor of Oleg.

---

[52] The Ugrians/Vengrians were the ancestors of the Hungarians.

Around 906, Oleg's preparations for his campaign against Constantinople were completed.

Leaving Prince Igor in Kiev to manage affairs during the time of his absence, Oleg embarked on his campaign against the Byzantines, having gathered many Varangians, Novgorod Slavs, Chuds, Krivichs, Mari, Polesians, Severians, Drevlians, Radimichs, Croats, Volhynians (or Dulebes) and Tivertsi. This Slavic war host was moved to Constantinople on ships, ferries, and horses. There were two thousand ships, upon each of which forty men were placed; eighty thousand men thus came by water while the cavalry went along the shore.

When Oleg reached Constantinople, the Byzantines barricaded the city with iron chains and shut and locked the city harbor. Oleg disembarked onto the beach and began to ravage the area surrounding the city, causing massive devastation; meanwhile, he dragged his boats onto the shore, fixed wheels onto them, and waited for a fair wind; when such a wind arrived from the field, he raised sail, and his war host sailed up to the city on dry land as though it were water. The sight of this frightened the Byzantines, who sent Oleg the following message of submission: "Do not destroy the city: we will pay you tribute in the form of whatever you desire." Oleg ceased his invasion. As was expected, the Byzantines carried out a regal spread of food and wine, but the wise Rus' prince did not take this gift, for he knew that the treacherous Byzantines would surely attempt to poison him. In terror, the Byzantines then cried out: "This is not Oleg, but St. Demetrius, whom God has sent upon us." (*RPC*, 64) Oleg also demanded a heavy tribute from the Byzantines: twelve grivnas for each man upon each of the two thousand ships, which, as we know, each housed forty men. The Byzantines agreed to pay it all and asked only for peace. Backing off from the city, Oleg sent his peace terms to the emperor.[53] Having agreed to the aforementioned tribute of twelve grivnas a head, Oleg also established that the Byzantines would pay tribute to the Rus' cities under his rule: Kiev, Chernigov, Pereiaslav, Polotsk, Rostov, Liubech, and others.

Exacting tribute was the usual custom of every victor in war, but that was not the purpose of Oleg's campaign. The main thing his ambassadors said to the Byzantines was:

The Russes who come hither shall receive as much grain as they require. Whosoever come as merchants shall receive supplies for

---

[53] Leo IV, the Wise (reigned 886–912).

six months, including bread, wine, meat, fish, and fruit. Baths shall
be prepared for them in any volume they require. When the Russes
return homeward, they shall receive from your Emperor food, an-
chors, cordage, and sails and whatever else is needed for the journey. (*RPC*, 64–5)

Thus, Oleg's primary demand was that each Rus' person would have the
right to come to Constantinople and be accepted as a well-to-do and re-
spectable guest. Oleg demanded, thenceforth, good treatment, especially
for merchant travelers, for at least half of the year, when they arranged
their merchant affairs. He demanded that they would be able to take as
many steam baths as was necessary since this was the first item of hospitality for a respected visitor coming from far away; finally, he demanded
that when any Rus' departed homeward, they would also be sent off de-
cently as guests, that they would be supplied with food and everything that
any person making a journey on a long path would need.

Essentially, the Rus' demanded that Rus' people visiting Constantinople would be treated as they had been in days of old.

This demand implied that the Byzantines had vainly looked upon the
Rus' people with disdain, calling them barbarians, when, on the contrary,
the Rus' people were much more gentle and courteous with their guests
than the Byzantines, and they demanded this courtesy be reciprocated.

During the time of the Khazar yoke over the Russian Land, when we
had no military forces and nobody in Constantinople would stand up for
Rus' merchants, the Byzantines had grown accustomed to treating us in the
aforementioned way—disparagingly and unfairly.

Like a wanderer accidentally finding himself in this large, bustling city,
a Rus' had to watch out for the hand of every Byzantine, bow to him, belittle
himself, or else obtain his essential goods by force, robbery, or theft, which
was dangerous and rarely successful, since the Byzantines, taking advantage of their power, would extract very cruel recompense from the Rus'
for even the slightest grievance. This is why, as soon as the Rus' sensed that
they were strong enough, they immediately embarked on a dashing foray
under the leadership of Askold and Dir to avenge their ill-treatment in
Constantinople and, by doing this, display their strength to the Byzantines,
as Oleg had done during his famous march on Constantinople.

The Byzantine emperor, of course, consented to Oleg's terms, but for
his part, asked:

If Russes come hither without merchandise, they shall receive no provisions. Your prince shall personally lay injunction upon such Russes as journey hither that they shall do no violence in the towns and throughout our territory. Such Russes as arrive here shall dwell in the St. Mamas quarter [the Monastery of Saint Mamas]. Our government will send officers to record their names, and they shall then receive their monthly allowance, first the natives of Kiev, then those from Chernigov, Pereyaslavl', and the other cities. They shall not enter the city save through one gate, unarmed and fifty at a time, escorted by an agent of the Emperor. They may conduct business according to their requirements without payment of taxes. (*RPC*, 65)

Then, at the peace negotiations, the emperor kissed the cross, and according to Rus' law, Oleg and his men gave obeisance with their weapons raised to their gods Perun and Veles, the god of cattle.

Oleg's ships were filled with wondrous goods. There were so many silks and other fabrics that on the return journey, Oleg ordered his men to sew their sails with pavoloki (a multicolored silk) and the rest of the array with printed cotton (calico). When they raised the sails of silk, misfortune struck: they were ravaged by a wind, whereupon the Slavs said, "Let us keep our canvas one; silken ails are not made for Slavs." (*RPC*, 65)

On their way out of Constantinople, the Rus' nailed their shields to the gate as a sign of their victory. Oleg returned to Kiev with great glory, bearing gold, clothes, vegetables, wine, and all sorts of textiles and other goods used and valued in the Russian Land.

The people, seeing Oleg's return with such rich bounty, and seeing along with this that his army returned unharmed in its entirety, i.e., that he acquired all these goods without sacrificing the blood of any of his people, were astonished by this and called him *Veshchiy* (the Sage or the Wise), which meant glorious, wondrous, great, prophetic.

The fifth summer after this glorious attack of Constantinople, in the year 911,[54] Emperor Constantine VII Porphyrogenitus took the throne, and Oleg again sent emissaries to the Byzantines to maintain the peace agreements with the new emperor.

Fourteen emissaries were sent to Constantinople, among whom five

---

[54] While Nechvolodov did write 911, historians say Constantine VII took the throne in 913, with Alexander serving briefly from 912 to 913, after Leo IV.

had been present at the first meeting.

The great vassals who had come were all renowned warriors, and having greeted the emperor, "the great Autocrat in God," in the name of Oleg, the great prince of the Rus', they started to explain the purpose of their coming:

> First, that we shall conclude a peace with you Greeks, and love each other with all our heart and will, and as far as lies in our power, prevent any subject of our serene Princes from committing any crime or misdemeanor. Rather shall we exert ourselves as far as possible to maintain as irrevocable and immutable henceforth and forever the amity thus proclaimed by our agreement with you Greeks and ratified by signature and oath. May you Greeks on your part maintain as irrevocable and immutable henceforth and forever this same amity toward our serene Prince of Rus' and toward all the subjects of our serene Prince. (*RPC*, 66)

Afterward, they began to discuss what would happen if there were to be any killings of Byzantines by Rus', or vice versa, and of other incidental terms between the Rus' and the Byzantines:

> Whatsoever Russ kills a Christian, or whatsoever Christian kills a Russ, shall die, since he has committed murder. If any man flee after committing a murder, in the case that he is well-to-do, the nearest relatives of the victim shall receive a legal portion of the culprit's property, while the wife of the murderer shall receive a like amount, which is legally due her. . . .
>
> If any Russ commit a theft against a Christian, or *vice versa*, and should the transgressor be caught in the act by the victim of the loss, and be killed while resisting arrest, no penalty shall be exacted for his death by either Greeks or Russes. The victim of the loss shall recover the stolen property. If the thief surrenders, he shall be taken and bound by the one upon whom the theft was committed, and the culprit shall return whatever he has dared to appropriate, making at the same time threefold restitution for it. (*RPC*, 66–7)

Finally, the Rus' proposed:

If a ship is detained by high winds upon a foreign shore, and one of us Russes is near by, the ship with its cargo shall be revictualed and sent on to Christian territory. We will pilot it through every dangerous passage until it arrives at a place of safety. But if any such ship thus detained by storm or by some terrestrial obstacle cannot possibly reach its destination, we Russes will extend aid to the crew of this ship, and conduct them with their merchandise in all security, in case such an event takes place near Greek territory. But if such an accident befalls near the Russian shore, the ship's cargo shall be disposed of, and we Russes will remove whatever can be disposed of for the account of the owners. Then, when we proceed to Greece with merchandise or upon an embassy to your Emperor, we shall render up honorably the price of the sold cargo of the ship....

From this time forth, if a prisoner of either nation is in durance either of the Russes or of the Greeks, and then sold into another country, any Russ or Greek who happens to be in that locality shall purchase the prisoner and return the person thus purchased to his own native country....

With respect to the Russes professionally engaged in Greece under the orders of the Christian Emperor, if any one of them dies without setting his property in order and has no kinsfolk there, his estate shall be returned to his distant relatives in Rus'. But if he makes some disposition of his goods, the person whom he has designated in writing as his heir shall receive the property of which he thus disposed....

If a criminal takes refuge in Greece, the Russes shall make complaint to the Christian Empire, and such criminal shall be arrested and returned to Rus' regardless of his protests. The Russes shall perform the same service for the Greeks whenever the occasion arises. (RPC, 67–8)

The Byzantines agreed to these terms; obviously, the terms demonstrated to the Byzantines that the Rus' were quite polite, educated, and reasonable. The contract was drawn up by the Byzantine emperor and his emissaries, whereupon the Rus' swore to uphold law and order of their country and not to stray from the established peace and warm relations between the nations.

The Byzantine emperor made the Rus' ambassadors a gift of gold and rare fabrics and insisted on showing them the city:

> [T]he beauties of the churches, the golden palace, and the riches contained therein. They thus showed the Russes much gold and many palls and jewels, together with the relics of our Lord's Passion: the crown, the nails, and the purple robe, as well as the bones of the Saints. They also instructed the Russes in their faith, and expounded to them the ·true belief. (*RPC*, 69)

And he released them back to their homeland with great honor. Thus, wise Oleg established relations between the Rus' and the Byzantines in year 911.

Two years later, in 913, after thirty-two years of princehood, Oleg was no more.

"And all the people wept with great cries," burying their prince, who was the first to gather the peoples of the Russian Land into one great state and brought great respect to the name of the Rus' with his successful campaigns and wise diplomacy.

The *Primary Chronicle* says that magi and wizards had foretold Oleg's manner of death, that he would die by way of his favorite horse; therefore, this horse was retired, and Oleg never again rode on it; when Oleg heard of its death and saw its bones, he put its hoof upon his head and while laughing, said, "So I was supposed to receive my death from this skull?" (*RPC*, 69) But at that very moment, he was fatally bitten by a snake that inconspicuously crawled out from the horse's skull.

Our great writer Alexander Sergeyevich Pushkin wrote the following ballad, "Song of the Wise Prince Oleg,"[55] based on this story:

> The wise Prince Oleg has set out to repay
>   Foolhardy Khazars with a vengeance;
> For pillage, their dwellings and pastures as prey
>   To fire and sword the prince pledges;
> In Tsargrad's fine armor, in front of a force
> Oleg heads out riding his favorite horse.
>
> Here comes from the woods, lost in thoughts of his own,
>   A warlock inspired like all sages,

---

[55] Written in 1822, *Song of the Wise Prince Oleg* has many English versions. This version, translated by Yuri Menis, maintains the rhythm and rhyme scheme of the original.

An old man in service of Perun alone,
        A harbinger of future ages,
In pleadings and witchcraft forever engaged.
The prince then rides over to talk to the sage.

"Now tell me, o wizard, the darling of Gods,
        How long shall I live on in comfort
"And what, to the joy of my foes, are the odds
        With earth before long I'll be covered?
"You don't need to fear me; let truth here be known.
"Speak up and you'll have any horse that I own."

"No magus has fear of the mightiest lords
        Nor welcomes their gifts when they're given;
"Authentic and free are our vatical words
        And matched to the wisdom of heaven.
"In darkness the future is hid anyhow;
"But I see the fate on your luminous brow.

"Now heed what I tell you and mark every word:
        To warriors glory is sacred;
"Your fame has been earned by your glorious sword;
        Your shield decks the gateway to Tsargrad;
"The sea and the earth both your orders await,
"And foes are but jealous of this wondrous fate.

"The ocean's high waves in a perilous string
        Brought on by the ominous weather,
"The arrow, the treacherous blade, and the sling
        Have spared you in every endeavor....
"You've suffered no wounds in your armor supreme;
"Your power is guarded by forces unseen.

"The horse of your choosing braves dangers and woes;
        Obeying the sovereign's bidding,
"He stands unperturbed by the arrows of foes,
        Then charges with speed unremitting.
"Nor weather nor battle will make him retreat....
"But trust me, your death shall ensue from your steed."

Oleg merely chuckled; however, his eye
        And forehead grew dark in reflection.

Still silent, he gets off his horse with a sigh
     And a look of profound dejection.
In parting he offers his well-earned respect
By stroking and rubbing his friend's slender neck.

"Farewell, my companion, you've served as you should;
     It's time for our ultimate breakup.
"Now rest and remember that never my foot
     Shall enter your gold-plated stirrup.
"Forget not your master; take solace henceforth.
"My dutiful servants, attend to my horse;

"Protect him with cloth and a good fluffy rug
     And walk him to my fairest pasture,
"Provide with choice grain and clean up with a scrub,
     And offer spring water hereafter."
Away goes the steed at the prince's odd whim;
Another good horse is delivered to him.

A feast of the prince and his soldiers is on
     To boisterous clinking of glasses.
Their locks are as white as the new snow at dawn
     The glorious kurgan amasses. . . .
The troops reminisce on the days of the past
And battles together they fought to the last. . . .

"And where is my mate?" asks Oleg amidst fun.
     "My favorite horse, once so mighty?
"Is he just as healthy, as light on the run,
     As dashing as ever and sprightly?"
He heeds their reply that a cliff high and steep
Has sheltered his stallion's unbreakable sleep.

Encompassed by sadness, the mighty prince sits
     Reflecting, "The presage is fiction?
"Old quack, you're a liar; you're out of your wits!
     I wish I had spurned your prediction!
"My horse would still bear me," he gravely bemoans
And wishes to look at his horse's dead bones.

The mighty Oleg rides along with his band
     As Igor and guests duly follow.

They see on a hill, by the Dnieper's steep bank,
    The horse's remains gleaming hollow;
They are covered with dust and showered by rains,
And winds sway the grass o'er the noble remains.

The prince put his foot on the skull of the steed
    And uttered, "Your sleep, friend, is lonely!
"Your master of old has survived you indeed:
    At my final feast, which comes promptly,
"You won't be the one, by a battle-ax cut,
"To shower my ashes with hot streaming blood!

"So that's what my doom was foretold to portend!
    Some bones that have threatened my passing!"
He spoke and at once from the horse's dead head
    A tomb snake slipped out to harass him;
A black ribbon wrapped all the way round his feet—
Caught suddenly off guard, the bitten prince screamed.

The goblets of brotherhood sparkle and foam:
    The feast for Oleg is in mourning;
Prince Igor and Olga sit by on their own
    As others share drink until morning.
The troops reminisce on the days of the past
And battles together they fought to the last.

Igor and Saint Olga

After Oleg, Igor, Rurik's son, sat on the throne of the prince. This was in 913. His first act was the pacification of the Drevlians, who had stopped paying tribute after Oleg's death. Igor conquered them and imposed a tribute larger than Oleg's. Then he subdued another rebellious Slavic tribe, the Ulichs, who lived downstream of the Dnieper, near the modern city of Aleshka; at this time, the subjugation had not fully taken hold on the city of Peresechen, so Igor's conquerors lay siege to it for three years and seized all the food. Then the Ulichs all moved away from the Dnieper and settled around the Bug and the Dniester.

After their departure, the great Varangian trade route was completely in the hands of the great prince.

But from Scandinavia, through all the Russian Land, there was still a route to another corner of the sea—to the far east, the then famous Caspian

Sea.[56]

As is known, the Khazars dwelled there. Many offenses were carried out against the Rus' people during the time of the Khazar yoke, not only by the Khazars themselves but by the people who lived under the rule of the Arabs in the Caucasus Mountains by the sea, which was a desirable destination for our merchants.

Thus came the time for the Rus' to show their strength and repay these long-standing insults.

After the subjugation of the Drevlians in 914, on five hundred boats, each carrying one hundred men, the Rus' army went down along the Dnieper into the sea; then, skirting from the south of the Crimean Peninsula, they went into the Sea of Azov; from there, they sent a message to the Khazarian khagan challenging him to allow them to pass into the Caspian Sea to take revenge against the Caucasian people for their long-standing insolence. The Khazarian khagan agreed, probably not considering himself strong enough to prevent them, and asked for half the wealth of their plunder upon their return. Having received this answer, the Rus' went through the Sea of Azov and up the Don until the Volga Pass, near the Khazar city of Sarkel, at the modern settlement of Kachalinskaya. From there, as Oleg had done at Constantinople, they had to outfit their boats with wheels to get over the Volga Pass and enter the Caspian Sea.

Here our daring heroes spread out in detachments along all the rich Volga and Transcaucasian coastline and began enacting cruel vengeance for all their former insults. "The Rus' spilled blood," says one Arab writer. "They took women and children alike, pillaged property, sent horsemen to attack and burn towns and cities." The tribes who dwelled around this sea cried out in horror, and the Rus', having ransacked this rich coastline, withdrew to the oil sands around the city of Baku, where there were still fire worshippers living, and they settled down for some rest on the outlying islands nearby.

Then, having recovered from the strike, the invaded peoples armed themselves, got onto boats and merchant ships, and set out to the islands. But the Rus' did not sleep and responded with such a rebuff that a thousand of their attackers were massacred and drowned. After this victory, the Rus', burdened with great booty, began their journey home and, as per their agreement with the Khazarian khagan, gave him half of their goods in exchange for their passage into the Caspian Sea. However, the Khazars had

---

[56] This is the Volga trade route.

decided to deal with our ancestors in the following treacherous way. In Atil, they had gathered a large force and attacked the returning Rus'. The cruel slaughter went on for three days, and almost all of us were killed in the end. One thousand and five of them escaped and went up to the Volga, but a Finnic tribe called the Burtas and the Volga Bulgars completely finished them off. It is unknown how many of the brave seafarers returned home. But without a doubt, someone brought news to the Motherland of how so much Rus' blood had been spilled on the Volga in such a treacherous way. Nowhere and never had the blood of the Rus' been shed without harsh revenge; all that was needed was to wait for an opportune moment.

But another great sorrow was to befall the Russian Land after this unfathomable tragedy.

In 915, from Central Asia, a hostile tribe arrived in our southern Russian steppes called the Pechenegs.

It was without a doubt at the behest of the Byzantines, who, upon seeing the strength of the Rus' as well as the Bulgars on the Dunya, and not wanting to count on weakened Khazaria, dispatched the Pechenegs against the Slavs, following the example of Emperor Justinian. At first, Igor made peace with them, and they went straight for the Bulgars, but then new hordes of them arrived and settled in eight groups along the coast between the Don and the Dunya, of course blocking the Rus' from the Varangian trade route.

Obviously, this was a disaster for the newly formed Rus' state. From the time of the Pecheneg's arrival, our ancestors could only go along the Dnieper to the Black Sea either by conquering the Pechenegs or making a deal with them. Thus, just five years after the Pechenegs' arrival, Prince Igor would start a lengthy war with this tribe.

This war would sometimes turn peaceful for a few years, and then we could freely go into the Black Sea. The Byzantines were generally always friendly with the Pechenegs and artfully incited them sometimes against us, sometimes against the Bulgars, and also against the Hungarians.

The Pechenegs were an insatiable and greedy nation: they would shamelessly beg the Byzantines for expensive gifts in exchange for their assaults on the Slavs. At the same time, they were also warlike and ferocious and were outstanding mounted archers.

Upon the Hungarians, they promptly carried out such cruelty that it would seem they refused to fight with them any further, but of the Rus' the Pechenegs always lived in fear, for they often would render rather harsh defeats against them.

After the affair of the Pecheneg departure from Kievan Rus' to the Black Sea, the Byzantines, little by little, soon began to once again behave insultingly toward Rus' people in Constantinople and treat them with disdain because they reckoned that we wouldn't be able to replicate the raids of the city that had happened in the days of Askold and Oleg. However, the Byzantines were mistaken in their estimations. Having established peace with the Pechenegs in 941, Igor set out for Constantinople with a large force. He had no less than a thousand ships. According to Rus' fashion, he quickly came up to the city, landed on both shorelines of the Bosporus and laid waste to the whole coast, rendering what was the customary military action of the time: burning settlements, churches, and monasteries and mercilessly killing the locals.

The Byzantine navy soon came out, armed with devices from which they could shoot the then notorious Greek fire. These devices were built onto every ship's stern, bow, and sides. The Byzantine navy met with Igor's ships at the Sparks (Iskrest), which the Rus' called the torch-lit towers, or the lighthouses, that stood on the rocks to the south of the Bosporus.

The Rus' had surely lured the Byzantines out into the open sea, hoping they could not only successfully split them up but also capture their enemies alive. There was total calm on the sea, which appeared to be favorable for the Rus'. Still, at the same time, this calm turned out to be ruinous for them since, in a wind, the Byzantines wouldn't have been able to throw their Greek fire from their boats onto ours; it was by way of the still weather that this fire was able to operate without any impediment. It was chiefly made of oil and would burn even in water. As soon as the boats were close to each other, the Byzantines let loose the fire from all sides. The Rus' boats and men were completely covered in oil, and all their supplies ignited in flame, which caused fire of the utmost strength. Because of the fire, the Rus' started to jump into the sea, thinking it better to drown than to be burned to death. Some, burdened by chainmail and helmets, immediately sank to the bottom, and others burned while floating in the waves of the sea itself. The only ones to escape this ruin were those who managed to sail back along the Asiatic coast of the Black Sea in the shallow waters, where the Byzantine ships couldn't venture due to their large size.

However, the remaining Rus' were still quite numerous, and due to this, disembarking on the shores of Asia Minor, could spread their raids out far along the coastline and also deeper into the country in search of great plunder. When they were knocked off of the footpath by Byzantine land regiments, the Rus' would retreat to their few boats in the shallows and, in this way, fared successfully against the Byzantines over the course of an entire year. The shallow water was a kind of fortress for them in that the whole time they lived and slept on their boats. Finally, September came. The local stock had depleted, and the Rus' decided to head home, to which end they set off one calm night. But the Byzantines anticipated their departure and were watching the sea keenly. In the morning, we were overtaken by the large Byzantine ships, and a second sea battle took place, from which few Rus' made it home; most of the participants in the homeward rush died, and a few were taken captive. In Constantinople, in the presence of foreign ambassadors, all the Rus' prisoners were beheaded.

Thus concluded Igor's unlucky excursion against Constantinople in 941.

The home-returning Rus' told of the unfortunate events that befell them from the previously unknown Greek fire, which was as if "lightning from heaven, and [the Byzantines] had set them on fire by pouring it forth, so that the Russes could not conquer them." (RPC, 72)

Naturally, forgiving the Byzantines for our misfortune was impossible, and to punish them dearly, Igor, upon his return home, immediately began to gather a new large force and sent out a call for Varangian soldiers. The war preparations of the Rus' spanned three years.

During this time, when the call to war was resounding throughout the country and even across the seas, Igor's son Svyatoslav, the future avenger of all the ill-treatment of the Rus' people, was the heir to the princehood of his father. The whole Rus' force and the Varangians were gathered over the sea in 944. Besides Varangians, Igor had also taken Pechenegs, and in order to assure their loyalty, took hostages from them as well. After this, his huge army set out on their boats and horseback.

The Chersonites were the first to learn of this excursion and sent word to Constantinople saying that "the Russes were advancing with innumerable ships and covered the sea with their vessels." (RPC, 72–3)

The Bulgars, then also allied with the Byzantines, sent news from their country that "the Russes were on the way, and that they had won the Pechenegs for their allies." (RPC, 73)

Seeing the inevitable disaster, the Byzantine Emperor Romanos I Lekapenos hurried to arrange a non-hostile meeting with the Rus' and sent his best soldiers with a message for Igor: "Come no nearer, but rather accept the tribute which Oleg had received, and to the amount of which something should even be added." (RPC, 73) To the Pechenegs, he sent much gold and rare fabrics, thinking to buy them away from the Rus'.

By this time, Igor had only gone as far as the Danube. He convened his company and began to think. The company reasoned, "If the Emperor speaks thus, what do we desire beyond receiving gold, silver, and palls without having to fight for them?" (*RPC*, 73) Igor heard his company, distributed the gold and fabrics from the Byzantines among the whole army and ordered them home, and sent the Pechenegs to conquer the land of the Bulgars.

The next summer, the Byzantine emperor again sent word to Kiev, looking to rebuild the peace that had been established under Oleg.

"Tell me, what did your emperor say?" Igor asked when the Byzantine ambassadors appeared before him in person.

"The Emperor has sent us. He loves peace," answered the Byzantines, "and desires to maintain concord and amity with the Prince of Rus'. Your envoys have received the pledge of our Emperors, and they have sent us to receive your oath and that of your followers." (*RPC*, 76)

"Very well," said Igor.

On the morning of the next day, he went out with the ambassadors to the hill where Perun stood. There the Rus' placed their weapons before the idol: shields, swords, etc., and also gold (bracelets from their wrists and grivnas from their necks). And Igor swore along with those who were unbaptized, and the Christian Rus' swore over their synodical churches of Saint Ilya. Approving the peace and profitable treaty with the Byzantines, Igor rewarded the Byzantine ambassadors with Russian goods: valuable furs, servants, and wax.

Considering the monumental failure incurred three years earlier against the Byzantines at sea, Prince Igor sent a part of his company on a raid in the Caspian to avenge the betrayal the Rus' incurred in 914. The Arabs and the Armenians have preserved the stories of this raid. One Armenian writer says:

> At this time, from the north, there came the wild and marvelous Rus' people. Like a whirlwind, they spread all over the Caspian, and there were no means of resisting them. They put the city of Berd to the sword and seized all the property of its inhabitants. The native ruler laid siege to the city but was unable to do them any serious injury, for they were an invincible force. The women of the city, resorting to trickery, had started to poison the Rus'; but learning of this duplicity, the Rus' mercilessly exterminated the women and children.

Another writer, an Arab, says:

> Only one enemy was able to survive the Rus' hold of the city—this
> extraordinary abundance in the country of a great crop of garden
> fruit, from the consumption of which among the Rus' caused the
> widespread proliferation of illness, made worse by the Rus' being
> locked up in the fortress. Death crept into their ranks by the thou-
> sands in a few months. And when the snow fell, and the be-
> siegement by the locals of the country didn't let up, then the Rus',
> seeing the imminent ruin from the endemic disease, decided to
> break through and make for home. By night, they returned to their
> boats with their stolen booty and hastened back to their country.

This excursion, regardless of the successful escape, was not especially for-
tuitous for us in light of the many deaths from rampant illness.

In Kiev there took place yet another tragedy. With the onset of fall, Igor
set out, as usual, on his poliudie, for the collection of tribute and to carry
out trials and reprisals. Having arrived in the land of the Drevlians and
taken their tribute, he dismissed his company and, with a small detachment, headed for the city of Iskorosten (modern Korosten) in order to personally demand a tribute for himself. The Drevlians started to think and
conjecture about what to do with their prince Mal, and decided to kill Igor.
They attacked him, killed all his men, and lashed him to two trees they had
bent down to the ground, which tore him in half while alive when they cut
the bindings of the trees. Thus was how the life of Prince Igor unhappily
ended in 945.

In general, his entire life was not very fortunate: the unlucky first raid
in the Caspian, the arrival of the Pechenegs to the southern steppes, and
then the disastrous large boat excursion to Constantinople in 941. But regardless of all this tremendous adversity, Igor, throughout his long life, sto-
ically carried out the affairs of his father Rurik as well as Oleg the Prophet:
to unite the Russian Land and, in the event of defeats in military excursions,
never to lose spirit, but to gather forces anew and harshly dole out punishment against the enemy for their offenses. And he achieved a lot: Constantinople had to bow their heads to him and, paying a huge tribute, beg for
peace. With the Pechenegs, he managed to lock down an agreement and
even persuade them to join his side, then, as for the Caspian excursion in
Armenian territory, a part of the offenses against the Rus' people had already been avenged by the end of his life.

As for the offenses against the Rus' for which Prince Igor could not successfully reconcile in his life, as well as his shameful death at the hands of the Drevlians, these would also sooner or later be harshly repaid. With the Drevlians, justice would come about not long after.

At the time when Igor was inhumanly dismembered by the Drevlians, his wife, the Princess Olga remained in Kiev with their son Svyatoslav, just a few years old. The princess and the city, as well as the entire land, favored the warlord Sveneld to take the prince's place, and Svyatoslav was kept by his steward and tutor, Asmud.

The great princess received the first news of Igor's death from Drevlian ambassadors. The Drevlians had planned the killing of the Rus' prince to completely do away with his family in Kiev and thus concluded: "We have killed the Prince of Rus'. Let us take his wife Olga for our Prince Mal, and then we shall obtain possession of Svyatoslav, and work our will upon him." (*RPC*, 78)

Having thus made up their minds, the Drevlians sent Olga ambassadors—or matchmakers, rather—twenty of their best men, their oldest fighters. The ambassadors sailed to Kiev on boats along the Pripyat and the Dnieper and ordered Olga to announce their arrival.

The princess called them to her. "Have my kind guests arrived?" she asked.

"The kind guests have arrived, princess," the ambassadors replied.

"Tell me, on what business have you come?"

The Drevlians answered, "[Our] tribe [has] sent [us] to report that [we have] slain [your] husband, because he was like a wolf, crafty and ravening, but [our] princes, who had thus preserved the land of Dereva, were good, and [you] Olga should come and marry [our] Prince Mal." (*RPC*, 79)

"Your proposal is pleasing to me," Olga said, "indeed, my husband cannot rise again from the dead. But I desire to honor you tomorrow in the presence of my people. Return now to your boat, and remain there with an aspect of arrogance. I shall send for you on the morrow, and you shall say, 'We will not ride on horses nor go on foot; carry us in our boat.' And you shall be carried in your boat." (*RPC*, 79)

The ambassadors rejoiced and went to their boats, singing merrily, raising their hands, and exclaiming, "If you knew, O Prince of ours, what we have all arranged for you."

And Olga, in the meantime, ordered a large and deep pit to be dug out in the yard around her tower, which was filled with hot oaken coals. In the morning, she went up her tower and sent for her guests to be brought to her.

"Olga summons you to great honor," said the messengers from Kiev. (*RPC*, 79)

The ambassadors all complied with what had been said: they sat in the boats lounging and dignified and demanded of the Kievan Rus' that they be carried in on the boats. "Slavery is our lot," answered the Kievan Rus'. "Our Prince is killed, and our Princess intends to marry their prince!" (*RPC*, 79) They picked up the boats and solemnly carried the ambassadors—the matchmakers—to the royal tower. Seated in the boats, the Drevlian ambassadors looked proud and stately. They carried them into the princess' courtyard and threw them into the hot pit along with the boats.

"A great honor for you indeed!" Olga exclaimed, creeping up to the pit.

"This is worse than Igor's death," groaned the ambassadors.

Olga ordered them to be buried alive. Then she sent a message to the Drevlians "to the effect that, if they really required her presence, they should send after her their distinguished men, so that she might go to their Prince with due honor, for otherwise her people in Kiev would not let her go." (*RPC*, 79) The Drevlians and their prince Mal elected a new embassy of their most honorable men and sent them to Kiev.

As the new embassy approached, Olga had a banquet fixed for them and then heated the baths for them. The Drevlians went into the bathhouse and began to wash. Then the doors were shut and locked with them inside; thus, the bathhouse became scalding, and they were burned to death.

After this, Olga sent another message to the Drevlians: "I am now coming to you, so prepare great quantities of mead in the city where you killed my husband, that I may weep over his grave and hold a funeral feast for him." (*RPC*, 80)

The Drevlians began brewing mead, and Olga set out from Kiev lightly, with only a small retinue. Arriving at the corpse of her husband, she began to cry and, in the midst of her mourning, ordered the people to build a large grave. While it was built up into a large mound, the princess organized the funeral. After this, the Drevlian nobles and aristocrats sat down to drink. Olga told her men to make merry and drink their fill. All livened up, the Drevlians remembered their ambassadors.

"Wherever is our company, our men whom we sent to you?" they asked Olga.

"They are coming behind me with a company of my men, who have been assigned to take care of their belongings," the princess answered.

When the Drevlians had finished drinking as much as was their custom, the princess had her people drink to them, which meant that they had to drink half a glass for brotherhood, friendship, and each other's health, all of which were impossible to distinguish; this was custom. This was also called "drinking each other." When the Drevlians finally got drunk, the princess hurriedly left the feast, ordering the killing of all the Drevlians. They were cut down like grass; five thousand people perished in total. Olga then returned to Kiev and began to prepare an army to eliminate the remaining Drevlian powers.

The next summer in 946, Olga led a large and valiant force into Drevlian territory under the command of little Svyatoslav with his warlord Sveneld and the boy's uncle Asmud. The Drevlians also assembled and set out. The armies met face to face, and Svyatoslav, the four-year-old boy, started the battle first because the valiant princes of the Rus', according to the custom of fathers and uncles, always fought in from their company and always were the first to enter into battle.

Thus, Svyatoslav commenced the battle, throwing his spear at the Drevlians. The spear flew over his horse's ears and landed before her feet. But by doing this, his ceremonial act of prince was complete. Then Sveneld and Asmund exclaimed, "The prince has already begun battle; press on, vassals, after the prince." (*RPC*, 80) Afterward, a brutal victory was carved out by the Kievans, and the Drevlians were scattered into their cities and bunkered down for a siege. Olga and her son first went to Iskorosten, where Igor had died. The city knew that it would be shown no mercy, so it fought bitterly.

The great princess lay siege to the city for the entire summer and could not take it; then, she sent messengers into Iskorosten to say: "Why do you persist in holding out? All your cities have surrendered to me and submitted to tribute, so that the inhabitants now cultivate their fields and their lands in peace. But you had rather die of hunger, without submitting to tribute." (*RPC*, 80)

"We would be happy to pay tribute," the citizens answered, "yet you want to avenge the death of your husband."

"Since I have already avenged the misfortune of my husband," answered Olga, "twice on the occasions when your messengers came to Kiev, and a third time when I held a funeral feast for him, I do not desire further revenge, but am anxious to receive a small tribute. After I have made peace with you, I shall return home again." (*RPC*, 80–1)

"Take what you wish, princess," the Drevlians answered. "We are happy to give you honey and good furs."

"You have been made poor by the siege," Olga said. "You have neither honey nor furs; I wish only to exact a sacrifice to the gods from you, and I need a cure for my headache—from each of your households, I ask but three pigeons and three sparrows."

The people of Iskorosten were naturally quite pleased by the light tax and presented the birds to the princess with a bow. Olga announced they would now live in peace, for she would leave the city in the morning and set out for Kiev. Upon hearing the news, the citizens rejoiced anew and retired to their homes to rest peacefully. Meanwhile, Olga gave the pigeons and sparrows to some soldiers and ordered each bird to have flint and tinder covered with cloth and wrapped with a thread tied to them and, as dusk approached, to light the cloth and release the birds into flight. The birds flew to their nests—the pigeons to their cotes and the sparrows to their twig nests under the eaves. The city was at once lit up from all sides; in horror, the people fled the city walls, but then their true retribution began: some were killed, others enslaved, and the rest they burned alive.

After this, a heavy tribute was put on the Drevlians: two black martens and two squirrels, in addition to furs and honey, from each household.

This is how Olga exacted her revenge, as a good and faithful wife, for the death of her husband. For this harsh revenge, which she also oversaw with cunning and sapience, the people gave her the nickname the "wisest of all."

Such was the heathen side of Olga.

Considering herself prudent in the business of revenge for Igor's death, she considered herself just as prudent in managing Kievan Rus' during the time of Prince Svyatoslav's youth.

In that regard, the stately accomplishment for which she was especially exalted was the establishment of economic order in Kievan Rus'. The very next year after the burning of Iskorosten, the princess began to traverse the entirety of Kievan Rus' in person; she established order and justice in all the local affairs; she set up churchyards where traveling merchants could visit, set rent prices, defined hunting areas, and, by way of her great righteousness and sympathetic attitude toward less fortunate tribes, earned the love of the entirety of Kievan Rus'. "The sainted Olga always sought wisdom in this world," says Saint Nestor. (*RPC*, 83)

In searching and experimenting with ways to improve life in Kievan Rus' and traveling this whole land from end to end, Olga finally resolved to accept the Christian faith.

To this end, the princess, in 955, herself resolved to make the dangerous and perilous pilgrimage to Constantinople, where at this time, the co-

Emperors Constantine VII Porphyrogenitus and his son Romanos II ruled.

Olga joined a regular merchant caravan group, taking with her sixteen trusted *boyars* for her extended family,[57] eighteen ladies of the court, and other servants.

Upon the arrival to Constantinople of our noble caravans, the suspicious Byzantines would not admit Olga and her companions into the city for a long time, for they were not convinced of the purpose of her visit, which displeased her greatly.

Finally, on September 9th, our princess was solemnly taken in by the emperors into their magnificent palace, which had been built over six hundred years since the time of Saint Constantine the Great, Equal-to-the-Apostles.

When one descends toward Constantinople from the Black Sea, they must first go through a sea strait, the Bosporus, both sides with visibly populated shorelines. At the end of the Bosporus, to the right, there is a long sea bay called the Golden Horn. There is a great coastal nook between the Bosporus and the Golden Horn, and that is where Constantinople is. The whole city stands on seven hills. The imperial court was started on that very coastline and went higher and higher into the mountains; the imperial chambers stood on a high hill, and opposite them, also on a hill, the marvelous cathedral of the Hagia Sophia—the Wisdom of the Lord. All around the city are stone walls with quadrangular towers. The golden imperial chambers are visible to travelers descending from the walls closest to the hill, as is the golden palace-cathedral. And further, the cathedrals and chambers, churches and houses, and above them all, the great majestic Hagia Sophia cathedral, with its massive domes crowning the entire city. It was a wondrous spectacle.

Having reached the entrance to the imperial palace, the great Princess Olga of Kiev and her fellow travelers entered the great court, paved with marble and other such valuable stone; in the court, there stood enormous, monumental copper statues of famous emperors and great pillars of marble. Right in the middle was a huge, quadrangular through-pillar consisting of various columns and arches. A large cross towered above it with Emperor Constantine VII and his wife Empress Helena, looking to the east; the very same image of the cross could be seen on the special podium to the north of this great through-pillar, and to the east of it, there stood on another pillar a statue of Emperor Constantine the Great Equal-to-the-Apostles, with a

---

[57] Translator's note: *Boyars* are aristocrats who served and advised the prince/princess.

shining image around his head, which they say had been made of the very nails that were driven into the cross of our Savior. From one side, this court was joined to the great imperial palace and the other to the Hagia Sophia cathedral.

In this way, at the court, Princess Olga could see all that made the Byzantine Empire so strong and glorious. It was with a firm faith in the intercession of the Theotokos that her Sophia cathedral was erected on the same square, with a special baptismal font for all searching for the Holy Faith. High, exalted, and triumphant indeed was this kingdom with its Holy Cross, whose image ruled over the square. In the end, it also stood in the exaltation of the first Christian emperor, Saint Constantine Equal-to-the-Apostles.

Going out from the court into the palace, the great princess, along with her companions, proceeded through many great chambers, wonderfully decorated with jewels, silver, and gold, with intricate water basins, cast beasts, cleverly arranged for special times with gold and silver organs that would be played when choirs chanted the praise of the emperor. Then, finally, the princess came to the emperor's reception chamber, which had been built by Saint Constantine Equal-to-the-Apostles and was called the Great Golden Ward.

It had the appearance of a church and was oriented from west to east, and it stood out for its especially marvelous finery. Above the pillars of the chamber was an image of the Lord Almighty, seated on a throne, and the eastern section of the chamber had been built as an altar on a few stairs above and in front of the rest of the chamber, so that one could go up there on the golden marble staircase. This royal dais was separated from the rest of the chamber by four pillars, two on each side. Between the pillars there hung valuable curtains, which covered the sanctuary during regular times.

Beside this place stood a huge golden organ, glistering with jewels and embellishments, and it was called the royal organ. In other areas of the chamber, there were other organs made of silver. In the deepest part of this sanctuary, there was the royal altar—a golden throne, all spangled with precious stones, called Solomon's throne, after the king, for it was built in the same style as the throne of the Jewish king Solomon, son of David. The throne had steps with golden lions lying on each side. These lions were marvelous: at some famous time, they had stood up on their hind legs and roared as though they were alive. Above the throne sat two large golden birds who had once sung as though they were alive.

But even more marvelous were the golden poplar trees, or the syca-mores, which stood close to the throne, on which there were many more such golden jewel-adorned birds of various sorts, which had also famously once sung as though they were alive.

Like a banner of victory, the great golden cross of Emperor Constantine the Great, covered in jewels, towered over everything near the throne. At the foot of the throne, there was a golden seat for members of the royal house.

During the time of the receptions, there were golden royal robes and crowns hung up on the walls. The Byzantine Emperor Constantine VII had entered, dressed up in his rich royal garments, before Olga's arrival; he was deep in prayer for the land before the image of the Almighty Lord on the chamber's dome and then had seated himself on the throne of Solomon. At this time, the rich curtains impeded entrance into the chamber.

At the approach of our great princess, the curtains at the door were raised, and doorkeepers with golden staves in their hands admitted first the Byzantine nobles and officials by rank as each rank entered separately and were accommodated at the side of the chamber.

At last, the great princess entered, accompanied by such Rus' princes and eleven nobles.

Upon seeing the emperor, she paused. At this time, the organs and pipes were playing. Then, an elder Byzantine dignitary inquired after her health, and suddenly the two golden lions of the throne of Solomon roared, just as the birds on the throne and the trees sang their various birdsongs; at this, the lions on the steps of the throne stood up on their hind legs.

After this, the emperor was showered in gifts of precious sable furs from the Rus', and Olga entered into conversation with him.

When the princess, conversing with the emperor, went to leave the chamber, then again the organs would play, the lion's roar would be heard again, as would the birdsong, and the beasts would also move on the steps of the throne. From the emperor, Olga proceeded along the marvelous room to the reception chamber of the empress, who also greeted her from her throne and then asked Olga to pass by the royal bedchamber, where the emperor had gone; here, the emperor, the empress, and the princess could all converse more intimately.

After this discussion, on that exact day, a ceremonial feast was estab-lished in honor of the great Rus' princess.

At the time of this feast, two choirs of cathedral singers, one from the Church of the Holy Apostles and the other from the Hagia Sophia, were singing hymns in honor of the emperor's family, but just then another performance was decided on, consisting of dancing and various games. It opened with a hymn:

> God, who has now given you power in your hands, has given you free will and made you master of yourself! Great Archangel, descended from heaven, opened before the face of your brother-kingdom! The world, prostrated before the scepter of your right hand, praise be to the Lord, all favor to you, O king! He knows you as a blessed emperor, regal and just!

Then there was a dance after the choral singing, which continued until the feast's end.

At the end of the table in the princess' area, there were some desserts prepared on a small, golden dinner wagon, on golden plates and dishes that were studded with precious stones. Here in their places, there sat the co-Emperors Constantine VII Porphyrogenitus and his son Romanos II, the royal children, the emperor's daughters-in-law, and the Rus' princess.

Then, Olga was presented with a gift of jewel-studded golden dishes. More and more gifts were brought to her.

According to the story in the *Primary Chronicle*, Emperor Constantine VII, impressed by Olga's intelligence, said to her, "It would be fitting for you to rule in this city with us."

But our wise princess, sensing why the emperor would want this, answered him, "I am a heathen. If you want, baptize me yourself. Otherwise, I won't be baptized."

Then the emperor delegated her to the Patriarch Polyeuctus, who instructed her in the study of the Christian faith and, along with the emperor, baptized her, whereupon, afterward, Polyeuctus praised her with the words, "Blessed art thou among the women of Rus', for thou hast loved the light, and quit the darkness. The sons of Rus' shall bless thee to the last generation of thy descendants." (*RPC*, 82) Then the patriarch taught her about the various Church admonitions and ordinances, the prayers, the fasting, the almsgiving, and in the maintenance of chastity.

She sat with her head bowed and attentively listened to him, and then she spoke: "Verily, by what you have said, the Lord has saved me from a great and terrible trap."[58]

---

[58] This quote is similar but not exactly the same as recounted in the *Russian Primary Chronicle*,

After this, the emperor announced to her that he wanted to take her as his wife.

"How can you marry me, after yourself baptizing me and calling me your daughter? For among Christians that is unlawful, as you yourself must know," Olga answered. (*RPC*, 82)

"Olga, you have outwitted me," exclaimed this reckless emperor. (*RPC*, 82)

On Sunday, October 18th, Olga was for a second time ceremoniously received by the emperor and empress, given gifts, and then began her return journey to Kiev. Before her departure, she met the patriarch to request a blessing and said to him, "My people and my son are heathen. May God protect me from all evil!" (*RPC*, 82)

"Child of the faith," answered the patriarch, "thou hast been baptized into Christ and hast put on Christ. Christ shall therefore save thee." (*RPC*, 82) Then, the patriarch gave Olga a blessed crucifix, long kept in Kiev even after her reign.

Arriving in Kiev, Olga had brought a few wise priests with her and built a wooden church to Saint Sophia, decorated with icons sent to her by the patriarch.

Olga's companions returned to Kiev with her, many of whom, of course, were also baptized with their great princess. The greatness and purity of the Christian life which they had discovered in Constantinople naturally produced a great upheaval in their souls. They began influencing their closest people in order that they renounce paganism and accept baptism. Olga tried especially hard to influence her son Svyatoslav to accept Christianity. "How shall I alone accept another faith? My followers will laugh at that." (*RPC*, 84) His company not only laughed at converts to Christianity but sometimes would abuse them. All this deeply upset the great princess.

However, it wasn't very far in the future that the Holy Christian Faith would enlighten the whole Russian Land.

After her baptism, the great princess lived for another twelve years, throughout which she continued to travel around her motherland. Then, overlooking the terrain of modern-day Pskov and staying on the shore of the Velikaya River, where then there was a thick forest and many oak trees, she saw three beams of light, as if they were falling from heaven onto the

---

82: "Through thy prayers, Holy Father, may I be preserved from the crafts and assaults of the devil!"

steep opposite shoreline. The princess Equal-to-the-Apostles raised a cross at this site and prophesized that there would be a temple of the Holy Trinity there and a great and marvelous city would be erected. On that place where the great princess stood, chapels have now been built where there is a source of healing waters.

Figures for Chapter Three

79: (Above) Copper-cut etching, made
under the command of Empress Catherine
the Great for the introduction to the
Common Imperial History of Russia, kept in
the Imperial Academy of Arts.

80: (Right) *Saint Cyril Preaching
Christianity to the Slavs*, drawing
by the artist F. Bronnikov.

81: (Left) Zemovit, from a Polish armorial, *The Nest of Virtue*, 1550 edition.
82: (Center) Head of a small bronze statuette depicting, it is supposed,
Charlamagne, kept in the Carnavalet Museum in Paris.
83: (Right) Great Prince Rurik, from *The Great State Book* of 1672, kept in the Moscow
Archives of the Ministry of Foreign Affairs. An account of the Russian State
written at the behest of Tsar Alexei Mikhailovich by the Masters of Russia, with
the full National Treasury at their disposal, but given the absence of ancient
originals, these depictions are strictly suppositions up until Ivan the Terrible.

84: (Left) The Sineus Burial Mound near Beloozero.
85: (Right) *Askold's Raid of Constantinople*, M. Tichonov's illustration.

86: (Left) A Coin of Byzantine Emperor Constantine IX Monomachos with an image of Saint Mary of Blachernae. 87: (Right) Section of the Walls of Constantinople, corner tower by the Sea of Marmara.

88: The baptism of a Rus', "Christening with a Rose," from the fourteenth-century Bulgarian manuscript of *Codex Manesse*, in the Vatican Library in Rome, considered one of its greatest and most valuable texts, translated from the Byzantine script of the twelfth century and embellished with engravings and miniatures, doubtlessly copied from older forms. A few of these miniatures, touching upon the life of the ancient Rus', are for the present work, just as dear to us as those of the *Radziwiłł Chronicle* and the Madrid manuscripts of John Skylitzes.

89: *The Miracle of the Gospel.* Skylitzes, *Synopsis of Byzantine History.*
Labels are (top to bottom, left to right): the Rus' Prince; the Gospels;
a bishop; the Rus' Prince; the bishop throws the Gospel into the fire.

90: (Left) A Rus' druzhnik of the tenth century, from Strekalov,
Russian Historical Clothing. 91: (Right) Female clothing of a
pretty Russian woman of the tenth century, same source.

92: "And Oleg, howling, ordered wheels to be put on the boats; having
succeeded in catching the wind, sailed from the field and took the
city. Seeing this, the Byzantines were afraid." *Radziwiłł Chronicle.*

93: "And carrying breadstuffs and wine to him he took it not; for he took it to be
poison for his mouth. And the Byzantines were frightened and thought,
'We bring this not to Oleg, but to Saint Demetrius, sent to us from God.'
And Oleg exacted a tribute of two thousand boats, with twelve
grivnas per person and forty men per boat." *Radziwiłł Chronicle.*

94: "And having become swollen with silk cloth that had been tailored
by the Slavs, the Rus' sails were scattered to the wind; and the
Slavic sailors said 'this cloth bears a thickness that is too
great, it is not a fabric for the Slavs.'" *Radziwiłł Chronicle.*

95: (Left) The Rus' fastening their shields to the gate of Constantinople, by the
Russian artist F. Bruni, from Rezov, *Essays on Events of Russian History*.
96: (Right) A Vlanga-Bostan tower from the south side walls of Constantinople.

97: A depiction of a lion hunt on a casket of bone, a precious Byzantine work from
the tenth or eleventh century, kept in the sacristy of Troyes Cathedral, France.

98: Byzantines working in a field, from a Byzantine manuscript of the eleventh
century, kept in the National Library of France in Paris.

99: *Oleg and the Magician*, a painting by Viktor Vasnetsov.

100: (Left) *Oleg and the Snake*, a painting by Viktor Vasnetsov.
101: (Right) Prince Igor, as depicted in the *Great State Book.*

102: *The Fire-worshippers of Baku*, a painting by M. Mikeshina

103: Depiction of the Pechenegs. Skylitzes, *Synopsis of Byzantine History*.
Text: Byzantine warlord Vard Sklir with druzhina; Pechenegs.

104: Prince Igor and the battle of the Rus' against the Byzantines at
Constantinople, drawings made for the introduction of Empress Catherine the
Great's *History of Russia*.

105: (Left) A ship with Greek fire contained in clay pots, from an ancient
Arab manuscript, stored in the National Library of Paris.
106: (Center/Right) Catapults for the throwing of Greek fire, same source.

107: Illustration of a sea battle in a tenth or eleventh-century Byzantine
manuscript, kept in the library of the Cathedral of Saint Mark in Venice.

108: *The Oath of Igor*, drawing by the artist V. P. Vereshchagin.

109: Illustration of the Holy Mother with the Savior and saints with
Armenian facial features in ancient Armenian robes, from an
Armenian Bible from the year 989, kept in Echmiadzin.

110: Image of the ruins of the ancient Armenian capital, Ani, in the Caucasus.

111: (Left) Drevlian ambassadors being carried in the boat, illustration by the artist
I. Izhakevick.   112: (Right) "And carried thusly to Princess Olga upon a boat, the
brigands were so thrown down along with it. And Olga went up to them and
spoke, 'What better honor befits such as you?' They then spoke, 'Igor's
death was the making of more than us,' and thus were they
ordered to be buried alive." *Radziwiłł Chronicle.*

113: The burning of Iskorosten, painting by the artist G. P. Kondratenko.

114: Tsargrad (Constantinople)

115: The Hagia Sophia Cathedral in Constantinople in the time of the emperors.

116: Interior of the Hagia Sophia Cathedral in Constantinople in modern times.

117: (Left) Icon of the Holy Mother, a splendid work of the tenth or eleventh century, made of gold and precious vitreous alloy (enamel), kept in the sacristy of Saint Mark's Cathedral, Venice. 118: (Right) Byzantine cloth of the tenth century with an embroidered image of the Byzantine emperor in celebratory robes. One of the women depicted is carrying his crown to him, the other his battle helm. Found in the tomb of Gunther, bishop of Bamberg, in the eleventh century.

119: (Left) *The Morning Visit of a Byzantine Empress to the Graves of her Ancestors*, a painting by the artist Valentin Sergeevich Smirnov in the Tretyakov Gallery, Moscow. 120: (Right) The Holy Mother with the Savior, ivory carving of Byzantine craftsmanship, tenth or eleventh century, kept in the Centraal Museum in Utrecht.

121: Ark made of ivory of Byzantine origin, tenth or eleventh century, from a series of carvings depicting the life of King David, kept previously in the Kircherian Museum, Rome.

122: The emperor's regalia in the palace of Constantinople, from the *Codex Manesse*.

123: Baptism of Saint Olga. "The Russian princess went with
Constantine to the emperor's Basilica and was baptized."
Skylitzes, *Synopsis of Byzantine History.*

124: And she spoke thusly to the emperor: "If I should be baptized,
then I want that you should baptize me yourself; for if so, I
shall have the emperor as my patriarch." *Radziwiłł Chronicle.*

125: (Left) Blessed Saint Princess Olga, an ancient Byzantine icon of the
thirteenth–fourteenth century, from Obolensky, *On the Primary Chronicle.*
126: (Right) Crucifix and hat of Saint Olga, kept in the Trinity Cathedral, Pskov.

127: Sepulcher of slate stone, opened during excavating the foundation of
the former Church of the Tithes in Kiev. By all appearances,
it contained the remains of Saint Olga within it.

CHAPTER FOUR

Svyatoslav: His Childhood and Initiation into Battle

While Princess Olga was preparing herself to receive holy baptism and make a long journey to Constantinople, Svyatoslav was growing up and maturing. From his early years, he did things befitting a prince. As a four-year-old lad, he bravely led his royal guard to battle against the Drevlians to avenge his father and was the first to throw his spear. Warfare had been the first act of his life; moreover, warfare was honorable, daring, and just, and as per pagan custom, it was also sacred since he was avenging his father.

Since Svyatoslav had already proved himself brave, daring, and honorable as a young child, he remained so for the rest of his life.

After becoming fatherless in his fourth year, his wise mother decided that the responsibility of Svyatoslav's rearing should be transferred from the feminine palaces to the hands of his uncle and, thus, to the *druzhina*.[59] As per the custom of those times, children were given *postrigi*, ceremonial cutting of the first hair, a custom which stemmed from deep antiquity and consisted of shaving one's head and leaving a stripe of long hair Svyatoslav would wear throughout his life. Then the child would be mounted on a horse, and the king's whole druzhina would feast and celebrate the occasion. Both the druzhina and the foreign guests that would be invited to the festivities would get rich gifts, which included gold and silver, expensive furs, pavoloki, clothes, and especially horses. This was the boy's initiation into the war band, into princehood, into the warrior caste. That's why little

---

[59] Translator's note: A group of boyars who served the prince/princess.

Svyatoslav fought the Drevlians on a horse—he had already been initiated as a warrior.

Had his father remained alive, of course, he wouldn't have been leaving the care of his mother that soon, but now he was a fully-fledged prince. He was the only prince in Kievan Rus' and thus had to be immediately handed over to the druzhina, which became his father, tutor, and guardian.

This is why, as a son of the druzhina, Svyatoslav didn't yield to his mother when she was trying to convince him to accept Christianity, especially since he spent his childhood not in Kiev, but in Novgorod, whose people demanded to have him there because they wanted the prince to live with them and had born special hatred for Kievan Christians since the days of Askold. Svyatoslav's druzhina was very well picked, with ranked warriors and champions from all over Kievan Rus', regardless of the Slavic tribe they belonged to. They were the true sons of their great motherland and devoted supporters and friends of their prince. Svyatoslav didn't differentiate himself from his druzhina in any way and carried over all the difficulties and hardships of military campaign life along with his men. He never traveled with excessive luggage, such as luxurious food, fine drink, and soft bedding to entertain himself while on a campaign. He wouldn't even bring a cauldron to cook food, but would consume tender cuts of horsemeat, game, or beef, which would be fried on coals, perhaps even on sword or spear, and also ate thusly. He didn't bring a tent, preferring to rest on a simple cloth and a saddle under the night sky. Thus lived his whole druzhina. That allowed him and his guard to move swiftly and lightly, like a leopard, from country to country, and send messages to his enemies saying "I am coming for you" confidently.

Svyatoslav's Campaigns

Having grown up and matured, and gathering many brave men, Svyatoslav led his first campaign along the Volga Basin in 964, where the Rus' army that was returning in 914 after their Caspian campaign had been treacherously ambushed by Khazars, Burtas, and Volga Bulgars. Now the grandchildren, as per the pagan custom, went to avenge their grandfathers.

Leaving Kiev by boat through Desna, Svyatoslav had the boats carried by land to the Oka River to travel along its coast to the Volga. At that time, this area was controlled by Vyatichi, a Slavic tribe that had yet to swear allegiance to the Kievan Rus' prince.

"Who do you pay tribute to?" asked Svyatoslav.

"We pay tribute to the Khazars," answered the Vyatichi.

Svyatoslav remained silent and sailed on. The wise prince realized that it would be foolish to subjugate the Vyatichi, which by doing so would turn them against him and leave them behind him at the same time, while he still had to move forward along the Volga; the campaign could have been unsuccessful, so it was wiser to meet them on the return trip as friends, rather than as enemies.

This first campaign of Svyatoslav continued for over three years and was extraordinarily successful; after it took place, as per the Arab historians, there was no trace remaining of the Volga Bulgars, the Burtas, or Khazars. Svyatoslav razed the principal city of the Volga Bulgars, sacked Khazarian Sarkel (or White Vezha) on the Don, and then, descending to the south, subjugated the warlike tribes of the Iazyges and the Kasogi, which lived in the Northern Caucasus in modern Kuban province. Finally, victorious Svyatoslav, on his return journey, made the Vyatichi his subjects and made them pay him tribute. His warriors also brought a tremendous amount of booty from the glorious eastern campaign.

Ever since then, the rich Volga ceased to be a Khazar or Volga Bulgar-held river and became a river ruled purely by the Rus'.

But Svyatoslav would not remain in Kiev for long. Shortly after his glorious campaign, there came an envoy (Kalokyros) of the Byzantine Emperor Nikephoros II Phokas, a famous noble and son of a Corsican governor.

Kalokyros brought Svyatoslav many gifts, including twenty-seven pounds of gold, and requested help on behalf of the emperor against the Danubian Bulgars. Under the previous few emperors, the Byzantines had paid an annual tribute to the Bulgarians. When Nikephoros II came to the throne and won glory by way of victory over the Arabs, he found it unacceptable to pay tribute to the Bulgars; so, when their envoys came to Constantinople, he ordered them to be insulted and slapped them on their cheeks; then he waged war on them but proved not to be strong enough to defeat them by himself. Then he sent Kalokyros with gifts to request help from the Rus' prince. Kalokyros, a man of bravery and cunning, witnessed the might of the Rus' and realized that with their help, not only victory over Bulgars could be attained but the Byzantine throne itself as well. So he started planning things somewhat differently than how he was instructed by Emperor Nikephoros II. He wanted to become emperor himself with the Rus' help and offered the prince the entirety of the Bulgar land in return for his help.

A brave, courageous, and ambitious project was something that Svyatoslav certainly desired. He figured that conquering the Bulgarian Empire would put another great Slavic tribe under the hand of the Rus'.

In August of 967, Svyatoslav, along with sixty thousand brave men, descended on the usual Rus' route through the Dnieper to the Black Sea, then reached the Danube and, after swift deployment on land, attacked the Bulgars, who, unable to handle the attack, retreated into their fortress at Dorostopol,[60] while their ruler Tsar Peter I was so crushed by the sudden Rus' attack that his hands and legs became paralyzed.

The Rus' raided along the Danube, just like they raided along the Volga years earlier, and returned home with a lot of booty to pass the winter. The following year, in 968, Svyatoslav again sailed along the Danube and swiftly, like a snow leopard rushing from one place to another, took eighty Bulgarian settlements. After that, he took another throne in Pereyaslavets on the Danube. Kalokyros remained with him and continued his schemes to gain the Byzantine throne. However, Emperor Nikephoros II found out what was being planned against him by the cunning Kalokyros. Nikephoros II also realized that he had made a big mistake by sending the Rus' against the Bulgars since, in so doing, he had gained himself a far more dangerous neighbor than the Bulgars. Thus, abandoning his pride, he sent envoys to make peace with the Bulgars, reminding them that both the Bulgars and Byzantines were Christians and thus must live together as friends and kin. In addition to that, as an act of friendship, he asked the Bulgarians to send brides of their aristocratic lineage to marry the sons of the previous Byzantine emperor Romanos II.

The Bulgarians, of course, made peace and allied with the Byzantines with great enthusiasm.

Their first duty against their common enemy—the Rus'—was to hire the Pechenegs so that they would attack Kiev and make Svyatoslav leave Pereyaslavets.

And so it happened.

In the summer of 968, the Pechenegs crept up to Kiev and laid siege to it in great numbers.

Princess Olga was trapped in the city along with her three grandsons. The druzhina, for some reason, was staying on the other side of the Dnieper and was unaware of the imminent danger. Things in Kiev took a sharper

---

[60] Located in modern-day Silistra, Bulgaria, the Dorostopol fortress was on the Danube about 80 miles northeast of Preslav. Also called Dorostolon.

turn as the local population remained without access to food or water since it was impossible to reach the shores of the Dnieper. They needed to inform the army on the opposite shore, but how could they do that with the Pecheneg's encircling the city?

Finally, one young Rus' lad volunteered his services. He was still a boy, too young even to be considered an adolescent. Able to speak Pecheneg, he stealthily snuck through the city wall into the field and, with a leash in his hands, started walking among the enemy soldiers and asking, "Did anyone see my horse?" The Pechenegs assumed he was one of them and began to assist him. Thus he reached the shore of the Dnieper where he quickly threw his clothes off, jumped in the river, and swam to the other side. The Pechenegs, realizing the deceit, began releasing arrows at him but couldn't hit their mark as he was already too far, while the Rus' from the other side rowed over on boats and picked him up.

He told them, "If we don't go to the city by tomorrow, people there will want to surrender to the Pechenegs."

To that, a Rus' captain named Pretich replied, "We must come up in boats, somehow sneak Olga and the princes out, and withdraw to this side; otherwise, Svyatoslav will kill us once he is back."

Everyone agreed, so at the dawn of the next day, they piled into their boats and blew their trumpets, and the people in the city started cheering back. The Pechenegs assumed that it was Svyatoslav himself and retreated from the city; meanwhile, Olga and her grandsons managed to get to the other side in the boat. After seeing this, the Pechenegian princes asked to meet with Pretich. They rode from their camps toward each other.

The Pecheneg asked, "Who is this who has come?"

Pretich answered, "The people from the other side."

"Are you the prince?" the Pecheneg asked again.

"No, I am one of his men," Pretich answered, "and I have come as a fore-runner, and under me, there is a regiment of innumerable fighters."

Then the Pecheneg prince answered the captain, "Be my friend."

He agreed. They exchanged gifts: the Pecheneg gave Pretich a horse, sa-ber, and arrows, while Pretich gifted the Pecheneg armor, a shield, and a sword. After that, the Pechenegs retreated from the city but remained en-camped close enough to prevent the Russians from watering their horses in the Dnieper.

Nevertheless, because of the young hero's courage and cunning, the city's fall was avoided. It is immeasurably sad that his name was never preserved in the chronicles. The Kievan Rus' immediately sent a message to notify Svyatoslav: "Oh Prince, you visit and frequent foreign lands. But while you neglect your own country, the Pechenegs have all but taken us captive, along with your mother and your children as well. Unless you return to protect us, they will attack us again, if you have no pity on your native land, on your mother in her old age, and on your children." (*RPC*, 86) Upon hearing this, Svyatoslav immediately mounted his horse along with his retinue and rode swiftly from the Danube to Kiev, embraced his family, and routed the Pechenegs away from there.

However, Svyatoslav did not remain there for long. Peaceful life in Kiev wasn't his fancy. He constantly thought of Bulgaria. There another nest could be made for the Rus'; there great and honorable deeds awaited the prince.

Finally, in the spring of 969, Svyatoslav told his mother and the boyars, "I do not care to remain in Kiev, but should prefer to live in Pereyaslavets on the Danube, since that is the centre of my realm, where all riches are concentrated; gold, silks, wine, and various fruits from Greece, silver and horses from Hungary and Bohemia, and from Rus' furs, wax, honey, and slaves." (*RPC*, 86)

To that, the princess, already infirmed from age and illness, replied, "Can't you see I am ill? Why do you want to abandon me? Bury me first, and then go where you please!" And so she died a few days later. Her children, grandchildren, and other people greatly mourned her. Christians mourned her, losing their last source of support in Kiev; even pagans mourned her, losing the wise leader of the Russian Land.

Before dying, the Blessed Princess Olga Equal-to-the-Apostles willed that pagan rituals not be held upon her death, but that she should be buried under Christian doctrine, which her priest did. Additionally, she sent money to the Byzantine patriarch to pray for her soul. Saint Olga was buried near Askold's grave. Her incorrupt remains were placed in a small rock casket,[61] buried in the foundations of the Church of the Tithes in Kiev.[62]

After mourning for his mother, Svyatoslav prepared to leave Kievan

---

[61] Incorruptibility is the term used to describe a body (usually who is in the process of becoming a saint) who is found to have not decomposed. In some cases, incorrupt saints have been unearthed in perfect condition. In other cases, some decomposition occurs akin to drying, but the body is otherwise intact, with the skin present and face recognizable.

[62] Also called the Church of the Dormition of the Virgin and originally the Church of Our Lady, it was the first stone church built in Kiev, built by the order of her grandson Vladimir the Great from 989 to 996 at the site of the death of martyrs Theodore the Varangian and his son John. Olga was officially canonized and named Equal-to-the-Apostles in 1547.

Rus'. In Kiev, he crowned his eldest son Yaropolk, who was nine or ten years old at the time, and his other son Oleg was enthroned over the Drevlians.

When Svyatoslav was ready to go to his cherished Pereyaslavets on the Danube, the Novgorodians approached him, asking him to give them a prince, because they preferred the rule of a prince over rule by governors. "If you will not come to us, then we will choose a prince of our own," the Novgorodians also said. (*RPC*, 87)

"If only someone would be willing to join you," said Svyatoslav and relayed their plea to his sons. Yaropolk and Oleg refused.

Then Dobrynya, governor of Novgorod, said to the Novgorodians, "Seek Vladimir!" who was Svyatoslav's son born from Malusha, his concubine as well as councilor, sister of Dobrynya, making him Dobrynya's nephew.

"Give us Vladimir," said the Novgorodians.

"Here you go," said Svyatoslav, passing the infant from one hand to another. And thus, enthroning his sons, Svyatoslav went onwards with his men to the Danube, to his Pereyaslavets.

In his absence, things had drastically changed. The Bulgarians had become close allies with the Byzantines and managed to take over the surrounding countryside and the city of Pereyaslavets.

When longboats carrying Svyatoslav's warriors appeared on the Danube, the Bulgarians sailed out from the city in great numbers, and a fierce battle began. The Bulgarians initially gained the upper hand, attacking the Russians from multiple fronts. Seeing this, Svyatoslav cried, "Here is where we fall! Let us fight bravely, brothers and companions!" (*RPC*, 87) After hearing the prince's speech, his warriors concentrated their strength and, by evening, had taken the city in one final assault. After that, Svyatoslav, in his fashion of swift attacks, like a pouncing wildcat, began taking Bulgarian cities one after another, until he had taken the capital city of Preslav and captured the Bulgarian Tsar Boris II as well as his whole family and court. Then, after finding out that the Byzantines were to blame for this, enraged, he ordered a message to be sent to them: "I am coming against you; I want to take your city, just like I took Pereyaslavets."

After receiving Svyatoslav's declaration, Emperor Nikephoros II began hastily preparing the defense against the enemy and the fortification of Constantinople. He had an iron chain set up to block the straits to prevent Rus' access from the sea. Amid these preparations, Nikephoros II received harsh news that Arabs had defeated his armies in Near Asia, and following that, in the December of 969, he was assassinated in his own palace.

His assassins were the Empress Theophano herself and his general John I Tzimiskes, who gained the Byzantine throne after that. Armenian by lineage, his name meant "small." Despite his short stature, however, the new emperor was a skilled warrior and an extremely agile and strong man. Ascending to the throne in the forty-sixth year of his life, he still retained his virility and wasn't afraid to charge enemy ranks by himself; with the strength of a giant in his arms and legs, he was able to fell multiple enemies and then swiftly retreat to his men. He greatly surpassed other men of his time in various athletic feats such as jumping, ball games, spear throwing, and archery. Placing four horses next to each other, he could jump over them and mount the last one. He was such a good marksman that he could fly an arrow through a ring. Such was John I Tzimiskes, against whom Svyatoslav would now have to compete.

Loyal to his word to capture Constantinople, the Russian prince, in the spring of 970, crossed the Balkan Mountains, taking Philippopolis, and advanced further to Constantinople. Then John I Tzimiskes, seeing the Rus' offensive and learning about the successes of the Arabs over his troops in Near Asia, along with the fact that his kingdom had been suffering from famine for three years, decided to bide time, seeking peace with Svyatoslav and sending his strongest army against the Arabs.

To find out how many troops Svyatoslav had, the Byzantines sent envoys to Svyatoslav, saying they could not fight him and were ready to pay tribute to each man in his whole druzhina, which is how they sought to learn how many men he had. Svyatoslav perceived their intentions and, to conceal his lack of manpower, said that he had twenty thousand men, when in reality he only had ten. Upon discovering the Rus' numbers, the Byzantines didn't give tribute but gathered an army of a hundred thousand men and attacked Svyatoslav. Witnessing the great disadvantage in number, the Rus' druzhina's spirits faltered. But Svyatoslav's didn't.

Before the battle, he spoke to his warriors: "Now we have no place wither to flee. Whether we will or no, we must give battle. Let us not disgrace Rus', but rather sacrifice our lives, lest we be dishonored. For if we flee, we shall be disgraced. We must not take to flight, but we will resist boldly, and I will march before you. If my head falls, then look to yourselves." (*RPC*, 88)

"Wherever your head falls, there we too will lay down our own," was the response of the druzhina to their great prince, and after fierce combat, the Byzantines were routed. (*RPC*, 88) Svyatoslav advanced to Constantinople, taking and razing enemy cities on his way.

Seeing this, John I Tzimiskes gathered his council of nobles in the royal palace and told them, "What shall we do? We can't fight Svyatoslav."

"Send him gifts," said the nobles, "and you will see what he likes more, gold or expensive silks." So Tzimiskes sent Svyatoslav gold, silks, and wise men, whom he ordered to "get a good look at his face."

Svyatoslav was informed that Byzantine envoys had arrived with great humility. He ordered to let them in; the Byzantines arrived, bowed, and put gold and silks before him. Svyatoslav, after looking around, ordered his men to "hide this." After the envoys returned to the emperor, who had again gathered a council, they told him, "As we gave the gifts to him, he didn't even look at them and ordered them to be hidden."

Then one noble told the emperor, "Try him a second time; send him arms." (RPC, 88) And so they sent Svyatoslav a sword and various other weapons, which he accepted, praising and marveling at them, and ordered a bow and his gratitude sent to John I Tzimiskes.

When the envoys returned and said what happened, after thinking about it, the nobles said this to the emperor: "This man must be fierce, since he pays no heed to riches, but accepts arms. Submit to tribute." (RPC, 88–9)

After that, Emperor Tzimiskes sent envoys to Svyatoslav: "Don't go to Constantinople but take as much tribute as you want." And he sent him as much tribute as Svyatoslav had wished; Svyatoslav also took tribute for his fallen warriors, saying that "their families should receive it." (RPC, 89) It is likely that Tzimiskes and Svyatoslav even met in person. Then, after taking so much tribute, Svyatoslav returned to Pereyaslavets with great honor.

After repelling the imminent danger to Constantinople and paying a massive tribute to Svyatoslav, Tzimiskes immediately started gathering a vast army to finally crush the Rus'. He started hastily rallying his regiments from Near Asia, where they fought the Arabs. He gathered only the bravest men for his personal guard, calling them and their regiment the Immortals.

Svyatoslav was also not resting on his laurels: the Rus' druzhina was joined by a host of subjugated Bulgars, called to the aid of the Pechenegs and Hungarians, again going from Pereiaslav to Adrianople, spreading terrifying desolation and returning to the Danube.

As soon as the spring of 971 came, John I Tzimiskes put up his red banners and marched against the Rus'.

From his palace, he went to pray in the Church of the Holy Saviour in the Country (the Chora Church), then to the famous Hagia Sophia, and then to the Church of Saint Mary of Blachernae, the savior of Constantinople from the very same Kievan Rus'.

From the Palace of Blachernae, the emperor marveled at his fireboats, numbering three hundred, watching their skilled and organized sailing, and rewarded the sailors and warriors with money, ordering them to go to the Danube and prevent the Rus' from retreating home. His ships were sailing up the Danube when the emperor reached Adrianople by land. Here, he found out that the Rus' were nowhere nearby and that the narrow and dangerous passes in the Balkan Mountains, known as the *myshki*, had been left without guards by Svyatoslav. He quickly traversed those narrow passes with his Immortal regiment, followed by fifteen thousand infantry and thirteen thousand cavalrymen. The rest of his massive army, with siege engines and supplies, followed slowly behind.

Having traversed the mountain passes, Tzimiskes ambushed the Russian detachment stationed at the Bulgarian capital of Preslav, where the Bulgarian Tsar Boris II was staying with his wife, two children, and the famous Byzantine Kalokyros, who had been plotting to seize the throne of Constantinople with Svyatoslav's help.

After a terrible battle, Tzimiskes took Preslav, and the remaining brave Rus', numbering about seven thousand, retreated to Pereyaslavets. Kalokyros himself rode to the fortress of Dorostopol on the Danube in order to warn Svyatoslav, who was there at that time.

After approaching the Bulgarian Tsar Boris II and promising his help against the Rus', Tzimiskes ordered his army to attack, hoping to take Pereyaslavets, where our brave men were besieged.

However, overcoming the Rus' did not seem possible; the emperor joined the assaults, but with no success: the Byzantines fell against the city like wheat. Then he ordered the walls of the city to be set on fire from all sides.

To avoid dying in the fire, the Rus' marched into the field, and in a fight to the death, all seven thousand fell; only General Sveneld fought his way through and left to rejoin Svyatoslav.

After taking Pereyaslavets, Tzimiskes spent the Holy Pascha (Easter) there and sent prisoners to Svyatoslav to tell him of what happened and to decree to the Rus' prince that he could choose one of the two: either lay down his arms and, after asking forgiveness for his audacity, immediately leave Bulgaria, or prepare to defend himself against certain death.

Dorostopol

Svyatoslav, upon hearing this news, decided to make peace with Tzimiskes near the fortress of Dorostopol.

Dorostopol was the place on the Danube where Emperor Constantine-Equal-to-the-Apolstles saw the sign of the cross in the sky before battle and heard the voice say, "With this you shall win." Thus, Dorostopol, now known as Silistra (Bulgaria), was built by him to commemorate this miracle.

Tzimiskes reached Dorostopol in a few days, retaking Bulgarian cities and towns that willingly separated themselves from the Rus' and surrendered to him without a fight.

Then, to prevent more treason from the Bulgarian population, Svyatoslav ordered all the noble and rich Bulgars, numbering about three hundred, to be beheaded and the rest to be imprisoned in dungeons.

When Tzimiskes approached Dorostopol, Svyatoslav let out his whole host. He only had sixty thousand men; the emperor had far more. After forming a wall with shields and spears, the Russians met the Byzantines, like two indestructible walls clashing. A fierce battle began, but no side could gain the upper hand. The initiative passed from one side to another a dozen times. At last, the emperor, after lowering the imperial banner, took his cavalry reserve and attacked the Rus' from the rear. The Rus', unable to counter the enemy cavalry due to a lack of their own, retreated behind the city walls.

The Byzantines were singing songs of victory and were rewarded by their emperor, but at the same time, they had to fortify their camp, setting up moats and ditches, because they were afraid of another Rus' attack. After one unsuccessful assault on the city, they began moving their fireships closer to the walls. After witnessing the fearsome ships on the Danube, the Byzantines started cheering while the Rus' moved their longboats closer to the walls, and on the next day, protected by long shields and armored in mail, they sailed again to face the Byzantines. Again the battle switched initiative from side to side many more times until finally, one Byzantine soldier killed a brave Rus' general with a spear, causing our men to retreat behind the walls again.[63]

---

[63] Byzantine historians John Skylitzes and Leo the Deacon assert that Sveneld (Sphangel) was killed here, but the Rus' chronicles do not and mention him several times afterwards.

With the arrival of the fireships that blocked the entrance to the Danube, Svyatoslav realized that he needed to hold at all costs and fortified the walls with an additional deep moat. But the Rus' lacked the most important thing: food. Getting it would require some desperate measures.

And so, one dark night, during a fearsome thunderstorm, two thousand valiant Rus' manned small boats and fearlessly embarked in search of food. They searched fruitlessly along the river's shores and were on their way home. That's when they saw a Byzantine supply train: men watering horses, gathering wood, and foraging. They stealthily left their boats, flanked the Byzantines by moving through the forest, and then ambushed them, returning to the city with many spoils. Upon hearing this news, Tzimiskes was stunned. He declared that his generals would face the penalty of death if this were to happen again. After that, the Byzantines besieged the Rus' with even greater effort, ditches were dug, and guards were dispatched to the river shores to prevent more raids to finally make Svyatoslav succumb to hunger. The Byzantines saw no other way to defeat him.

Nevertheless, the Rus' continued their daring raids, inflicting heavy casualties on the Byzantines. During one of those raids, when the Rus' were attempting to destroy some Byzantine siege engines, a general rode against them who was a close relative of the emperor, named John Kourkouas. He had been into the hops and fell off his horse. The rich and intricate armor, gilded with gold, led the Rus' to believe it was the emperor himself. They attacked him and chopped him into small pieces along with his armor; his severed head was impaled on a spear and placed atop a tower as a way of bragging about having slain the emperor himself. Encouraged by these events, the Rus' once again took the field and prepared for battle. The Byzantines advanced against them with all of their forces. The first man among the Rus' after Svyatoslav was the brave General Ikmor; he was lowborn and had achieved his rank only through courage. Ikmor fiercely slashed through the Byzantine ranks, slaying them without mercy left and right. At this time, one of the Byzantines' strongmen by the name of Anemas drew his sword and, spurring his horse with great fervor against the Rus' giant, struck him so powerfully that he cut off his head and arm and sent them flying far onto the ground. This sudden death of the brave Ikmor greatly affected our warriors, who retreated behind the city's walls.

After this battle, the Byzantines, while checking the corpses of our warriors, were surprised to find many women in men's clothing among them, who fought as bravely and passionately as their husbands and relatives.

When night came along and the moon had risen, the Rus' entered the field, gathered their dead, and burned them in a pyre after sacrificing prisoners and women, as per pagan custom. Then, according to the words of the Byzantines, after this bloody sacrifice, the Rus' put roosters and small children into the current of the Danube, most likely those whose mothers fell in battle earlier that day.

After these customs and sacrificial rites had been observed, the sun rose and the day began. Svyatoslav and his men began pondering what to do next. Some quietly advised taking to their ships and fleeing under cover of darkness. Others suggested pleading for peace since outrunning fireships seemed impossible. All unanimously suggested ending the war. Then Svyatoslav, with a deep-hearted sigh, spoke to his druzhina:

> If we give the Byzantines their way now, then where shall be the glory of the Rus' sword that tirelessly vanquished our enemies; where shall be the glory of the Rus' name, which bloodlessly conquered whole nations? We inherited brave deeds from our fathers and grandfathers! Let's stand strong. Saving ourselves by flight is not our custom. We either live and be victorious or die with glory. The dead do not know shame, but if we flee the battle, then how would we look our people in the eyes?

Thus spoke Svyatoslav.

His brave warriors couldn't argue with his courageous speech, and all excitedly decided to lay down their bones for the glory of the Rus' name. In the meantime, the night had passed, and dawn had broken.

On July 24th, 971, early in the morning, all the Rus' left Dorostopol and chained the city gates to ensure that they would never return. Then a ferocious battle ensued. The day was hot and humid. By midday, the Byzantines, tormented by heat and thirst, began to retreat; while suffering from the same conditions, the Rus' began furiously chasing them down. Then Tzimiskes appeared with his Immortals to aid the Byzantines; he ordered his troops be brought water and wine. The Byzantines returned to battle again. The battle, however, was still fairly equal: not a single side had yielded. Then the Byzantines slyly retreated. The Rus' rushed after them. But it was only a cunning trick to lure our lads further into the field. Then an even more ferocious battle ensued, during which the Byzantine general Theodor fell off his horse. The Rus' tried to kill him, while the Byzantines tried to save him. The general was also skillfully defending himself. He grabbed a Rus' by his belt and swung him from one side to another like a light shield, deflecting swords and spears. Finally, the Byzantines saved their hero, and both armies, without yielding to each other, ceased the battle.

Seeing that the Russians couldn't be defeated, Tzimiskes decided to resolve the conflict by personal combat and sent Svyatoslav a challenge to a duel. This message was relayed to Svyatoslav from the Byzantine emperor: "Better to have one death to end the struggle than to doom whole groups of our people to extermination. Whichever one of us wins, let him take everything."

But Svyatoslav did not accept the challenge, suspecting some kind of treachery from the cunning Tzimiskes; he sent him a condescending reply: "I know what's good for me better than my enemy. If your emperor is tired of living, then there are plenty of other ways that lead to death. He can choose whichever one he likes!" Then the bloody massacre resumed with renewed rage.

For a long time, it was unclear who would get the upper hand. The Byzantine warrior Anemas, having recently vanquished the glorious giant Ikmor, then attacked Svyatoslav himself, who, in rage and ferocity, was issuing orders to his regiments. After speeding up his steed with measured strides in different directions, he charged our prince and, wounding him in the shoulder, threw him to the ground. Only mail armor and shield saved Svyatoslav from death. But Anemas died with his horse under blows from Rus' spears and swords. After that, in a terrifying rage, the Rus' charged the Byzantine ranks, which were, at last, unable to stand the extraordinary onslaught of Svyatoslav's warriors and began to retreat. Then the emperor, with a spear in hand, rode out with his Immortals against the fleeing Byzantines and ended the retreat. Drums were beating, trumpets were blowing, and the Byzantines, along with their emperor, turned their horses and marched at the Rus'.

Then a severe storm approached from the south, raising dust and rain right in the face of the Rus' host, and someone on a white horse appeared ahead of the Byzantine regiments, encouraging them to assault the enemy; in a miraculous way, they were able to pierce the Rus' lines. Nobody had seen that warrior among the Byzantines before or after the battle. They looked for him for a long time after, as the emperor wanted to reward him. Then a rumor spread that it was the great martyr Theodore Stratelates, to whom the emperor had prayed for protection and aid since the battle occurred on his feast day. They also said that in Constantinople, a young girl who was especially devoted to God had seen the Theotokos in a dream, who told the fiery warriors accompanying her, "Bring me Theodore the martyr!" The warriors instantly brought forward a brave young man. Then the Theotokos said, "Theodore! Your John (the emperor) battles Scythians in dire conditions; rush to his aid! If you are late, then he will be in danger." The warrior obeyed and departed immediately. Thus the girl's dream ended as well.

Led by faith in divine intervention, the Byzantines pushed the Rus' back to the city walls. Svyatoslav himself, who was wounded and bleeding, would have perished had it not been for the coming night.

Despite his scorn and anger over the collapse of his army's ranks, Svyatoslav understood that the battle was lost, and thus, desiring to preserve the remains of his druzhina, sent peace terms to the emperor the following day; the conditions were thus: the Rus' would give the Byzantines Dorostopol and return their prisoners; they'd leave Bulgaria and return home on their ships; and in exchange for this, the Byzantines would let them through. Then the Byzantines would freely allow the import of bread from Kievan Rus' and would treat Russian merchants courteously.

Tzimiskes eagerly accepted the peace offer, since he only thought that he had won against the Rus' due to a miracle, and sent each member of the Rus' host two measures of bread. In total, twenty-two thousand men received bread; thus, from Svyatoslav's host of sixty thousand, thirty-eight thousand courageous men had fallen.

Tzimiskes was so happy about the end of the war against unbeatable Svyatoslav that he built a marvelous church over the nearby grave of Saint Theodore and sanctioned a large budget for its maintenance. The city itself, where his relics remained, was renamed from Euchaneia to Theodoropolis. Then in Constantinople, within the palace grounds, he built a new church for our Savior without sparing any expenses on its luxurious design. Furthermore, he gathered an extensive tithe from the people. Finally, he ordered the minting of Byzantine coins with the image of our Savior and the words "Jesus Christ King of Kings" on both sides, which was unheard of before, and which was also done by successive emperors.

Thus was his victory over Svyatoslav considered—the powerful Byzantine Emperor John I Tzimiskes, a brave and skillful warrior and military leader, had achieved victory over the Rus' under the command of Svyatoslav.

A few days after peace was reached, before the Rus' departed for home, some former enemies met on the shores of the Danube.

Tzimiskes came mounted on a horse, with weapons gilded with gold, followed by a regiment of cavalrymen in shining armor. The Byzantine Leo the Deacon, who witnessed the meeting, writes:

> [Svyatoslav] arrived sailing along the river in a Scythian light boat, grasping an oar and rowing with his companions as if he were one of them. His appearance is as follows: he was of moderate height, neither taller than average, nor particularly short; his eyebrows were thick; he had grey eyes and a snub nose; his beard was clean-shaven, but he let the hair grow abundantly on his upper lip where it was bushy and long; and he shaved his head completely, except for a lock of hair that hung down on one side, as a mark of the nobility of his ancestry; he was solid in the neck, broad in the chest and very well articulated in the rest of his body; he had a rather angry and savage appearance; on one ear was fastened a gold earring, adorned with two pearls with a red gemstone between them; his clothing was white, no different from that of his companions except in cleanliness. After talking briefly with the emperor about their reconciliations, he departed sitting on the helmsman's seat of the boat.[64]

Thus was Svyatoslav. Like a simple warrior, he sat in his longboat with his druzhina's oarsmen and worked the oar as they did. And in this simplicity and brotherly unification lay the great power of Svyatoslav.

By his example, many successive Rus' rulers always considered Rus' warriors their brothers and, when circumstances required, never hesitated to share their difficult work and last piece of bread with them and would risk their lives on the field of battle with them.

Death of Svyatoslav

After parting with the Rus' prince, John I Tzimiskes hurried to Constantinople, where he was greeted with festivities. Svyatoslav and his men sailed back to the Dnieper in their logboats. They wanted to reach Kiev the usual way, through the Dnieper's narrows. However, his old general Sveneld advised him to ride around since the Pechenegs often sat in ambush there. But Svyatoslav didn't listen to Sveneld's advice; he put too much faith

---

[64] Leo the Deacon, *History*, Book IX, 199–200.

in the Byzantine emperor's word, who even promised to send envoys to the Pechenegs so they wouldn't attack the returning Rus'. But the typical scheming of Byzantines was witnessed even here: the Pechenegs were informed that "Svyatoslav returns home to Kievan Rus' with a small druzhina, having taken from the Byzantines many riches and immeasurable wealth." So when the narrows were reached, Svyatoslav discovered they were already full of Pechenegs. It was impossible to go through them, so they decided to winter on the Dnieper, a little below the narrows, in Beloberezhie. But the Rus' didn't have enough bread, and a great famine came, and they had to sustain themselves on fish only.

In the spring of the following year, 972, Svyatoslav set out for the narrows, where the Rus' were expected by the Pecheneg khan Kurya, who ambushed them and killed the whole druzhina, including Svyatoslav. Escaping to Kiev on horseback, only General Sveneld survived, without a doubt having been tasked by Svyatoslav beforehand to go there and gather a host. Thus perished Svyatoslav, the most warlike of Rus' leaders, in the thirty-second year of his life, having ruled for twenty-eight years.

The Pecheneg khan Kurya who killed him made a chalice out of his skull, which he gilded with gold and drank from in memory of his victory over the Rus' prince.

Yaropolk and the Strife with His Brother

After Svyatoslav's death, Yaropolk, who sat in Kiev, became the eldest in the princely line. He was no older than fifteen at the time. The younger brothers were Oleg in Drevlian lands and Vladimir in Novgorod. Of course, all affairs were carried out not by the princes but by the boyars behind them. Yaropolk would soon inherit the great power which was held by his father's general Sveneld. Once, Sveneld's son Lyut entered Drevlian land while hunting after some beast. It has to be said that hunting was considered to be an important and favorite pastime for both princes and boyars, and forests were certainly brimming with various beasts: bears, moose, giant bison, black martens, wild boars, deer, and goats were in great abundance.

Oleg left to hunt on the same day, and upon discovering that this Lyut whom he had met was Sveneld's son, ordered him to be killed. This was in 975.

Of course, Sveneld used all of his power to avenge his son and, two years later, convinced Yaropolk to raise levies and march on his brother in the Drevlian land. Both hosts met, and Yaropolk's forces overcame those of Oleg. Oleg rushed to escape with his men, and at the entrance to the town of Ovruch, there was a big stampede on the bridge among the retreating forces, and Oleg was pushed into the moat and crushed by falling horses and human corpses.

When Yaropolk entered Ovruch, he ordered that his brother be found, but he couldn't be found anywhere until finally, one Drevlian said, "I saw he was pushed off the bridge." They began tossing horses and human corpses out of the moat and finally found Oleg's body. When he was carried out and laid out on a carpet, Yaropolk wept bitterly over his brother's corpse and said to Sveneld scornfully, "See the fulfillment of your wish." (*RPC*, 91) After burying Oleg near Ovruch, Yaropolk took possession of the Drevlian land.

When rumor of fratricide reached Novgorod, Vladimir and Dobrynya sensed danger. By the rules of blood feud, Vladimir had to bring vengeance to Yaropolk for his brother's death, and knowing that his brother expected that, Vladimir realized Yaropolk would try to kill him too. In such circumstances, Vladimir, seeing his weakness against Yaropolk, decided to cross beyond the sea to his relatives—the Rus' Varangians—to gather a big host and avenge his brother's death.

Yaropolk, on the other hand, after Vladimir's departure to the Varangians, put his governor in Novgorod and became the ruler of all Rus'.

While Vladimir was gathering his army among the Varangians, Yaropolk marched against the Pechenegs to avenge his father's death, subjugated them, and made them pay him tribute. Then the Byzantines approached him with a tribute of their new Emperor Basil II; this Basil took the throne following John I Tzimiskes, whose life had ended very painfully from the poison with which he was assassinated.

Yaropolk graciously accepted the Byzantine envoys and reestablished the old peaceful and loving relations. In Kiev at that time, many Christians were among them, of course, also being cherished guests. Yaropolk himself was raised by his grandmother, the wise lady Olga, in Christian custom and hadn't been baptized only because she was afraid of the wrath of his father, Svyatoslav. Yaropolk's wife was also Christian; she had been an Orthodox nun, captured by Svyatoslav and given over to his son because of her extraordinary beauty.

During those friendly meetings between Yaropolk and the Byzantines, Vladimir, having spent the preceding three years overseas, had brought with him a Varangian force, and his first act was to chase away Yaropolk's governors from Novgorod, ordering them to tell his brother, "Vladimir is coming for you, prepare for war." Thus had spoken his father Svyatoslav when he went against his enemies; thus, his son started the campaign against his brother.

Furthermore, not only did Vladimir wage war on Yaropolk, he also decided to steal his bride. Since he had been married to a Byzantine lowborn, Yaropolk, in 980, had also become engaged to the beauty Rogneda, the daughter of Prince Rogvolod of Polotsk (not of Rurik's dynasty).

As he prepared to wage war against his brother, Vladimir sent Rogvolod emissaries to also ask for the hand of his daughter. Rogvolod, conflicted by the choice of which brother to give his daughter to, asked her which one she would prefer. The proud Rogneda replied, "I will not draw off the boots of a slave's son, but I want Yaropolk instead." (*RPC*, 91) This response was also relayed to Vladimir, which insulted not only the young prince, but also his uncle, Dobrynya, the brother of Malusha, who had been called a slave by Rogneda.

To wash away the insult with blood, Vladimir gathered his Varangians, Novgorodians, Chuds, and Krivichs and marched on Polotsk. After a battle with Polotskians, Vladimir took the city, killed her father and two brothers in front of Rogneda, and then forced her to marry him; of course, all of this was masterminded by Vladimir's uncle, Dobrynya, because the prince himself was still very young—no older than sixteen or seventeen years old.

After avenging Rogneda's insult to his mother's memory, Vladimir marched on Yaropolk to avenge the death of Oleg.

Yaropolk no longer had the old man Sveneld; General Blud had taken over the elder boyar's position.

This Blud was a traitor who secretly sided with Vladimir and conspired with him, and he gave his great prince some advice that would lead to his demise.

When Yaropolk found out from his banished governors that his younger brother had come back from overseas, he wanted to immediately gather his armies and march against Vladimir since he was very brave. Blud, instead, convinced Yaropolk not to gather troops and that Vladimir would not be able to fight him.

"It cannot happen," he said, "that Vladimir would attack you. Such would be to say that a titmouse would fight an eagle. We have nothing to fear and no reason to gather our armies. This would be forlorn work for you and your warriors." As a result of this cunning advice, when Vladimir descended on Kiev, Yaropolk didn't have an army, so he couldn't meet him in the field, and fortified himself inside the city.

Vladimir had, in the meantime, sent his men to Blud and begun luring him, saying, "Be my friend; if I kill my brother, I will regard you as my father, and you shall have much honor from me. It was not I who began to fight with my brother, but he, and I was for that reason overcome by fear, and therefore have come out against him." (*RPC*, 92)

Blud replied to Vladimir that he would help with all of his heart, and they began conspiring together. Then it turned out that Kievans supported their prince. Then Blud came up with a new idea: he began smearing Kievans, telling Yaropolk that they were conspiring with Vladimir against him and calling to Vladimir, saying, "Come to the city; we will hand over Yaropolk." Thus convincing Yaropolk that he would be in great danger if he remained in Kiev, Blud then offered him to secretly flee to another town, closer to the Pechenegs. Yaropolk agreed and fled to the town of Rodnya,[65] on the Ros River, while Vladimir took Kiev without a battle and besieged his brother in Rodnya, where famine soon began since Blud had intentionally not prepared any provisions. This famine was so fierce that people began using "famine as in Rodnya" as a saying.

Having placed Yaropolk in a desperate circumstance, Blud told him, "Do you see what a large force your brother has? We cannot overcome them. Make peace with your brother." (*RPC*, 92) Yaropolk was forced to agree to this, and Blud sent a message to Vladimir: "Your wish has been granted; I'll bring you Yaropolk, and you can think of how to kill him."

Then, upon receiving this news, Vladimir went into his father's castle hall and sat with his druzhina, while Blud sent Yaropolk to him, instructing him to say, "I'll take what you give me." Without suspecting any treachery, the naive Yaropolk set out to his younger brother in Kiev, while his loyal bodyguard Varyazhko sensed danger and told his prince, "My Prince, they will kill you. Flee rather to the Pechenegs and collect an army." (*RPC*, 93) But Yaropolk didn't listen to him and went to his brother. As soon as he walked through the palace doors, the two Varangians standing at the sides impaled him with their swords, while Blud shut the doors instantly so that none of his druzhina would see the unfortunate Yaropolk. Loyal Varyazhko, seeing that his prince was dead, fled from the court to the Pechenegs and so persistently made war against Vladimir alongside them to avenge

---

[65] Not to be confused with the modern city of Rodnya along the Volga near Moscow. This Rodnya lies south of Kiev on the west bank of the Dnieper where it is joined by the Ros River, near the modern town of Kaniv, Ukraine.

his prince's death that Vladimir could barely manage to call him back to his side after swearing an oath never to do him any ill.

Vladimir the Pagan

After defeating his brother, Vladimir governed from Kiev and became the ruler of all of the Russian Land. His first act was to marry a beautiful Byzantine, the former nun that was his brother's widow. As a fearsome heathen, who conquered Kiev with his pagan Novgorodian druzhina, Vladimir began to oppress Christians, who were rather numerous in Kiev by that time, even though they had already had their church, Saint Ilya, since the time of Igor.

As for state matters, Vladimir, despite his youth, proved himself to be as stoic and courageous a prince as his father Svyatoslav. The Varangians that came to him from the sea, upon settling in Kiev, came to be very unruly and even demanded that Vladimir force the Kievans to pay tribute to him. He told them that they must wait a month; in a month, however, upon selecting the best, smartest, and most courageous men among those Varangians and giving them cities to govern, he refused the rest of the tribute and suggested they enter into the Byzantine emperors' service, which they did.[66]

After that, Vladimir waged several successful campaigns. He defeated the Poles and took from them the towns of Peremysl, Cherven, and others, where Red Rus' was situated, thus adding them to Russian Lands.

Then the Vyatichi refused to pay tribute, but Vladimir subjugated them immediately. After this, Vladimir campaigned against the Yotvingians, a warlike tribe living northwest of the Drevlians, and achieved complete victory over them.

Finally, in 984, Vladimir very successfully defeated the Radimichs. He sent his general against them, whose name was Wolf's Tail (Volchiy Khvost), and who defeated them on the river Pischan.[67] Russians from then on began to ridicule the Radimichs, saying that they "run from wolves' tails."

Remaining a devout pagan, Vladimir built many idols to thank the gods

---

[66] This Varangian mercenary force of the Byzantine's was known as the Varangian Guard.
[67] While both Nechvolodov and the *Primary Chronicle* do say "Pischan" here, it's unclear which river this is meant to be. The location of this battle was likely where the tributary river Pronya meets with the Sozh River, at the location of modern Slawharad, Belarus, formerly called Prupoy.

for his successes. On a hill close to the castle, he built a giant statue of Perun with a silver head and a golden mustache.

Dobrynya, sent as governor to Novgorod, was just as devout a pagan and built a giant statue on the shores of the Volkhov. "And the people of Novgorod offered sacrifice to it as if to God himself," the *Primary Chronicle* says. (*RPC*, 94)

While building shrines, Vladimir took many wives in addition to Rogneda and the Byzantine one, taken from Yaropolk. In total, according to various accounts, there were eight hundred of them. Proud Rogneda, insulted by this neglect by her husband, decided to murder him.

Once when Vladimir came to her and went to sleep, she took a knife and would have stabbed him if he hadn't woken up in time and grabbed her hand. "From my sorrows did I raise my hand against you," responded Rogneda to her angry husband, who asked her why she would want to kill him. "You killed my father and subjugated his land because of me. And now you no longer love me or this infant," she said, pointing at her young son Izyaslav.

Vladimir remained silent but ordered her to wear the royal dress she wore on her wedding day and sit on her immaculately garnished bed in her bedroom. He wanted to kill her with his sword as if it were a wedding ceremony. But Rogneda knew what her husband was thinking, and before he arrived, she did this: she gave little Izyaslav an unsheathed sword and instructed him what to say when his father entered.

When Vladimir entered, little Izyaslav stepped out with a big sword in his hands: "Father, do you think you are the only one walking around here?"

"Nobody expected you here!" exclaimed the stunned Vladimir, dropping his sword. Then he called his council and instructed them to decide for him.

The boyars thus decided: "Don't kill her because of the lad, but give her land to govern along with her son." Then Vladimir built a special town for Rogneda and named it Izyaslavl after her son,[68] while proclaiming her new name as Goreslava.

After this occasion, Vladimir continued his pagan lifestyle. In 983, upon returning from another victorious campaign again the Yotvingians, he decided to honor his gods especially well through a human sacrifice. They decided to cast straws on a young man and woman. The straw was

---

[68] Now called Zaslawye in the Minsk Region of Belarus.

drawn by a young Varangian, beautiful in the face as well as soul and also a Christian.[69] His name was John. This youngster lived with his father, Theodore, who was also a follower of the Christian faith. The pagans, happy that the straw was drawn by one of the Christians whom they especially disliked in Vladimir's time, went to his house to get the youngster; they declared that they had come for his son, to bleed him for the gods.

"These are not gods," answered his father, "but only idols of wood. Today it is, and tomorrow it will rot away. These gods do not eat, or drink, or speak; they are fashioned by hand out of wood. But the God whom the Greeks serve and worship is one; it is he who has made heaven and earth, the stars, the moon, the sun, and mankind, and has granted him life upon earth. But what have these gods created? They are themselves manufactured. I will not give up my son to devils." (*RPC*, 95)

When the men that were sent relayed his reply, the pagans were enraged and marched in great numbers to Theodore's house and demanded he hand over his son. "Give us your son as a tribute to the gods!" screamed the crowd.

"If they be gods," answered Theodore, "they will send one of their number to take my son. What need have you of him?" (*RPC*, 96) Then enraged people set his house on fire and killed both Varangians.

Eventually, the Church of the Tithes was built on that spot, and the relics of the martyr John were moved to the Caves of Saint Anthony in the Kiev Monastery of the Caves, where they reside now. Those without children come to pray there for fertility, but where Theodore's relics are is unknown.

The murder of the Varangians, John and his father Theodore, created a strong impression on Vladimir.

Since then, he began thinking of spiritual matters more and became more estranged from paganism. Of course, he must have seen the advantage of the Christian faith over his own, all the more so since in Kiev, there were many Christians among the merchants and other citizens since the times of Askold and Olga. They were even present within the prince's druzhina; their pure life was clearly in stark contrast with the pagan lifestyle.

The prince's doubt in the pagan faith, which he had ferociously followed, soon became known to everyone. And so, he accepted visits by the

---

[69] John, or Ioann, and his father Theodore, or Feodor, were ethnically Scandinavian but lived in Kiev after Theodore finished his mercenary service with the Byzantine Empire, during which service he converted to Christianity.

Volga Bulgars who followed the Islamic faith, the Khazars of Jewish law, the Germanic peoples who had accepted Catholicism and submitted to the pope, and, finally, the Greek Orthodox, the Byzantines. They praised their faith and tried to convince the great Rus' prince to convert to their law, as well as the rest of the Rus' people.

"Though you are wise and prudent," said the Volga Bulgars, "you have no religion. Adopt out faith, and revere [Muhammad]."[70] (*RPC*, 96)

"And what is your faith?" asked Vladimir.

"We believe in God," they answered, "and Muhammad tells us: practice circumcision, don't eat pork, don't drink wine, and after death, Muhammad will give everyone seventy beautiful wives."

After listening to them carefully, Vladimir decided, "Drinking is the joy of the Russes. We cannot exist without that pleasure." (*RPC*, 97)

Then came the Germans from the pope, who started convincing him to accept Catholicism. "And what are your commandments?" asked Vladimir of them.

"Fasting according to one's strength," answered the Germans. "But whatever one eats or drinks is all to the glory of God, as our teacher Paul has said." (*RPC*, 97)

"Depart hence," retorted Vladimir. "Our fathers accepted no such principle." (*RPC*, 97)

After the Germans, the Khazar Jews came to Vladimir. To denigrate the Christian faith, they told Vladimir that the Christians worship the one they crucified. "But we believe," they continued, "in the one God of Abraham, Isaac, and Jacob." (*RPC*, 97)

"And what are your laws?" asked Vladimir.

"Circumcision," answered the Khazars, "not to eat pork, not to eat hares, and observe the Sabbath."

"And where is your land?" then asked Vladimir.

"In Jerusalem," he received as an answer.

"Do you live there now?" the prince continued.

"God was angry at our forefathers," said the Jews, "and scattered us among the gentiles on account of our sins. Our land was then given to the Christians." (*RPC*, 97)

"How can you hope to teach others while you yourselves are cast out

---

[70] This translation cited of the *Russian Primary Chronicle* uses the spelling "Mahomet." As earlier, the surrounding quotations without a citation are paraphrased by Nechvolodov, and the editors prefer the modern spelling of "Muhammad."

and scattered abroad by the hand of God? If God loved you and your faith, you would not be thus dispersed in foreign lands. Do you expect us to accept that fate also?" (*RPC*, 97)

Finally, the Byzantines sent Vladimir a learned man. He began to describe the lies and falsehoods of other religions orderly. Islam he described in such a way that Vladimir spat and said, "This is a vile thing." (*RPC*, 98)

Then he spoke of Catholicism, that it is the same faith as the Orthodox one, but with errors, and they serve unleavened bread as a sacrament, yet the Lord ordered us to serve leavened bread because when he broke bread, he said to his disciples at the Last Supper, "This is my body, broken for you."

After listening to the wise words of the learned man, Vladimir said, "The Khazar Jews came to me and said the Germans and Byzantines worship the one they had crucified."

To this, the Byzantine replied, "Of a truth we believe in him. For some of the prophets foretold that God should be incarnate, and others that he should be crucified and buried, but arise on the third day and ascend into heaven. For the Jews killed the prophets, and still others they persecuted. When their prophecy was fulfilled, our Lord came down to earth, was crucified, arose again, and ascended into heaven. He awaited their repentance for forty-six years, but they did not repent, so that the Lord let loose the Romans upon them. Their cities were destroyed, and they were scattered among the gentiles, under whom they are now in servitude." (*RPC*, 98)

After attentively listening, Vladimir asked the Byzantine, "Then why did God descend to earth and accept such suffering?"

Then the learned man said that if he wanted, he could tell him everything in the order of how it happened, so he retold him the whole Holy Scripture: on the creation of the world; on the pride and self-love of Satan; on how Satan was banished from the heavens; on the life of Adam in paradise; about how Eve was created to be his companion and how first sin occurred, and how Adam and Eve were banished from paradise; how Cain murdered Abel; how men, upon growing in numbers, had forgotten God and begun to live like beasts, and how God punished them later; how, from the righteous Noah and his three sons, all other nations came to be, and then he told of what happened after the deluge, all the way to the arrival of our Lord Jesus Christ on earth and his acceptance of the suffering, and then his miraculous Resurrection from the dead and his Ascension. And this is how the Byzantine wise man concluded his tale: "God hath appointed a day, in which he shall come from heaven to judge both the quick [living] and the dead, and to render to each according to his deeds; to the righteous, the

kingdom of heaven and ineffable beauty, bliss without end, and eternal life;
but to sinners, the torments of hell and a worm that sleeps not, and of their
torments there shall be no end." (*RPC*, 109)

Having told him this, the Byzantine wise man showed Vladimir an inscription that depicted God's Judgment: to the right were righteous men
joyously walking to the heavens; to the left, sinners were going into eternal
suffering. After a sigh, Vladimir pondered what he had heard and said,
"Happy are they upon the right, but woe to those upon the left!" (*RPC*, 110)

"If you desire to take your place upon the right with the just, then accept
baptism," answered the Byzantine. (*RPC*, 110)

Vladimir took these words to heart but answered, "I shall wait yet a little longer." (*RPC*, 110) Then he called his druzhina and the eldest citizens of
Kiev to council and told them, "Behold, the Bulgars came before me urging
me to accept their religion. Then came the Germans and praised their own
faith; and after them came the Jews. Finally the Greeks appeared, criticizing all other faiths but commending their own, and they spoke at length,
telling the history of the whole world from its beginning. Their words were
artful, and it was wondrous to listen and pleasant to hear them. They
preach the existence of another world. 'Whoever adopts our religion and
then dies shall arise and live forever. But whosoever embraces another
faith, shall be consumed with fire in the next world.' What is your opinion
on this subject, and what do you answer?" (*RPC*, 110)

"You know, oh Prince," said the boyars and elders, "that no man con-
demns his own possessions, but praises them instead. If you desire to make
certain, you have servants at your disposal. Send them to inquire about the
ritual of each and how he worships God." (*RPC*, 110)

The Baptism of the Kievan Rus'

These words pleased the prince, and he selected ten men of a kind and
wise nature, who first went to the Volga Bulgars, then to the Germanics,
then to the Byzantines. Upon their return, all the boyars from his druzhina
and city elders gathered again. The envoys told of what they saw in the different countries: "When we journeyed among the Bulgars, we beheld how
they worship in their temple, called a mosque, while they stand ungirt. The
Bulgar bows, sits down, looks hither and thither like one possessed, and
there is no happiness among them, but instead only sorrow and a dreadful
stench. Their religion is not good. Then we went among the Germans, and
saw them performing many ceremonies in their temples; but we beheld no

glory there. Then we went to Greece, and the Greeks led us to the edifices where they worship their God, and we knew not whether we were in heaven or on earth. For on earth there is no such splendor or such beauty, and we are at a loss how to describe it. We only know that God dwells there among men, and their service is fairer than the ceremonies of other nations. For we cannot forget that beauty. Every man, after tasting something sweet, is afterward unwilling to accept that which is bitter, and therefore we cannot dwell longer here." (*RPC*, 110)

Then the boyars spoke and said, "If the Greek faith were evil, it would not have been adopted by your grandmother Olga who was wiser than all other men." (*RPC*, 110)

"Where shall I accept baptism?" then asked Vladimir.

"Wherever you would like," answered the druzhina.

This was in the year 988.

At that time, Vladimir had a conflict with the town of Korsun, which belonged to the Byzantine emperors, and he campaigned against it.

Upon reaching the city, the Rus' besieged it and built a mound by the city wall to get over it. But the Byzantines dug beneath their wall and would take the earth that the Rus' piled up there. Thus Vladimir's endeavor did not progress. But then, among the population of Korsun, there was a friend of the Rus' named Anastasius. He sent an arrow to our camp with a note, saying, "There are springs behind you to the east, from which water flows in pipes. Dig down and cut them off." (*RPC*, 112)

Happy with this message, Vladimir exclaimed, "If Korsun surrenders, then I will accept baptism." So then the well was dug out, and the thirst-tormented Korsunians surrendered in a few days.

On his entrance to the city, Vladimir immediately sent envoys to the co-emperors and brothers Basil II and Constantine VIII with these words: "Behold, I have captured your glorious city. I have also heard that you have an unwedded sister. Unless you give her to me to wife, I shall deal with your own city as I have with Kherson [Korsun]." (*RPC*, 112)

Alarmed and grief-stricken, the emperors replied, "It is not meet for Christians to give in marriage to pagans. If you are baptized, you shall have her to wife, inherit the kingdom of God, and be our companion in the faith. Unless you do so, however, we cannot give you our sister in marriage." (*RPC*, 112)

Vladimir replied, "I've already tested your faith and am ready to accept baptism; I like this faith and its rites which the wise men you sent me spoke of." Constantine VIII and Basil II were overjoyed by this response and began to beg their sister Anna to marry Vladimir. They sent envoys to him to inform him to baptize himself before they sent Anna. Vladimir said, "Let the priests that bring her baptize me." With great difficulty, the brothers convinced their sister to comply and sent her to Korsun with the priests.

Anna's parting with her brothers was very upsetting. "It is as if I were setting out into captivity," she lamented; "better were it for me to die at home." (*RPC*, 112)

Her brothers cheered her up by saying, "Through your agency God turns the land of Rus' to repentance, and you will relieve Greece from the danger of grievous war. Do you not see how much harm the Russes have already brought upon the Greeks? If you do not set out, they may bring on us the same misfortunes." (*RPC*, 112)

Escorted by the priests, Anna boarded a ship with tearstained eyes, bid farewell to her cherished motherland, and sailed to Korsun, where the citizenry solemnly greeted her. At that time, in God's design, Vladimir had become so badly ill in his eyes that he couldn't see anything, which brought him much sorrow. He didn't know what to do. Upon finding out about this sickness, Anna sent word to him that to rid himself of this malady, he should accept baptism soon.

Upon hearing this, Vladimir said, "If this proves true, then of a surety is the God of the Christians great." (*RPC*, 113)

Then his baptism came. After an announcement, the Bishop of Korsun, along with the priests that came from Constantinople, baptized the great prince. As soon as hands were laid on him, Vladimir instantly regained his sight. Having been touched to the depth of his soul by this, he exclaimed, "I have now perceived the one true God." (*RPC*, 112)

After the baptism, during which Vladimir was given the Christian name of Basil, the wedding with Anna immediately followed, and then, taking the queen with him,[71] along with Metropolitan Michael, who had been appointed for the Rus', and Anastasius, and priests along with holy vessels and parts of the relics of Saint Clement and his disciple Phoebus, the great prince returned to Kiev. From Korsun, they also dispatched two giant copper statues and four copper horses of great Byzantine workmanship to Kiev. Korsun itself was handed back to the Byzantine emperors, as a dowry

---

[71] Anna was a Porphyrogenita, a legitimate daughter born in the special purple chamber of the Byzantine Emperor's Palace. While she became princess of Kiev by marrying Vladmir, due to her noble birth as the daughter and sister of Byzantine emperors, she was referred to as a queen.

payment for their sister, as per the ancient Slavic custom of paying either wine or dowry for the bride.

Upon arrival to Kiev, Vladimir's first order of business was to baptize his sons and relieve his pagan wives of their spousal responsibilities.

He sent the following word to Rogneda: "Now that I am baptized, I must have only one wife whom I have taken, a Christian one, and you can pick a husband from my princes and boyars, whichever you wish."

But Rogneda Rogvolodovna was not like that. She, in turn, sent Vladimir the following: "I was always a queen and will remain a queen and won't be anyone's slave. And if you decided to take baptism, I can also become Christ's bride and assume the appearance of an angel." At that time, her ten-year-old son Yaroslav was with her, lame from birth, which is why he could not walk up to that day.

Upon hearing his mother's words, he said, "You are the true queen of queens and lady of ladies since you would never back down. You would be a great wife." Upon saying that, Yaroslav stood on his feet and started walking from that point forward, and then Rogneda took monastic vows and was named Anastasia. In total, she had six children from Vladimir: his sons Izyaslav, Yaroslav, Vsevolod, and Mstislav, and daughters Mstislava and Predslava.

After releasing his pagan wives, Vladimir, upon his arrival to Kiev, began to purge the city of pagan idols; some were chopped into pieces, some were burned, and the main one, Perun, was tied to a horse's tail and dragged from the mountain, and twelve men were obliged to hit it with sticks, to desecrate it before the people. When it was dragged to the shore and thrown into the water, many shed tears and followed the floating idol along the shoreline. After destroying the idols, they began proselytizing the Christian faith, and the metropolitan that had arrived from the Byzantine Empire and the other priests walked and preached God's word around Kiev. The great Prince Vladimir himself took part in that preaching. At last, when everyone was ready, he ordered everyone who wasn't baptized to come to the Dnieper.

There, on August 1st, 988, the greatest event in the history of Kievan Rus' occurred—she received her Holy Baptism.

Kievans, young and old, entered the waters of the Dnieper. Some walked deep, some not; younger ones closer to the shore, and infants were held in their arms. The rite was carried out by Metropolitan Michael and the Byzantine priests who came with Anna.

The godfather of this nation was the prince himself, who stood there on the shore.

The *Primary Chronicle* says:

> Vladimir, rejoicing that he and his subjects now knew God himself, looked up to heaven and said, "Oh God, who has created heaven and earth, look down, I beseech thee, on this thy new people, and grant them, oh Lord, to know thee as the true God, even as the other Christian nations have known thee. Confirm in them the true and inalterable faith, and aid me, oh Lord, against the hostile adversary, so that, hoping in thee and in thy might, I may overcome his malice." (*RPC*, 117)

The Rule of Saint Vladimir

After the baptism, Vladimir immediately ordered the building of churches in places where idols used to stand throughout the whole city. On the hill where Perun stood, they built Saint Basil's Church in whose name Vladimir had been baptized in Korsun. On the spot where the two Varangians—Theodore and John—had been killed by an enraged crowd, Vladimir ordered the building of a luxurious church, in honor of the Theotokos, by masters from the Byzantine Empire who were summoned for this task. When the construction of this church was completed, Vladimir ordered one-tenth of the income from his lands to be spent on its maintenance, which is why it was called the Church of the Tithes,[72] and Anastasius, the Korsunian, managed it.

This marvelous church was built and decorated in the style of Constantinople. Twenty-five towers were built outside of it, and inside there were many columns made out of expensive marble, jasper, and other stones; the walls were covered in durable paintings. In front of the church, from the western side, the two copper statues and four copper horses were placed in the style of Constantinople.

Along with the building of God's churches, the first order of Vladimir after his baptism was the creation of schools for the study of the written word, since Christianity, aside from faith, also brought literacy and science.

Vladimir, the godfather of his people, as per the duty placed by the

---

[72] Originally it was called the Church of Our Lady and then the Church of the Dormition of the Virgin, though because of the tithe, the name the Church of the Tithes stuck.

church on godfathers, was obliged to immediately start teaching his children the Christian faith and all the other wisdom in the glory of God and all of the Russian Land. After him, all Russian rulers, inheriting power over the land from their predecessors, also inherited the duty of godfather over the people, which is why they have always been leaders of the Russian Orthodox Church and education.

To begin the education of the people, Vladimir gathered the children of the best of the lowborn men of Kiev and sent them to newly-created schools under the guidance of priests. Because of this, many mothers would cry and mourn their children as if they were dead, for the people were still in darkness. However, the children who went to those schools would become future priests, church workers necessary for rituals, and educators of the flock in science.

After the baptism of Kievans, Vladimir sent priests, along with men from his druzhina, to different ends of the Russian Land to preach the Gospel and baptize the people. To the north, along the great Varangian trade route, Metropolitan Michael was sent, along with Dobrynya, Vladimir's uncle, and Anastasius the Korsunian.

The people that lived along the path would accept baptism without resistance. Still, in Novgorod, a nest of ancient paganism that always disliked Kiev and its Christians, the Christian faith's introduction proved difficult. When they found out that Dobrynya was coming to baptize them, they assembled a town meeting, and all swore not to let him into the city and to not give their idols to destruction. As soon as Dobrynya arrived, they took up weapons and went to the great bridge. Dobrynya began trying to convince them with pleasant words, but they refused to listen and set up siege engines; the Novgorodians were especially agitated by the Christian sage Bogomil, nicknamed Nightingale for his way with words. On the merchant side, the appointed Bishop of Novgorod, Joachim, Korsunian by birth, would walk along with the priests and proselytize among the people as much as they could; in two days, they baptized around a hundred people. On the other side of the river, the Novgorodian commander Ugonyaj rode everywhere, exclaiming, "It is better for us to die than to give our gods to destruction," and excited the people to the point where they looted Dobrynya's house and killed his wife and some other relatives. Then Dobrynya sent his commander Putyata to that side of the river with five hundred men. Putyata secretly sailed on boats, took Ugonyaj and the other instigators, and sent them to Dobrynya's to be killed. After that, people battled Dobrynya ferociously and destroyed the Church of the Transfiguration of the Savior that belonged to the Novgorodian Christians, who existed in the city in small numbers.

To assist Putyata, Dobrynya also arrived with his men and began setting houses on fire on another shore. The Novgorodians became afraid and began putting out the fires, while the local nobility finally sent envoys to cease hostilities. Dobrynya, of course, agreed to peace but ordered all the idols to be immediately destroyed: the wooden ones to be burned and the stone ones to be broken and thrown into the river. Seeing this, the men and women screamed and pleaded on behalf of their gods to stop. Dobrynya sardonically replied, "You shouldn't feel bad for them; if they can't defend themselves, what good can they provide to you?" and sent a decree that everyone should become baptized. At the same time, Governor Vorobey, who had been raised with Vladimir in his youth and had a marvelous way with words, began negotiating and persuading people to be baptized. Many went on their own accord, some had to be dragged by force, those already baptized were ordered to wear crosses, and those that didn't have them were led to the water. Thus the Novgorodians were baptized. People remembered this forceful conversion for a long time. Many years later, you couldn't infuriate Novgorodians more than by saying that "Putyata baptized them with a sword, while Dobrynya did so with fire."

After accepting Christianity, Vladimir not only forced it on his people, but also changed in spirit to an unrecognizable extent. From the time of his baptism, aside from the city elders, he would also invite bishops to his city duma, who would exert great influence on his decisions.

Vladimir was especially strong in matters of charity. Once in church, while listening to the Gospels, Psalms, and the book of the Wisdom of Solomon, as Saint Nestor's tale goes, he was most impressed by the following parts in those holy books, respectively:

Blessed are the merciful, for they shall be shown mercy. (Mt. 5:7) Sell what you have and give alms. (Lk. 12:33) Do not lay up for yourselves treasures on earth, where moth and rust destroy and where thieves break in and steal; but lay up for yourselves treasures in heaven, where neither moth nor rust destroys and where thieves do not break in and steal. (Mt. 6:19–20)

Blessed is he who considers the poor. (Ps. 41:1)

He who has pity on the poor lends to the Lord, and He will pay back what he has given. (Prv. 19:17)

Hearing that and wishing to live by Scripture, Vladimir ordered every poor and meek person to come to his court and take whatever they needed: clothing, food, and money from his coffers. Then he remembered those who were unable to reach his court due to their infirmity and elderly age. So Vladimir ordered special carriages to be set up and laden with bread, meat, fish, various vegetables, honey in some barrels, and kvass in others, to carry it all around the city and ask everywhere, "Are there any poor or ill ones, who cannot come to the prince's court?" and to give away where needed.

Upon becoming Christian, Vladimir became so charitable to people that he stopped executing and punishing criminals; as a result, there were now many thieves and murderers who took over the roads and began mercilessly killing and robbing all travelers, to the point where there was no safe passage to Kiev anymore.

Then the bishops themselves came to Vladimir and pleaded, "Robbers have grown in number; why won't you execute them?"

"I'm afraid of sin," said Vladimir.

"You've been installed by God," retorted the bishops, "to execute evil ones and spare the kind ones; therefore, you should execute the robbers, but truthfully and with a trial." Then Vladimir began executing robbers and eventually found a means of foregoing execution and began punishing criminals with a monetary fine—the *vira* (blood money).

Being honorable and executing the Gospels' commandments to be charitable, Vladimir, along with that, was a very generous and welcoming host; he and his queen always held lavish feasts—not only for church festivities but also every Sunday. To those feasts were invited: first of all the druzhina, and then captains (sotnik), sergeants (desvatnik), and other elected men of the city. On the prince's table, there was everything: meat from livestock and beasts, and everything was in abundance.

People nicknamed their well-tempered prince the Red Sun.

The prince especially loved his druzhina and never held anything back from it. Once his guests were drinking and began criticizing their prince: "Doom is upon us; he makes us eat with wooden spoons and not silver ones!" Hearing this, Vladimir instantly ordered silver spoons to be made. He said, "I can't gather a druzhina with silver and gold, but with my druzhina I'll gather gold and silver like my father and grandfather would find gold and silver with their druzhina."

Proselytizing the Christian faith and establishing order in the Russian Land, Vladimir, after his baptism, had lots of wars to conduct. He successfully campaigned against the Danubian Bulgars, sending Rus' troops to aid the Byzantine emperors.

Once, he sent a regiment of Rus' fighters numbering six thousand men to his brother-in-law, Emperor Basil II. This Basil, around the year 1000, took them with him to Armenia, where he had gone in peace and hosted envoys from Georgia and the Caucasus. Then this happened. One of the Rus' warriors was carrying forage for his horse. One of the Georgians took the forage from him. Then another Rus' came to his aid. The Georgian called his own, and they murdered the first Rus'. Then all the Rus' there, all as one, stood up to fight and killed every Georgian there. "Not a single noble Georgian remained alive that day; all paid with immediate death for their crime," writes one Armenian writer regarding this event. This shows why the Rus' have always been formidable; she has always repaid all the ills done to her and never left them unavenged. Even after her conversion to Christianity, the custom of blood feuds existed for a long time and was even codified in law.

The most difficult campaigns for Vladimir were against his closest neighbors—the Pechenegs. Since then, ever since they were led to Russian Lands by Varyazhko to avenge Yaropolk, they had constantly tormented Vladimir and marched near the border, which was very close to Kiev at that time.

In 992, the Pechenegs marched on Kiev from the Sula River; Vladimir confronted them on the river Trubezh, on a shore near Pereyaslavl. Finally, the Pecheneg prince rode out to Vladimir and said: "Send one of your warriors, and I will detail one of mine, that they may do battle together. If your man conquers mine, let us not fight together for three years to come. But if our champion wins, let us fight three years in succession." (*RPC*, 119)

Vladimir agreed and, upon returning to his camp, sent out the word, "Is there anyone who wants to duel a Pecheneg," but nobody stepped forth. By the next day, the Pechenegs had arrived and brought their warrior. Vladimir was saddened that he couldn't send anyone against the Pecheneg strongman, and then an old man came to him: "Oh Prince, I have a younger son at home. I came forth with four others, but he abides by the hearth. Since his childhood, there has been no man who could vanquish him. One day when I reprimanded him while he was tanning a hide, he flew into a rage at me and tore the leather to bits in his hands." (*RPC*, 120)

Vladimir rejoiced, sent for the youngest son of the old man, and told him what was going on; to this, he replied, "Oh Prince, I know not whether I be capable of this feat; wherefore let them test me. Is there no large and strong bull hereabouts?" (*RPC*, 120) So they found a bull, enraged it with hot steel, and let it loose. When he ran past the strongman, he grabbed it by the side and ripped its skin with its flesh, as much as he could grab.

Then the happy Vladimir said, "You are well qualified to do combat with the champion." (*RPC*, 120)

The next day, the Pechenegs came and cried, "Is there no champion present? See, ours is ready." (*RPC*, 120) Vladimir ordered the young warrior to arm himself, and then both warriors confronted each other. The Pechenegs let out their formidable giant, and when Vladimir's warrior stood out, the Pechenegs started laughing because he was of average height. Then they cleared a space between the enemy regiments and let the contenders fight. They grappled and began to firmly strangle each other until the Rus' finally grabbed the Pecheneg in his arms and squeezed him to death, then threw him on the ground; cries could be heard among the warriors, the Pechenegs fled, and the Rus' chased them. The joyous Vladimir founded a city where he stood, called Pereyaslavl, because the Rus' hero had taken the glory from the Pecheneg one; both father and son were anointed as noble boyars. Our glorious tanner's name was Jan Usmar (alt. Yan Usmoshvets).

In 995, once the three years had passed after this contest, the Pechenegs, as per the agreement, resumed combat and reached the town of Vasylkiv. Vladimir came out to confront them with a small druzhina and almost perished; the druzhina was routed and, along with a few men, only saved himself by hiding under a bridge. This was on the Feast of the Transfiguration of Our Lord, August 6th. In gratitude for saving him from inevitable death, Vladimir built a wooden votive church in Vasylkiv and then celebrated the Transfiguration for eight days; he brewed three hundred *provars* of mead, gathered boyars, governors, elders from all the cities, and many regular folks and gave gifts to all the poor. The next day, the great prince returned to Kiev and again celebrated a great holy day,[73] gathering countless people.

In two years, in 997, the Pechenegs again gathered in large numbers by our borders. Vladimir went to Novgorod to gather horsemen, and the Pechenegs, upon discovering that the great prince wasn't there, came and encircled Belgorod, which caused a great famine to come to the city. Finally, after eating almost all of the supplies and foreseeing their death from hunger, the Belgorodians, as per the words of the *Primary Chronicle*, gathered in

---

[73] This would have been the August 15th Feast of the Dormition of the Theotokos, called the Assumption in the West.

assembly and said, "We are about to die of hunger, and no aid is to be expected from the Prince. Is it not better to die? Let us surrender to the Pechenegs, and let them spare some, though they kill others. We are perishing of famine as it is." (*RPC*, 122–3) And so they decided.

Only one old man wasn't present at the assembly; when he asked why they were gathering, they said they wanted to surrender to the Pechenegs, so he sent after the elders and said, "So what did I hear, that you want to surrender to the Pechenegs?"

They answered, "What else can we do? Our men can't suffer hunger anymore."

Then the old man told them, "Listen to me: do not surrender for three days, and do as I tell you." (*RPC*, 123) They happily agreed to obey him, and he ordered, "Gather a handful of rye or barley or oats." When they had found it all, the old man ordered the women to prepare the liquid with which they brew porridge, put it into a wooden bucket, then to dig up another well and place that bucket there, then to look for honey; a bowl of honey was found in the prince's stores, and the old man ordered it to be poured into the bucket that was in the other well.

On the following day, they sent for the Pechenegs; the citizens came and told them, "Take hostages from us and send ten men of your own to our city, so they can see what is happening there." The jubilant Pechenegs, thinking that the Belgorodians wanted to surrender, took their hostages and sent their best men into the city to see what was happening. When they entered the city, the Belgorodians told them, "Why do you waste your strength? You cannot overcome us if you besiege us for ten years. We secure our sustenance from the earth. If you do not believe it, behold it with your own eyes." (*RPC*, 123) Then they brought them to one well, poured out the liquid, and brewed porridge; that porridge was brought to another well, and they poured honey from it and then began eating; they gave that dish to the Pechenegs as well.

They were stunned and said, "Our princes will not believe this marvel, unless they eat of the food themselves." (*RPC*, 123) The citizens poured another bowl and gave it to them, and the Pechenegs returned to the camp and told what they saw. The Pecheneg princes tried the dish, were surprised, exchanged hostages, retreated from the city, and went home.

The relentless attacks of the Pechenegs on Kievan Rus' caused Vladimir to fortify the borders and build towns upon the rivers Desna, Ostra,

Trubezh, Sula, and Stugne.[74]

Vladimir sent druzhinas made of the bravest and best men of the Novgorodians, Krivichs, Chuds, and Vyatichi, who were constantly ready to fight the Pecheneg incursions.

A tale about Prince Vladimir and the Pechenegs was recorded by the Saxon bishop Bruno,[75] who Pope Sylvester II sent to proselytize Christianity to the Pechenegs in the year 1000. To get to the Pechenegs, Bruno came to Kiev; Vladimir took him in graciously and tried to talk him out of it, and when Bruno insisted, he accompanied him to the borders and appointed him as an envoy in the peace negotiations with the Pechenegs.

This is how Bruno himself spoke of this to the Holy Roman Emperor:

After I had pointlessly spent a year among the Hungarians, I went to the most savage of pagans, to the Pechenegs; the prince of the Rus', Vladimir, lord of a big country of great wealth, showed me hospitality, delayed me for a month, trying to convince me to change my mind, as if I were someone who would throw his life away. When, however, he couldn't do anything about this and, on top of that, was frightened by a vision he saw of my unworthy self, for two days he and his warriors followed me to the borders of his country, which he surrounded with a fortified palisade. There he dismounted; my comrades and I went ahead, and he and his most noble warriors followed behind us. Thus we crossed the border.

The prince stopped on a hill. I carried a cross myself, which I hugged with my hand and sang the famous hymn, "Peter, if you love me, then herd my sheep." When I finished singing, the prince sent us one of his advisors with this offer: "I have escorted you to the place where my land ends, and enemy land begins. I beg of you, in the name of God, not to lose, to my dishonor, your young life: I know that tomorrow before three o'clock, you will suffer a harrowing death with no reason or benefit." I sent him this reply: "Let the Lord open heaven for you, as you opened my path to the pagans." Thus we parted and went for two days without being seen. On the third day—that was a Friday—three times: in the morning, afternoon, and at nine o'clock, were we bound by our necks and sent to

---

[74] It is unclear what the modern names of the rivers Ostra (Остру) and Stugne (Стугнѣ) are; they are likely smaller tributaries and known by different names today.
[75] Saint Bruno of Querfurt (c. 974–1009)

be executed, and every time we were left unharmed by the hands of our enemies.

After spending five months among the Pechenegs, among terrifying dangers, Bruno managed to baptize thirty men and reached peace between them and the Rus', as Vladimir sent one of his sons as a hostage to the Pechenegs.

One of the best-known events of Vladimir's rule was the beginning of the minting of gold and silver coins, which grew in quantity due to the growing trade.

Vladimir had twelve sons in total.

They ruled as princes in the following cities:

1. Vysheslav (c. 977–c. 1010),[76] the eldest, from a Varangian wife Olava, in the most esteemed city after Kiev—Novgorod (988–1010)
2. Izyaslav (c. 979–1001), from Rogneda—in Polotsk (989–1001)
3. Svyatopolk (c. 979–1019), from Yaropolk's Byzantine concubine Irina—in Turov on the river Pripyat (988–1015)[77]
4. Yaroslav (c. 983–1054), from Rogneda—first in Rostov (988–1010), and upon Vysheslav's death, in Novgorod (1010–1034)[78]
5. Boris (c. 986–1015), from the Byzantine Queen Anna—in Rostov (1010–1015)
6. Gleb (c. 987–1015), also from the Byzantine Queen Anna—in Murom (1013–1015)
7. Svyatoslav (c. 982–1015), from Malfrida—among the Drevlians (990–1015)
8. Vsevolod (c. 984–1013), from Rogneda—in Vladimir-Volynsky (c. 1000)
9. Mstislav (c. 983–1036), also from Rogneda—in Tmutarakan (990–1036), near the Azov Strait to the Black Sea[79]
10. Stanislav (c. 985–1015), from a Czech woman—in Smolensk (988–1015)

---

[76] Lifespans are added here by the editors for the benefit of the reader, though Nechvolodov did not include them, per his style.

[77] Nechvolodov does not include here that he was also Prince of Kiev from 1015 to 1019.

[78] Nechvolodov does not include here that he was also Grand Prince of Kiev from 1019 to 1054, notably the first Grand Prince, or Velikiy Knyaz.

[79] Nechvolodov does not include here that he was also Prince of Chernigov from 1024 to 1035 and is more widely referred to as Mstislav of Chernigov, though some other sources claim he was not the son of Rogneda but of another wife.

11. Sudislav (d. 1063), from Adela—in Pskov (1014–1036)
12. Pozvizd (b. before 988)—where he ruled and who his mother was is unknown.

Vladimir's favorite sons were the youngest ones—Boris and Gleb, from Queen Anna.

Toward the end of his life, the older great prince had to suffer many sorrows: in the year 1011, his cherished Queen Anna died, and then many sorrows were brought by his eldest sons—Svyatopolk and Yaroslav.

We saw that Vladimir at the beginning of his rule fought Poles and took from them the cities of the Red Rus': Peremysl, Cherven, and others. This was in 981.

The feud with the Poles ended with Vladimir's son, Svyatopolk, marrying the daughter of the Polish king Boleslaw the Brave. However, having given his daughter's hand to the Orthodox prince, Boleslaw started to try and influence Svyatopolk—through his daughter—to accept Catholicism. Soon Svyatopolk gave in since it was also in his interest that he ruled Turov, a city so close to Polish land. Then Boleslaw began instigating Svyatopolk to rise against his father. Because of that, Vladimir imprisoned his son and his son's wife for some time.

The imprisonment of Boleslaw's daughter served to be the cause of another war against the Poles in 1013, which, however, ended quickly, as Boleslaw feuded with the Pechenegs, whom he was going to send against the Rus', and went back to Poland.

Yaroslav, as we know, was Rogneda's son and inherited her pride and independence of character. When he arrived in Novgorod, people liked him. He had many difficult memories of his mother in Kiev, and Novgorodians, as we know it, didn't like anything Kievan: Oleg had moved the capital to Kiev; from Kiev, there came the baptism of fire and sword by Dobrynya and Putyata; and finally, Novgorodians had to pay a huge tribute of two thousand grivnas a year to the prince of Kiev for the needs of the whole state. They especially disliked this tribute and often yearned for a courageous and proud ruler who would declare independence from Kiev. Yaroslav seemed to be this man. With his mother's milk, he gained enmity to any sort of dependence, and remembering what they had suffered under his father when he was a pagan, Yaroslav, of course, could bear him no tenderness or affection.

And so, convinced by the Novgorodians, he decided not to pay tribute to Kiev in 1014. The old great prince was furious.

"Repair the roads and build bridges," he said and ordered his armies to prepare for a campaign. (*RPC*, 124)

Upon finding this out, Yaroslav also began preparing for war and sent for a Varangian host to come to his aid. But the father-on-son war did not actually play out.

Vladimir fell ill. At the same time, he heard that the Pechenegs were moving against the Rus' again, so he sent his favorite son Boris against them while leaving his least favorite son Svyatopolk by his side, who recently came out of imprisonment.

His illness, in the meantime, became worse, and on July 15th, 1015, Prince Vladimir the Great passed away.

He died in the village of Berestove, near Kiev. Svyatopolk rolled his body into a rug, as per the custom with dead men, put it in a sleigh, and brought it to the Church of the Tithes in Kiev, where countless people gathered in tears.

Everyone mourned—the boyars for the defender of the land, and the poor and meek for their protector and provider. With cries, they put the body into a stone casket and buried him.

Thus passed away Vladimir the Great, who baptized the Rus', famous for his stately mind, Christian kindness, and piety. The Orthodox Church canonized him and gave him the title of Equal-to-the-Apostles. His relics, which were entombed in the Church of the Tithes, near the body of Queen Anna, who died four years earlier, were, during a Tatar invasion, hidden with the casket and then rediscovered in 1631; some of them were taken from the casket. Now the head of the prince Equal-to-the-Apostles is in the great Kiev Monastery of the Caves, his jaw is in the Moscow Cathedral of the Dormition, and his hand is in Saint Sophia Cathedral in Kiev.

Figures for Chapter Four

128. Hunting deer with a leopard, from a Byzantine manuscript of the tenth century, stored in the French National Library in Paris.

129: The young prince with his patron-uncle, drawing by S. I. Yaguzhinsky

130: *Bulgar Ruins*, from Svinyin, *Paintings of Russia*.

131: Bulgar emperor and his family, from a very ancient
Bulgar Gospel, owned by Lord Zush in English.

132: Svyatoslav and his druzhina kill a Bulgar, from the *Codex Manesse*.
Svyatoslav is depicted in the top and bottom thumbnails in the long
clothes of a Byzantine emperor (in the original red patterned design).

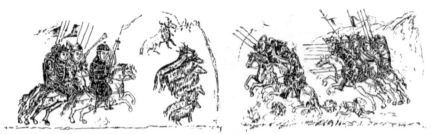

133: (Left) *Captives of the Rus'*. Russians capture Bulgarian livestock. From the *Codex Manesse*. 134: (Right) The pursuit of the Bulgars, same source.

135: (Left) The Russians go to Dorostopol
136: (Right) Acquiescence of the Bulgars of the City

137: Lad with a bridle, the savior of Kiev, from a rare book
from the early nineteenth century, *The Pictorial Karamzin*.

138: (Left) The Taking of Pereyaslavets, from the *Codex Manesse*.
139: (Right) Tsarina Theophano lifts John Tzimiskes, hidden in a basket,
up to the palace, to then assassinate her husband, the Emperor
Nikephoros Phokas. Skylitzes, *Synopsis of Byzantine History*.

140: (Left) John Tzimiskes sends emissaries to Svyatoslav, same source as fig. 139.
141: (Right) Byzantine warriors, from a rare ninth-century Byzantine
manuscript kept in the National Library in Paris.

142: Svyatoslav shares words with his army before the Battle
of Adrianople, an illustration by the artist Lissner.

143: John Tzimiskes sends gifts to Svyatoslav, from the *Radziwiłł Chronicle*.

144: Negotiations between John Tzimiskes and Svyatoslav.
Skylitzes, *Synopsis of Byzantine History*.

145: Meeting between Svyatoslav and John Tzimiskes.

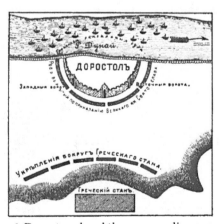

146: Dorostopol and the surrounding area.

147: Feast of Svyatoslav before the final Battle of Dorostopol.

148: Svyatoslav deliberates with his druzhina.
Skylitzes, *Synopsis of Byzantine History*

149: Waverings in the Battle of Dorostopol, from the same source as fig. 148.

150: The fight between Svyatoslav and Anemas.

151: (Left) The Seal of one of the members of Anemas's family. From the collection of Gustave Schlumberger. 152: (Center) Saint Theodore Stratelates, from a Greek manuscript of the tenth century, kept in the Vatican library in Rome. 153: (Right) Coin with an image of the Savior, recaptured by John Tzimiskes after the Battle of Dorostopol.

154: Meeting between Svyatoslav and Tzimiskes according to the writings of Leo the Deacon, from a painting by the academic A. F. Solntzev in the Imperial Museum of Alexander III in Saint Petersburg.

155: Pechenegs encircle Svyatoslav and kill him along with his druzhina. Skylitzes, *Synopsis of Byzantine History*.

156: (Left) An ancient royal hunt, painting by Nicholas Roerich.
157: (Right) A bison, photograph taken in the Beloberzhsky woods.

158: A tenth-century bear hunt, illustration by Nikolay Samokish,
from Kutepov, *Great Prince's, Tsar's and Emperor's Hunting in Russia*.

159: The Demise of Oleg Svyatoslavich, from the *Radziwiłł Chronicle*.

160: Vladimir sends emissaries to Prince Rogvolod of Polotsk
to ask for the hand of his daughter Rogneda.

161 and 162: Blud betrays Yaropolk.

163: (Left) Christians in Kievan Rus' at the time of their persecution by Vladimir,
illustration by the artist Nikolay Karazin. 164: (Right) "Father, do you think you
are the only one walking around here?" The young Izyaslav defending his mother
Rogneda against his father Vladimir, illustration by the artist Medvedev.

165: (Left) The killing of John and Theodore. *Radziwiłł Chronicle.*
166: (Right) Vladimir learns about God.

167: (Left) Image of Saints Dmitry and George the Victorious, carved onto planks of black slate and 168: (Right) Fragment of a lithographic stone with a convex image of extremely fine Byzantine craftsmanship of the tenth or eleventh century, both discovered during an excavation in Korsun, kept in the Hermitage Museum.

169: (Left) Seal of an eleventh-century imperial viceroy of Korsun
170: (Right) Silver seal of Emperors Basil II and Constantine VIII

171: Excursion of Queen Anna from Constantinople to Korsun. *Radziwiłł Chronicle.*

172: *Baptism of Saint Volodymyr* and 173: (Right) *The Baptism of Kyivans*, both murals by Viktor Vasnetsov in the St. Volodymyr's Cathedral in Kiev.

174: The main items discovered during the excavation of the old Church of the Tithes conducted in the 1830s by the venerable Evgeny, Metropolitan of Kiev: I) Ancient bell from the time of Saint Vladimir; II) Fragment of an ancient mural; III and IV) Inscriptions on the southern wall of the church; V) Remains in the granite of a red slate at the base of the church, belonging apparently to Saint Olga; when the grave was exhumed for the first time by Metropolitan Evgeny in the first instance, while air had not entered the chamber, one could see the appearance of Saint Olga's face, which then dissolved; VI) Remains in the grave of Saint Vladimir; the real head is missing since it is kept in the Kyiv Pechersk Lavra, along with handmade tassels, one of which is known to reside in Saint Sophia Cathedral in Kiev; VII) View of the church, erected in the 1830s on the spot of the old Church of the Tithes; VIII) Silver ingot of a very high grade (the currency of the time); IX) Saint Vladimir's tomb of red-black stone; X) Plan of the church from above.

175: (Left) Exterior view of the excavations of the foundations of the great prince's palace in Kiev, apparently belonging to Saint Vladimir and built, perhaps, by his grandmother Saint Olga. A mass grave was discovered next to the base of the palace.
176: (Right) Crucifix of Byzantine craftsmanship from the tenth century, discovered in a mass grave at the base of the palace apparently belonging to Saint Vladimir. By all appearances, this crucifix was taken by Saint Vladimir from Korsun and given to him in the Church of the Tithes, where it had served as the altarpiece carried out during processions. Very likely, this cross was hoisted into the Dnieper River during the baptism of Kievan Rus'. The cross is forged from iron and covered with a silver sheet on both sides; in the corners, there were relics underneath glass; one of them has been preserved. Buds of precious stones can be seen along the edge; in the center is an image of Saint Theodor. Kept in the Museum of the City of Kiev.

177: (Far Left) Neck scapular, byzantine craftsmanship, a Kievan treasure.
178: (Right Three) Ancient earrings (in the middle, two images of Sirina, the bird of paradise) of outstanding craftsmanship by Rus' masters in the Byzantine style. Found in Kiev during excavations by Zhitomirsky and taken into the famous collection of A. V. Zvenigorodsky.

179: Mothers mourn their children going to school, from the *Radziwiłł Chronicle*.

180: (Left) Ruins of a church in the city of Ani, the former capital of Armenia, tenth–eleventh century.   181: (Right) Ruins of a cathedral in Kutaisi, built in 1003 by King Bagrat III of Georgia, a tributary to Byzantine Emperor Basil II.

182: Stone chapel in Upper Svaneti in the Caucasus Mountains, under the dominion of King Bagrat III of Georgia in the tenth century. Divine Liturgy is still performed in it to this day.

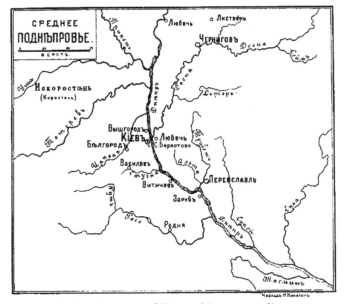

183: Russian map of Kiev and its surroundings

184: *Testing the strength of Jan Usmar*, painting by Grigoriy Ugryumov
at the Imperial Academy of Arts in Saint Petersburg.

185: (Left) The construction of the votive church in Vasylkiv by Saint Vladimir
From the *Radziwiłł Chronicle*.   186: (Right) Vladimir gathers an army.

187: (Left) Belgorodians store porridge and honey in the well to fool Pechenegs.
188: (Right) Belgorodians serve the porridge and honey from the well to Pechenegs.

189: Saint Vladimir.   190: A silver coin of Saint Vladimir.

191: Vladimir sends Boris against the Pechenegs, from a handwritten Lives of
Saints Boris and Gleb of the fourteenth century from Saint Basil's Cathedral,
kept in an ancient printing chamber of the Moscow Synodical Typography.

192: Svyatopolk takes the corpse of Saint Vladimir down into the
lower chamber and lays it out on a sleigh. Likhachyov,
Exterior Life of the Holy Russian Princes Boris and Gleb.

CHAPTER FIVE

The Killing of Boris, Gleb, and Svyatoslav by Svyatopolk

After the demise of his father, Svyatopolk took up his place in Kiev as before and immediately began distributing gifts to the townspeople—elegant clothing and money. He felt that the Kievans' hearts were not with him, so he wanted to coax them into his favor. In reality, the Kievans were incapable of overlooking Svyatopolk's allegiance to Catholicism and the insurrection against his father. As with the deceased Vladimir, the Kievans favored Prince Boris, who was barely past his youth, handsome, and of a pure Christian heart.

Having been raised by his Christian mother and his dear younger brother Gleb, he had read many books with youthful diligence, especially *The Lives of the Saints*. According to legend, while reading of the suffering of the martyrs, Boris broke down in tears and prayed, "Lord Jesus Christ! Honor me that I may partake of the holy works of your saints; teach me to walk in their footsteps. I pray to you, O Lord, let not my soul be carried away by the vanity of this world, fill my heart with light, that it should know you and your commandments; grant me this gift, as you have granted it to those who have pleased you."

He was called from Rostov, his appanage, by his sick and aging father, after he had been, as we know, sent by him to pursue the Pechenegs and, after returning from the vain excursion, stayed to rest on the banks of the Alta River. Here he learned of the death of his blessed father. By this news, he was stricken with great sorrow; he wept bitterly over his father, saying, "Oh light of my eyes, nevermore shall I enjoy your good teaching nor your wisdom."

His father's war band, having learned of the demise of their great prince, appealed to Boris with the following words: "Your father's army and war band are with you; go to Kiev and take up your father's throne, for it is what everyone expects of you."

Boris answered, "Be it not for me to raise my hand against my elder brother. Now that my father has passed away, let him take the place of my father in my heart." (*RPC*, 126)

Then, to remove any great cause for concern on the part of his older brother, and also to demonstrate to the army that he had no intention of taking action against Svyatopolk, Boris on the Alta River sent the army and the war band home and remained alone with his servants.

However, Svyatopolk, not trusting his brother and expecting some insidious ploy, decided to kill him. To this end, he sent a message to Boris to say that he desired his love and to offer him a greater amount of land than Boris had inherited from their father. Having sent these words to his brother, Svyatopolk meanwhile went to Vyshgorod by night and, secretly calling upon the Vyshgorodian boyars—Talets, Elovich, Lyashko, and Putsha—asked them, "Will you be whole-heartedly devoted to me?"

Putsha and the Vyshgorodians answered, "We are ready to lay down our lives for you." (*RPC*, 126)

Then he commanded them, "Say no word of this to anyone, and go kill my brother Boris."

Putsha and his comrades set out by night to the Alta and, approaching the prince's tent, noticed that he heard matins.[80] This was Saturday evening, on July 24th, 1015. Having no regard for discretion, Svyatopolk could not conceal their intent, and Boris knew they had come to kill him. He ordered the priest to sing matins and read the sixth psalm and the canon. At the end of matins, he knelt before an icon and prayed, "Lord Jesus Christ, who in this image hast appeared on earth for our salvation, and won, having voluntarily suffered thy hands to be nailed to the Cross, didst endure thy passion for our sins, so help me now to endure my passion. For I accept it not from those who are my enemies, but from the hand of my own brother. Hold it not against him as a sin, oh Lord!" (*RPC*, 127) Then, having partaken of the Holy Eucharist and having said goodbye to everyone, Boris quietly lay in his bed.

The murderers approached while the prince lay praying; then they ran up to the tent and stabbed through it with spears, striking Boris. Along with

---

[80] A prayer chanted or sung after midnight.

the prince, they killed his faithful servant, a Hungarian named George; this gallant youth desired to protect the body of his beloved prince and ended up taking death along with him.

Boris, who, for his part, also dearly loved his servant, had given him a large golden grivna, so large that the murderers were unable to remove it from his neck quickly and cut off George's head to pilfer the gold from his corpse. They then killed many other youths. While Boris was still breathing, they wrapped him in the tent canvas, put him on a cart, and drove him away, sending news to Svyatopolk of the success of their mission. Svyatopolk, learning that his brother was still breathing, sent two Varangians to finish him; they killed him in the forest near Kiev by plunging a sword into his heart, took his body to Vyshgorod in secret, and buried it beside the Church of Saint Basil.[81]

Another fratricide followed this first one: Gleb, Boris' younger brother, who was staying in Murom. "Behold, I have killed Boris; now how can I kill Gleb?" Svyatopolk said, according to the *Primary Chronicle* (*RPC*, 128); but Gleb was far away, so Svyatopolk sent him a message saying, "Get here quickly, for your father calls to you; he is very sick." Gleb quickly got on his horse and set out with a small retinue.

When he reached the Volga, around modern-day Tver, his horse stumbled in a ditch and injured his leg. After this, the prince continued by water to Smolensk to get down to Kiev by way of the Dnieper.

As soon as Gleb arrived in Smolensk and took a rest, he received a message from Novgorod from Yaroslav: "Don't go; our father is dead, and Svyatopolk has killed your brother."

Gleb wept over his father's death but grieved for his brother, whom he loved dearly, even harder: "Woe is me, oh Lord! It were better for me to die with my brother than to live on in this world. Oh my brother, had I but seen thy angelic countenance, I should have died with thee. Why am I now left alone? Where are thy words that thou didst say to me, my brother? No longer do I hear thy sweet counsel. If thou hast received encouragement from God, pray for me that I may endure the same passion. For it were better for me to dwell with thee than in this deceitful world." (*RPC*, 128)

Then the assassins sent by Svyatopolk found him. Gleb's men saw them and drew their weapons; soon, two of them were dead; then Gleb said to the remainder, "Brothers, if we do not fight them, they will seize me and take

---

[81] According to footnote 121 of the *Russian Primary Chronicle*, nothing is known of the church mentioned beyond the tradition that it was built by Vladimir and burned in circa 1020.

me to my brother; if we fight them, they shall surely kill us all." The assassins, approaching the boat, seized Gleb, and their leader, Goryaser, immediately ordered them to slaughter the young prince; this act was carried out by his own cook, Torchin. Gleb's body was taken out of the boat and thrown among the trees of the dense forest.

Learning of Svyatopolk's villainous acts of violence with his younger brothers, Prince Svyatoslav, who was near Kiev staying in the country of the Drevlians, did not remain to quietly await such a fate and fled to Hungary. But Svyatopolk sent men after him, and Svyatoslav was killed in the Carpathian Mountains.

Then, according to the *Primary Chronicle*, Svyatopolk began to think, "I shall stop all my brothers and take all the power in Kievan Rus'." But he would encounter a terrible foe in the form of Yaroslav.

We left Yaroslav last while he was in preparations for the war with his father, for which he had gathered an army from the lands of Novgorod and had summoned a Varangian royal guard from across the sea.

These Varangians, erstwhile living idly in Novgorod, began to make mischief and ended up starting fights and riots everywhere, behaving violently not only to the inhabitants but to their wives as well. The proud Novgorodians had never suffered such insults and decided that it was time to put a stop to the violence of the Varangians. When the Varangians were in the marketplace, the Novgorodian guard broke in and killed all miscreants.

This was, of course, a dire and bloody predicament for Yaroslav, not only in that it had weakened the army, but also killed two of his guests, and especially with such guests who, as we know, were untouchable according to custom and whose relatives would suppose themselves entitled to the cruelest recompense possible. Yaroslav resolved to avenge them thusly.

It is true that he was Christian, but only recently Christian, and the custom of blood vengeance was so deeply entrenched in people's hearts that for a long time, even after taking baptism, it was tolerated by the law at that time.

Hiding his resentment and feigning indifference to the death of the Varangians, Yaroslav said of these affairs: "Such is life, I am indeed unable to resurrect the slain," and then invited the Novgorodians who were guilty of the murder of the Varangians to a field outside of town; here they were unexpectedly attacked. Those who managed to escape fled the town in terror.

Having completed his treacherous slaughter, Yaroslav received that very night some important news from Kiev: his sister, Predslava, informed her brother of the death of their father, and Svyatopolk, having taken control of Kiev, had already killed Boris and had sent assassins after Gleb. How it must have been for Yaroslav to receive this news!

First of all, news of Vladimir's death would have awoken deep regret, for he had not gone to see his old father in his dying days. Moreover, Svyatopolk's murder of innocent Boris and his dispatching death to Gleb indicated to Yaroslav that he was next in line.

In addition to all this, the prince had only just executed his faithful retinue, who, more than ever, would have been especially necessary in the dangerous and difficult times to come.

"Alas for my beloved retainers," Yaroslav lamented in light of these circumstances, "whom I yesterday caused to be killed! You would indeed be useful in the present crisis!" (RPC, 131)

The next day, Yaroslav called the remaining Novgorodians to assembly on the outskirts of town and, on the verge of tears, announced to them, "My friends and brothers! My father is dead, and Svyatopolk sits on the throne of Kiev and is murdering my brothers. I would like to make war with him; please help me."

And the honorable Novgorodians helped their prince, whom they fervently loved with ardent conviction. Themselves pagans, but a short time ago, they doubtlessly would have understood that the killing of the retinue the day before was Yaroslav paying a debt for the killing of the Varangian guests. "We can still fight for you, oh Prince," he heard in response, "even though our brethren are slain." (RPC, 131)

Deeply moved by this, Yaroslav bestowed many privileges then and there to Novgorod that no other city had. In his honor, these rights and privileges were subsequently called Yaroslav's Charter; unfortunately lost to us, but an area of Novgorod, Yaroslav's Square, has survived, where for many ensuing centuries, Novgorodians have gathered in the evening and conducted their business on the foundation of this charter.

Gathering three thousand Novgorodians and one thousand Varangians in 1016, Yaroslav set out against Svyatopolk, trusting the success of his campaign to divine will. "It was not I who began to kill our brethren, but Svyatopolk himself," he said. "May God be the avenger of the blood of my brothers inasmuch as Svyatopolk, despite their innocence, has shed the just blood of Boris and Gleb. Perhaps he will even visit the same fate upon me. But judge me, oh Lord, according to the right, that the malice of the sinful may end." (RPC, 131)

Svyatopolk's Battles with Yaroslav

Knowing that Yaroslav was moving against him, Svyatopolk began to gather a war host of Rus' and, to strengthen himself, gathered Pechenegs as well. Then he moved out to Liubech on the Dnieper. He remained on one side of the river while Yaroslav stationed himself on the other. For three weeks, the brothers remained in a standoff against one another, with neither one resolving to cross the river and attack. In those days, there was a custom of taunting one's enemies to goad them into acting at a disadvantage. Seeing that the main part of Yaroslav's force consisted of Novgorodian villagers and townspeople, Svyatopolk's commander, nicknamed Wolf's Tail, the very same man who in 984 defeated the Radimichs, went up to the river bank and chided the Novgorodians, calling them workers and tradesmen, not warriors: "Why did you come hither with this crooked-shanks, you carpenters?[82] We shall put you to work on our houses." (RPC, 131)

The Novgorodians, greatly offended by this taunt, went up to Yaroslav and said, "Tomorrow we will cross over to them, and whoever will not go with us we will kill." (RPC, 131)

Seeing the intention of his Novgorodians, Yaroslav sent a message to Svyatopolk's camp that night: "What shall we do? There is very little mead brewed, yet there are many guests."

This was the reply: "If there is little mead but many guests, then put it out in the evening!"

Yaroslav understood that it was necessary to begin the battle that night. The Novgorodians began crossing to the other bank in the evening and, so as not to think of who wouldn't be returning, had set the boats out and stacked them in regiments; they also, for the same reason, concealed their heads with towels. There was a frost. Svyatopolk's army stood between two lakes, with the Pechenegs situated behind one of them. Svyatopolk himself was feasting and drinking all night with his druzhina and knew nothing about the attack that was being planned.

After the crossing, the Novgorodians attacked Svyatopolk, and a great

---

[82] "Crooked-shanks" referring to Yaroslav being lame, either at that time or in the past. According to the Norse sagas, corroborated by archaeological examination of his remains, his lameness was caused by an arrow wound. However, in the *Primary Chronicle*, Yaroslav is said to be born lame and began to walk after Vladimir's baptism.

skirmish took place; in it, Svyatopolk and his druzhina were pressed up against one of the lakes and forced to step out onto the ice, which cracked, and Svyatopolk's people began falling under; the Pechenegs, waiting on the other side of the lake, were unable to lend any aid, so victory went to Yaroslav.

After the battle, Svyatopolk fled to Poland with his father-in-law, and Yaroslav took up the Kievan throne of his father and grandfather.

The Novgorodians were sent home and very generously rewarded: the townspeople were awarded ten grivnas each, the people from the surrounding lands one grivna, and their captains ten.

But Svyatopolk was still alive and soon made himself known. He immediately allied with his father-in-law, Boleslaw the Pole, and they made war against Yaroslav. Firstly, they sent the Pechenegs against Kiev, and there was a great slaughter in the surrounding area of the town; many houses were burned, and Yaroslav was barely able to drive back these steppe dwellers.

Next, having secured an alliance with one of Boleslaw's enemies—the German emperor Henry II (Holy Roman Emperor)—Yaroslav laid siege to the town of Brest in Poland, but the siege was a failure.

At this time, the German emperor had also been unsuccessful in his campaigns against Boleslaw and soon made peace with him, after which he supported the Poles in their attacks against the Rus'.

In 1017, Boleslaw embarked on a campaign strengthened by German, Hungarian, and Pecheneg forces.

They and Yaroslav returned to the West Bug River on July 22nd of the same year, having taken possession of the land from the Rus'. Then just as warlord Wolf's Tail had taunted the Novgorodians at Liubech, so here, on the Bug, did the warlord Yaroslav taunt Boleslaw, laughing at him, calling him an old man and a wageworker as he came up the river on the other side with his army. The future Grand Prince Yaroslav called him these insulting terms and shouted at him: "We shall pierce your fat belly with a pike." (*RPC*, 132)

The *Primary Chronicle* says:

For Boleslav [Boleslaw] was big and heavy, so that he could scarcely sit a horse, but he was crafty. So Boleslav said to his retainers, "If you do not avenge this insult, I will perish alone," and leaping upon his horse, he rode into the river and his retainers after him. (*RPC*, 132)

Inspired by these words and following the example of their duke, Boleslaw's retinue also charged the river behind him, catching Yaroslav's army completely by surprise since they didn't expect an attack. The Polish victory was thorough. Yaroslav narrowly escaped with just four men and set out to Novgorod with them; Boleslaw and Svyatopolk went to Kiev.

The Kievans shut themselves in and didn't want to take Svyatopolk and the Poles in; moreover, many people from the surrounding countryside had already come into the city to seek its defenses.

Boleslaw first wanted to take Kiev by starving them, but on August 14th, he attacked the city and rode in victorious within a few hours. According to the Polish chronicles, Boleslaw would, as he did everywhere, ceremonially mark his new acquisition of territory—in this case on the Golden Gate of Kiev—with a sword that had acquired so many nicks in its blade from being used to strike things so strongly that it had been given the nickname the Jagged Sword and would become the coronation sword of Polish kings.

Boleslaw would not remain in Kiev for long, however, regardless of the notch he made on his famous Jagged Sword by hitting the Golden Gate.[83]

When he came to the Russian Land, he thought he would take control of it as a conqueror of a subjugated land would. Finding Yaroslav's stepmother, wife, and sister in Kiev, he took one of them—Predslava (his sister), whom he had previously tried but failed to woo—hostage as revenge.

Next, he seized all of Yaroslav's property. Anastasius, the cunning Byzantine who fired the arrow with the note from Korsun into Vladimir's camp before the prince' baptism, lived with him in Kiev, where he was held in great honor and was in charge of the Church of the Tithes, went out to Boleslaw now quite graciously.

Trusting him, Boleslaw sent one half of his druzhina home, and the other half he dispersed into the city to look for food.

But in so doing, he was gravely mistaken.

The Rus' were by no means inclined to bear the insolent attitude that the Poles showed them and so began mercilessly slaying them everywhere. Even Svyatopolk helped them, for he had grown tired of his gorging father-in-law. He issued an order saying, "As many as there are Poles in the city,

---

[83] This is more legendary than historical. The Golden Gate was not built until 1037, and the Jagged Sword did not exist for another century or two. The name Jagged Sword even seems to be a misunderstanding of the Polish ceremonial sword Szczerbiec, which translates not to "jagged" but to "jagging," as in "a sword meant to jag other weapons," and it is smooth, without notches.

kill them."

Seeing the imminent doom of his Poles, Boleslaw ran away from Kiev after robbing the city clean, taking with him both the riches of the church and the prince, having taken two of Yaroslav's sisters—Predslava and Mstislava—his boyars, and numerous slaves. At the same time, to the plundered estate, he left his cunning new friend Anastasius, and on the way to Poland, he took back the Red Cities that had been taken from him by Saint Vladimir. Svyatopolk immediately took ownership of the princehood of Kiev after his father-in-law's escape.

Now we shall return to Yaroslav.

After his unexpected routing on the Bug River, he reached Novgorod with his four men and decided to ride even further, to the sea, to the Varangians.

But the valorous Novgorodians wouldn't again leave their favorite prince to misfortune and so did not allow him to go to the sea. Under the orders of Governor Constantine, Dobrynya's son, they scuttled the royal boats that had been prepared for the prince's escape, and they beseeched him, "We still want to fight Boleslaw and Svyatopolk." After this, money was immediately gathered for the war: from common men they took four coonskins, from the elders ten grivnas, and from the nobles eighteen grivnas. With this money, they hired Varangians and attacked Kiev.

Hearing of Yaroslav's excursion, Svyatopolk went to the Pechenegs and fetched a great host. Both armies returned to the Alta River at the same place where Prince Boris was killed. "My brethren," Yaroslav prayed to his brothers before the battle, "although ye be absent in the body, yet help me with your prayer against this presumptuous assassin." (*RPC*, 133) The fighting was vicious, more than had ever been seen in Rus'. Each host gained the upper hand three times, then lost it again; much blood flowed down the glen to the river. Finally, in the evening, Yaroslav emerged as the victor.

Overwhelmed by his defeat, Svyatopolk fled, carried on a stretcher, for he was weakened in all his limbs and bones, ceaselessly repeating the words, "Fly with me, they are pursuing us!" (*RPC*, 133)

So he fled across the Polish countryside and died in the wilderness among Czechs and Poles. This was in 1019. The Rus' people called him the Accursed.

After this, Yaroslav stayed in Kiev, where he "wiped away the sweat of his labors," as the *Primary Chronicle* says. (*RPC*, 134)

Yaroslav's Reign

His first act was to pay his final respects to his brothers Boris and Gleb. He would soon learn of Boris' burial place, but he would search in vain all year for Gleb's remains. Finally, only in the winter of 1020 would his body be accidentally found by trappers. The priests took him into a boat with candles and censures, and he was carried out to Vyshgorod, where he was buried alongside his brother.

After this, a general announcement was given which said that Gleb's body, though it lay for five years in the forest, had not been worn out by the weather, and neither animals nor birds had bitten into it; it was white and unfaded, as though still alive. Soon, the martyrs' graves came to be seen as holy and miraculous sites.

Under the advisement of Metropolitan John, Yaroslav decided to make the relics of the newly recognized saints available for public veneration, for they were sanctified by incorruptibility and were thus miraculous gifts. For this, they laid the foundations of a new church, and on July 24th, 1021, this church was consecrated, and the relics were displayed for the faithful people of the church.[84] During the Divine Liturgy celebrated there, before the confluence of countless nations, the lame, crawling to the sites of the saints, stood up, stayed standing, and walked in front of all the people.

The memory of the holy Passion-Bearer Boris is inseparable from his faithful servant Ephraim of Novotorzh. Ephraim, a Hungarian by birth, came into the service of Prince Boris along with his two brothers—Moses and George.[85] George, as we know, was alongside his lord at the banks of the Alta River and died by the spears of the assassins, who wanted to cover Boris' body with his. When he learned of the death of the prince and his favorite brother, Ephraim searched for George's body at the place of the murder, but only found the head that the villains had severed to take the golden grivna that Boris had given him from his neck. Ephraim picked up his brother's head and became a monk, retiring at the Tvertsa River in the village of New Torzhok. There he built a hospice, and when the relics of the saintly princes Boris and Gleb were put out for public veneration, he built a

---

[84] This was the Church of Saint Basil, which was later destroyed. Their surviving relics were then moved to the new Vyshgorod Cathedral, which was later renamed the Church of Saints Boris and Gleb.

[85] Moses is discussed further in Chapter Five on page 256.

stone church next to them and founded a monastery. The relics of the venerable Ephraim, retrieved in 1872, are resting open in the cathedral church of the Borisoglebsky Monastery in Torzhok. Along with them was the incorruptible head of his brother George, which was laid with him in his grave by decree of the venerable Ephraim.

Along with commencing his princehood by taking care of the debt incurred by his murdered brothers, Yaroslav met with some minor perturbance at the hands of his other relatives.

In 1020, Yaroslav's nephew Bryachislav, prince of Polotsk, the son of the same Izyaslav who, as a little boy, defended his mother Rogneda with a large sword from Vladimir's wrath, attacked Novgorod, ransacked the city, flooded many of the townspeople out, and, laden with rich treasure, returned to Polotsk. Learning of this, Yaroslav gathered forces and set out with astonishing speed along the route first taken by Svyatoslav, and within a day, had reached Sudom Creek, which flowed into the Shelon, a distance of about seven hundred versts (460 miles); here, he took everything of Bryachislav's all the way to Polotsk; he would soon be reconciled with him however, and added two towns to his territory.

Having straightened things out with Bryachislav, Yaroslav, over the next two years, carried out a much more tenacious war with his brother through Rogneda, Mstislav. This Mstislav, having been given the far-off town of Tmutarakan by his father,[86] had expanded his territory, victorious over Khazaria and the Kasogi,[87] who lived in the steppes near the Southern Caucasus. Mstislav was of a heroic nature, with a stout body, dark hair, and a handsome face, as well as being brave, gracious, and possessing forbearance. More than anything in the world, he loved his druzhina, and forsook no measure for their sakes.

In 1016, while helping the Byzantines, he severely destroyed the Khazaria and took the Khazarian khagan captive. In 1020, when Yaroslav reconciled with Bryachislav, Mstislav conquered the Kasogi.

It happened in this way. When Mstislav and his druzhina were matched with the Kasogi regiment, their prince Rededya, renowned for his strength, made a preposition to Mstislav: "Why do we destroy our forces by mutual warfare? Let us rather fight in single combat ourselves. If you win,

---

[86] Tmutarakan was situated on the Taman Peninsula, in present-day Krasnodar Krai, Russia, roughly opposite Kerch, along the Cimmerian Bosporus.
[87] Now known as the Circassians.

you shall receive my property, my wife, and my children, and my land. But if I win, I shall take all your possessions." (*RPC*, 134)

"Yes, it shall be so," answered Mstislav. Then Rededya added that it should be unarmed, a wrestling match. The two heroes grappled firmly. Rededya was strong and big, and Mstislav started to succumb. "Oh Theotokos, help me!" he exclaimed in prayer and thought. "If I conquer this man, I will build a church in your name." (*RPC*, 134) No sooner had he said this than at that very moment, he tackled Rededya to the ground, took out a knife, and stabbed him. Then, just as he had promised, Mstislav went to the Kasogi land, took it over, set up a tribute, and returned to Tmutarakan and built the church to the Theotokos that he had promised.

Thus Mstislav, who received the nickname the Bold, strengthened by the Kasogi regiment, decided in 1023 to seek out more territory after the death of his brothers and invaded the outskirts of Rus'. He had already demanded them for himself before, and Yaroslav gave them to Mur, but Mstislav thought that this wasn't enough.

While Mstislav was marching to Kiev, Yaroslav was in Novgorod, where he was working for the good of the nation. The matter at hand was that there was a famine in the Suzdal region; the pagan seers were causing worry among the people, instilling the belief that the elderly were drawing the wrath of the gods, and instructing people to kill them. All this caused a rebellion in the land, and some old women were killed. Yaroslav came to the aid of the unrestful populace, captured the seers, executed some of them, imprisoned the others, and subdued the country, saying that it is only God and not people who can send disaster and death to the world as punishment for sins—old women have nothing to do with it. Afterward, he led the people along the Volga down to the Bulgars for bread, which, after having received it, the land returned to life and was quieted.

Learning of Mstislav's hostilities, Yaroslav started to gather a host in Novgorod and sent an emissary overseas to hire Varangians. These Varangians came to him under the command of the warlord Yakun the Blind,[88] who wore a bandage of golden cloth over his eyes.

By then, Mstislav had reached Kiev, though the Kievans barricaded themselves and refused to let him in. Then he went to Chernigov.

Having amassed his Novgorodians and Varangians, Yaroslav set out against his brother; Mstislav also began moving toward him, and both regiments met at Listven, forty versts (twenty-six miles) north of Chernigov.

---

[88] Or Jakun, from the Old Norse Hákon. Historians believe him to be Hákon Eiríksson (d. 1029).

Mstislav deployed his army in the evening. A terrible thunderstorm broke out that night; lightning crashed, thunder rumbled, and rain poured down. Then the daring Prince Mstislav said to his druzhina, "We shall attack them; this is our chance." However, Yaroslav was also not idle; by all appearances, his Novgorodians and Varangians also wanted to take Mstislav by surprise. Both armies met, and there was a terrible clash. The great storm also would not let up. Finally, Mstislav rushed with his druzhina against the Varangians, who gave up and fled; the blind Yakun, in his hurry, even lost his golden eye cover and ran straight home across the sea. Yaroslav even had to retreat and make for Novgorod. Then Mstislav sent a message with the retreating army that they should tell Yaroslav on his behalf: "Stay in your Kiev, for you are the elder brother, and let this Chernigov region be mine." But Yaroslav, recalling his battles with Svyatopolk, did not answer the call immediately and sent his regents to Kiev. It was only a year later that he would gather a large army in Novgorod, set out to Kiev, and secure peace with Mstislav; the brothers rode out for Gorodets,[89] near Kiev, and carved up the Russian Land along the Dnieper. Mstislav would acquire for himself the eastern half, with his throne in Chernigov, and Yaroslav would have the western half, with Kiev. In 1025, "they thus began to live in peace and fraternal amity," says the *Primary Chronicle*. "Strife and tumult ceased, and there was a great calm in the land." (*RPC*, 136)

After the reconciliation with his brother, Yaroslav began working hard to bring order to state affairs and defend the borders from his neighbors, whose attention to Rus' had been drawn during the fraternal strife.

First of all, he had to punish the Poles for their having kept house in Kiev with Boleslaw and Svyatopolk.

As soon as Boleslaw died in 1025, there was insurrection all over Poland. The Red Cities were also caught up in this—Peremysl, Cherven, and others who no longer wished to live under the Polish yoke. Yaroslav and Mstislav sent them help, and in 1030, they took them back from the Poles and then invaded Poland, where they took many slaves.

That same year, Yaroslav expanded his power to the western coast of Lake Pskov and built the town of Yuryev in honor of his Christian name.

In 1036, Mstislav set out hunting, fell sick, and died. All his property was bequeathed to Yaroslav, who, from that point forward, became the sole

---

[89] On the east bank of the Dnieper at its junction with the Desna.

ruler of the Russian Land.[90]

In the same year, 1036, the grand prince went to Novgorod, where he installed his eldest son Vladimir as regent and appointed the famous preacher Luka Zhidyata as bishop. While staying in Novgorod, Yaroslav learned that the Pechenegs had embarked on Kiev in great numbers. He immediately went out against them with Varangians and Novgorodians, who, on arrival, united with the Kievans. The battle against the Pechenegs happened near Kiev, where Saint Sophia Cathedral now stands.

The slaughter was terrible, but by evening, Yaroslav had completely defeated the Pechenegs, who fled in terror in all directions.

The defeat of the Pechenegs was so thorough that from that time onward, they never again attacked the Rus'.

The next year, Yaroslav established a stronghold in Kiev and built Saint Sophia Cathedral at the place of his great victory against the Pechenegs.[91] He then built the Church of Saint Irina in Kiev and the Monastery of Saint George. Finally, in 1037, he built the Golden Gate, with the Church of the Annunciation above it, the same Golden Gate against which, according to the Polish legend, Boleslaw had allegedly made a notch on his Jagged Sword in 1018.

A great deal of work and care went into the construction of Saint Sophia Cathedral: Byzantine craftsmen and architects were brought in for it. This cathedral has been maintained quite comprehensively into modern times, regardless of remodeling quite later. At first view, this was a long stone building, built in part from enormous brick slabs and raw stone; its length was fifty-two arshins (120 feet), and width was around seventy-six arshins (177 feet), with a height approaching seventy arshins (160 feet). On the north, west, and south sides, stone galleries were built, supported by thick pillars; a tripartite altar, semicircular, with windows and two thresholds next to it. The cathedral was consecrated with five domes, the largest of which was placed in the middle. There was a parvis put up on the outside, from which on two sides, the northern and the southern, two staircases

---

[90] Nechvolodov's note: The only brother who remained alive was Sudislav, who stayed in Pskov and had, according to Nestor, been disowned by Yaroslav and remained silent.

Editors' note: According to Nestor, in the *Russian Primary Chronicle*, 137, Sudislav was imprisoned by Yaroslav in 1036 "because he had been slanderously accused." In 1059, Yaroslav's sons freed Sudislav and forced him to take the monastic habit, which is likely what Nechvolodov meant by he "remained silent." Sudislav settled in the Monastery of Saint George in Kiev where he died in 1063.

[91] Named after the Hagia Sofia (Holy Wisdom), not a specific saint named Sophia.

lead up to the choir loft.

The cathedral's interior was richly decorated with art and a special mural, a so-called *musia*, or mosaic. This mosaic mural consisted of small multicolored stones arranged on the wall so that the desired image would be
seen. The wonderful mosaic is extremely durable, and its images have been
preserved in Saint Sophia Cathedral ever since: on the arch of the main altar, the Theotokos, with raised hands, called the Immovable Wall; with an
image of the Last Supper underneath it; and a few other images further below; on the altar there are columns as well, with a depiction of the Annunciation, an angel with a branch pointing to the Theotokos. The mosaic image in the dome has also survived.

The walls of the stairway leading from the parvis into the cathedral
were done by a regular painter, depicting a few scenes of royal life: boats,
banquets, hunting, and others. These images, restored a little over the
years, exist to this day; in fig. 212, we see fools dancing and playing flutes,
sopels, harps, copper plates, and large balalaikas of some kind. One of them
supports a pillar on his back which is being climbed by a teenage fool. Fig.
213 has images of various scenes of a hunt. Unfortunately, it is unknown
exactly which place in the cathedral this depiction of Yaroslav's famous
family in fig. 214 was originally installed.

Besides Kiev, by order of Yaroslav, his son Vladimir erected a Cathedral of Saint Sophia in Novgorod in the same style as the Kievan one, only
smaller, and on the site of the original oak church that had burned down in
1045. This cathedral suffered the greatest devastation from the invaders
and their fires. Still, a part of its ancient, well-known mosaic art had survived, as well as the invaluable gates of the cathedral's western side, the so-
called Korsunian Gates.

In 1031, in Chernigov, Mstislav the Bold had also built the Holy Transfiguration Cathedral, which stands indestructible to this day. In recent
times, this cathedral has been especially revered for housing the incorrupt
and miraculous relics of Saint Theodosius Uglitsky, Archbishop of Chernigov.

After the rout of the Pechenegs, Yaroslav had to carry out a few more
wars; he sent out to fight the Yam, a Finnic tribe who lived in modern-day
Finland, and asserted Rus' dominance along the offshoots of the Northern
Dvina.

Next, he led a few excursions against the Lithuanians and Yotvingians
to punish them for raids they had been making on our borders.

Finally, in 1043, Yaroslav undertook a campaign against Constantinople as well. The cause of this excursion was as follows. After the baptism of Saint Vladimir, the Byzantines lived with the Rus' quite peacefully and faithfully observed the treaty established under Oleg and Igor. But on one occasion, some Rus' and Byzantines argued over a trade; some scuffling took place, and a Rus' was killed. Despite his advanced age, Yaroslav was hotheaded and unappeasable. He was enraged by this offense and gathered a great army, outfitted it with boats, and sent it to Constantinople under the command of his son Vladimir, along with two generals: Vyshata and Ivan Tvorimirich.

The Byzantine Emperor Constantine IX Monomachos, learning of the Rus' plans for war, immediately sent a message to Yaroslav offering peace, saying that such a minor event shouldn't merit the termination of the good and long-established peace and the outbreak of war between the two great nations.

But Yaroslav, the Byzantines said, having read the emperor's message, cast the letter aside with disdain and sent Constantine IX a proud and scornful reply. The Byzantines obviously considered the death of the Rus' merchant to be an unimportant affair and desired only to take his goods and his money, but the Rus' don't shed their blood lightly and consider some offenses unforgivable, especially when they come from smarmy Byzantines. A Rus' head lost in Constantinople always agitated the whole Russian Land, and the whole of that land, never mindful of the danger, would gather as one to take revenge for its blood having been shed.

Having received such an answer from Yaroslav, Constantine IX began preparing his defenses: fearing their insubordination, he first took all Rus' in Constantinople captive and sent them to isolated areas. Then, he armed his ships and army and deployed them at the entrance of the Black Sea at the Bosporus, where the Rus' would usually stop, a small marina at the Sparks (Iskrest) lighthouses. The Byzantines and Rus' stood against each other, but the battle did not start. Emperor Constantine IX again sent his emissaries to ask for peace. Prince Vladimir of Novgorod also dispatched them rudely, saying that there would be no peace unless each Rus' warrior were to receive three pounds of gold. Emperor Constantine IX was, of course, unable to provide that much gold, so the battle began.

This is how Michael Psellus, a Byzantine who was there with Emperor Constantine IX, described the battle:

[93] ... He himself [Constantine IX], with a picked body of senators, spent the night at anchor in the actual harbour, not far from the shore. A clear declaration of war at sea was made to the barbarians by a herald, and when day broke Constantine set his fleet in battle array. The enemy also put to sea from the port on the other side. They sailed out as if they were leaving a military camp, complete with fortified rampart. When they were well out from the land, they arranged all their ships in line, so that they formed a continuous chain stretching across the water from the harbour on one side to the harbour on the other. They were now ready to attack us, or, if we made the first assault, to repel us. It was a sight that produced the most alarming effect on every man who saw it. For my own part, I was standing at the emperor's side. He was seated on a hill which sloped gently down to the sea, watching the engagement from a distance.

[94] Such then was the order of battle on their side and ours. No attempt was made to join combat, however, for each fleet remained motionless, with line intact. A considerable part of the day had already passed, when the emperor signalled two of our big ships to advance slowly on the enemy. They sailed forward line abreast, moving beautifully, with the pikemen and stone-throwers cheering aloft and the hurlers of Greek fire standing by in good order ready to shoot. At this, several of the Russian vessels left their line and bore down on our ships at full speed. Then, dividing in two, they circled round each of the triremes and hemmed them in, while they tried to hole them below deck with long poles. Our men, meanwhile, engaged them with stones from above and fought them off with their cutlasses. Greek fire, too, was hurled at them, and the Russians, being unable to see now, threw themselves into the water, trying to swim back to their comrades, or else, at a loss what to do, gave up all hope of escape.

[95] Thereupon a second signal was given and more triremes put out to sea. Other ships followed or sailed alongside. It was our fleet now that took courage, while the enemy hove-to in amazement. When the triremes neared the barbarians, the latter lost all coherence and their line broke. Some had the fortitude to stay where they were but the majority fled. Suddenly the sun attracted a mist off the lowlying land (most of the horizon consisted of high ground) and the weather changed. A strong breeze blew from east

to west, ploughed up the sea with a hurricane, and rolled waves down on the Russians. Some of their ships were overwhelmed on the spot under the weight of tremendous seas; others were driven far away and hurled on to rocks and precipitous coasts. A certain number of these latter were hunted down by our triremes. Some they sank in deep water, with the crews still aboard. The fighting men in the triremes cut others in half and towed them, partially submerged, to nearby beaches. So a great massacre of barbarians took place and a veritable stream of blood reddened the sea: one might well believe it came down the rivers off the mainland.[92]

This is what the Byzantine Michael Psellus says about this nautical battle, about which he indicates that the storms aided the Byzantines more than anything. Cast out by the storm, the Byzantines gathered up the bodies of the Rus' then took their clothes and other items from the deceased.

Prince Vladimir's boat was also destroyed in the storm, and he nearly died. However, General Ivan Tvorimirich managed to get him onto his boat just in time. The Rus' who had survived returned home, some by foot along the river bank, others on the remaining boats. The total number that went on the bank after the storm was six thousand; they were naked, hungry, having no supplies and no leaders since none of the prince's druzhina wanted to walk with them, preferring instead to return by boat.

Then the gallant Vyshata, Yaroslav's general, seeing how many fighters had been left without a leader by the will of fate, exclaimed out of pity: "I shall not go to Yaroslav, but with them," and stepped off of his boat onto the bank. "If I survive, it will be with the soldiers," he said, bidding farewell to Prince Vladimir, "and if I perish, it will be with the Prince's retainers," whereupon he took command over the naked and starving soldiers. (*RPC*, 138)

Meanwhile, the Byzantines set out in pursuit of the Rus' boats. Upon learning of this, Vladimir turned around, fought the Byzantine ships, and gloriously destroyed them: four of them were captured with all their crew, and a Byzantine general committed suicide. After this, Vladimir returned to Kiev and his father with great honor.

But this was not the fate of the noble Vyshata. He made it as far as Varna with his sick, crippled, and barely clothed and shodden army. A Byzantine general had been expecting them there. Our soldiers made to fight but were

---

[92] Psellus, *Chronographia*, Book 6, §93–5.

destroyed; moreover, eight hundred of them, including Vyshata himself, were taken captive, after which they were taken to Constantinople and blinded.

The unfortunate end of the excursion here written of did not diminish the significance of the Rus' in Constantinople: Prince Yaroslav was too strong and mighty, and the Rus' army was too brave and undaunted. Moreover, the Byzantines couldn't subsist without Rus' allegiance: bread, furs, honey, fish, wax, amber, gold—all these were imported from the Rus', so the Byzantines were quite happy when the old peace with Yaroslav came to be renewed.

According to this peace, Vyshata and the blind druzhina were released back to their motherland, where they were, doubtlessly, received with great honor; one could find many blind men in Kievan Rus' following this.

Afterward, in order to strengthen the peace with the Rus', Constantine IX Monomachos had his daughter marry Vsevolod, who was Yaroslav's favorite son.

In addition to the Byzantine emperor, all the well-known kings and land-owning nobles of the time sought the honor of becoming related to the great Rus' prince.

Yaroslav himself was married to Ingegerd, daughter of the Swedish king Olof. Yaroslav's sister Maria Dobroniega he had given in marriage to Duke Casimir I, who had taken up the throne of Poland after Boleslaw the Brave; and Casimir's sister Gertrude was married to Yaroslav's son Izyaslav. One of Yaroslav's daughters, Elisaveta, was married to King Harald III of Norway. For a long time, Yaroslav hadn't agreed to give up his daughter because Harald had wooed her during the time of his exile from the country. Still, through his bravery and loyal service to Yaroslav and the Byzantine emperor, for whom he had conquered many cities, Harald finally managed to convince the great Rus' prince to consent to his daughter's marriage. Since then, the Norse have a traditional and hallowed song that they sing, which Harald had composed in fiery passion for his wife— the beautiful Elisaveta Yaroslavna. The other daughter, Anna Yaroslavna, became the wife of King Henry I of France and the mother of Phillip, the future king of France, whose rule of France would begin in childhood and last for many years. The French have preserved her handwritten signature to this day: "Queen Anne" on one of their state charters. "In it, Queen Anne," says one French academic, writing of this charter, "unpleased with the custom at that time for the generally unlettered to put a cross next to their name which had been written out for them by the scribes, signed her name herself in Russian."[93] In the town of Reims, where French kings were coronated, there is a Gospel that has been kept to this day, with which Yaroslav the Wise had blessed his daughter when sending her to France. French kings have since sworn their oaths on this Gospel, which would appear to French visitors unfamiliar with Slavic languages to have been written in some completely unknown language. On July 22nd, 1717, when Emperor Peter the Great rode through Reims and saw the cathedral's sacristy, the Gospel was displayed alongside a note written in an unknown language. To the great astonishment of those present, the great Russian tsar, taking it in his hand and seeing the Church Slavonic script, began to read it right then. Yaroslav's third daughter—Anastasia—was married to King Andrew I of Hungary, and of the sons of Yaroslav, two were married to German countesses of well-known lands.

Yaroslav's court, encircled by the sheen of greatness, served as a refuge for forlorn sovereigns and possessive princes: Saint Olaf II, the king of Norway, deprived of his throne, had lived in our land at one time. Yaroslav received him with the utmost friendliness and wanted to grant him control of a region, but he would soon return to Norway, leaving his young son Magnus with us; next, the sons of the English King Edmund, Edmund and Edward, would come to stay with us, having been exiled from England by the Danish conqueror Cnut the Great. Later on, the Hungarian princes Andrew and Levente also sought refuge with Yaroslav and ended up recruiting the service of the Varangian Sigmundr (Simon), who had been exiled from his fatherland by his uncle, Yakun the Blind,[94] who, as we know, fought at Listven.

Such was the brilliance with which Yaroslav the wise ruled the Rus' until the very end of his princehood. His acts were praised all across the nations of Europe, and the rules he established in Kievan Rus' served as an example to many. The coin minted for him—"Yaroslav's silver"—served as the monetary format for northern lands—Sweden, Norway, and others.

In 1054, feeling the approach of death, Yaroslav gathered his children and, as a precaution against any strife between them:

---

[93] Translator's note: While the word "Безграмотность" in Russian is translated as "illiteracy," it does not mean that the queen was necessarily illiterate, but simply that she may not have known the Latin script and didn't want to leave only a crude mark next to her name that scribes had written out, instead opting to write her name in Russian.

[94] His brother Afreki likely cooperated with Olaf II of Norway, and so Yakun (Jakun/Hákon) banished his nephew Sigmundr after Afreki's death, when Sigmundr would have been about twelve years old.

While he was yet alive, he admonished his sons with these words: "My sons, I am about to quit this world. Love one another, since ye are brothers by one father and mother. If ye abide in amity with one another, God will dwell among you, and will subject your enemies to you, and ye will live at peace. But if ye dwell in envy and dissension, quarreling with one another, then ye will perish yourselves and bring to ruin the land of your ancestors, which they won at the price of great effort. Wherefore remain rather at peace, brother heeding brother. The throne of Kiev I bequeath to my eldest son, your brother Izyaslav.[95] Heed him as ye have heeded me, that he may take my place among you. To Svyatoslav I give Chernigov, to Vsevolod Pereyaslavl', to Igor the city of Vladimir, and to Vyacheslav Smolensk." Thus he divided the cities among them, commanding them not to violate one another's boundaries, not to despoil one another. He laid upon Izyaslav the injunction to aid the party wronged, in case one brother should attack another. Thus he admonished his sons to dwell in amity. (*RPC*, 142–3)

Soon after this, the grand prince, already quite sick, yet not having ceased managing affairs of state, set out with urgency to Vyshgorod and perished there on February 19th, 1054, in the arms of his favorite son Vsevolod. He died seventy-six years after his birth, universally respected and loved, and greatly mourned by the nation.

His body was laid in a tomb of bright marble, where he rests to this day, in the aisle to the right of the altar in the Saint Sophia Cathedral in Kiev.[96]

The grateful Rus' nation honored his memory, naming him *the Wise*.

Verily Yaroslav had employed no small amount of wisdom nor sacrifice to create a great and powerful Rus'.

---

[95] Izyaslav was the eldest living son at the time, as the firstborn Vladimir of Novgorod (b. 1020) had died in 1052.

[96] While true at the time of original writing, the remains of Yaroslav the Wise are no longer at Saint Sophia's, having been either lost or stolen likely during the Second World War in an attempt to protect the remains from the Soviets, though since being discovered as missing in 2009, they have yet to be recovered.

The Condition of Kievan Rus' at the Time of Yaroslav's Death

The long internecine war between the brothers lasted many years. Indeed, the fortune of war had far from always been in his favor. Severe defeats had come his way from the Poles during his conflicts with Svyatopolk and from his brother Mstislav at Listven. Lastly, his Byzantine campaign wasn't exactly successful. But the wise Yaroslav overcame these hard times with his firm character and sharp wit, and by the end of his life, all had turned out as best as one could hope.

Yet apart from wars undertaken for the defense and strengthening of Rus' power and glory, Yaroslav had given no small part of his labor to the improvement of domestic affairs and the rulership of the Russian Land. Due to his love for the construction of churches, monasteries, chambers, and other buildings, the Kievans accepted him as a "lodgeman,"[97] that is, as a hunter and a builder. What's more, Yaroslav oversaw the evangelization of the people with love and diligence.

His time was marked by the spread of the Orthodox faith over virtually all of the Russian Land and the construction of many churches and monasteries.

As a devout Chrisitan, Yaroslav was ashamed that his uncles, Yaropolk and Oleg, had died unbaptized; thus, he exhumed their remains and, after baptizing them, returned them to their graves.

He raised his children according to the Christian faith with the utmost assiduousness. His wife, Ingegerd, who took the baptismal name Irina,[98] differed from him only in a greater intensity of faith, as well as his eldest son Vladimir, who ruled Novgorod, where he performed many labors for the construction of the Cathedral of Saint Sophia, and who, thirty-three years after his birth, was buried in the parvis of Korsun Cathedral alongside his mother, who before her death had taken the name Anna with her

---

[97] Translator's note: The word Nechvolodov uses here is "хоромец," which seems to derive from an archaic word used for almost all buildings in general. The point he seems to be making is that Yaroslav understood construction and hunting very well, which were two of the chief passions of Kievan society. It is unclear whether this was an official acceptance into some kind of guild or if it was simply a sign of respect to the prince.

[98] Translator's note: She had already been baptized in Sweden but took the name Irina because it was more common in the spheres of Kievan Rus' and the Byzantine Empire. The way this is expressed in Russian is clear, but in English requires clarification.

monastic tonsure.[99] The remains of Yaroslav's son Prince Vladimir of Novgorod and Yaroslav's wife Anna became famous for their incorruptibility, and on the day of the celebration of Russia's thousandth year in 1862, they were installed in silver shrines in the same cathedral. The Orthodox Church recognizes them both as saints.

In the time of Yaroslav's princehood, the generation of those children had been brought up who had learned literacy under Saint Vladimir and whose mothers had mourned their being taken into Church schooling as though they were dead. Now, these children had been placed everywhere as priests and bishops. Yaroslav continued the actions of his father: in Novgorod, he too took children who lived with the elderly and sent them to learn literacy and the teachings of the Church.

The grand prince, having been schooled in the written word, read theological books himself both day and night. He tirelessly sought them everywhere and, of course, collected all of the ones he could find in the language of the Slavs and the Bulgars. Not content with this alone, however, he would seat himself in the tower with a plethora of translators and force them to translate and transcribe in great numbers the books of the Greek language to distribute them throughout the churches. Given his zeal for literature, the grand prince decided to lay the foundation of the oldest Russian storehouse of books in the Novgorod Cathedral of Saint Sophia.

Following the example of Yaroslav and his family, all of Russian high society would take to learning and literacy in earnest; since writing had not been very well known up until that time, the understanding of letters was considered the most honorable undertaking, since the very first clergy of the prince and the literate priests would dedicate their free time to this activity above all things. Yaroslav's favorite son, Vsevolod, studied five languages by himself, and his other son Svyatoslav collected books wherever he could and piled them up in his chambers. Under his order, to this very day, his collected writings entitled *Izbornik of Svyatoslav*, adorned with invaluable drawings, have been preserved. A Gospel dating from the same period has also been preserved, with marvelous drawings and adornments written for the Novgorodian vicar Ostromir. It bears the title *The Ostromir Gospels*.

---

[99] Princess Ingegerd (Irina), due to her devout faith, took monastic vows (called tonsuring, which often involves a ceremonial cutting of the hair) before her death in 1050. As such, she took the name Anna, after the grandmother of Jesus.

The *Primary Chronicle* describes how strongly the love of literacy developed in Yaroslav's time:

> For as one man plows the land, and another sows, and still others reap and eat food in abundance, so did this prince [Yaroslav]. His father Vladimir plowed and harrowed the soil when he enlightened Rus' through baptism, while this prince sowed the hearts of the faithful with the written word, and we in turn reap the harvest by receiving the teaching of books. For great is the profit from book-learning. Through the medium of books, we are shown and taught the way of repentance, for we gain wisdom and continence from the written word. Books are like rivers that water the whole earth; they are the springs of wisdom. For books have an immeasurable depth; by them we are consoled in sorrow. They are the bridle of self-restraint. (*RPC*, 137)

Apart from the promulgation of Orthodoxy and education, Yaroslav also proved himself as a statesman, to whom it is attributed the first set of Russian laws ever written under the name *Russkaya Pravda* (Rus' Justice).

All his gifted aptitude for literary production went into the *Russkaya Pravda*, as well as rules for punishment, the extraction of levies, and state revenue.

This collection is quite interesting because, judging by the punishments it lists, it is possible to understand the values that were then promulgated in Kievan Rus'.

From the laws laid down in the *Russkaya Pravda*, we can see that regardless of the acceptance of Christianity, ancestral revenge under Yaroslav was still considered completely legal, for such violence was a custom of the ancient Aryan pagans. The *Russkaya Pravda* gives only one qualification, that in seeking revenge for an insult, it wouldn't be that the entire family of the offended party is involved, but only his closest relatives: a brother for a brother, a father for a son, a son for a father, and a nephew for an uncle. If it should happen for some reason that no vengeance is taken in the form of killing or maiming, then a vira (blood money), consisting of various amounts depending on the victim, would be paid to the prince, depending on the nature of the offense and the station of the aggrieved party; thus, the murder of a free person would cost forty grivnas, and for one of the prince's men, eighty grivnas. If a dead body were concealed in any town of the land so that the murder shouldn't be discovered, the whole town would pay vira to the prince; this vira was called a *dikoi*. According to the *Russkaya Pravda*, arsonists and horse thieves were to be punished especially harshly—they were the most hated enemies of the populace then as now. To the prince, there seemed to be a deluge of these types of criminals, so they were to be exiled and their houses and property seized.

Investigations of cases were always taken very carefully: witnesses were called, both parties would be heard, and only then would a final verdict be issued. If for some reason any witness or case should appear uncertain, then whether accused of murder or the theft of more than a single grivna, they would be put to the test of iron: swear an oath, either standing on a red-hot piece of iron or holding it with two fingers. For less important cases, a water test would be used: the accused was made to take a few steps into a strongly flowing river; if he appeared apprehensive or had any inhibitions, he would lose the case. Monetary penalties of various sizes were the most common outcome, the size being dictated by the gravity of the offense; in the event that he didn't have the funds to pay the fine imposed on him by the court, he would be given into slavery.

We have seen that the closest assistant to the princes of Kievan Rus' in all matters was his druzhina. The druzhina consisted of both older men, or boyars, as well as younger men who were called *gridas* (the word *gridnitza* would also come from this word, which meant the chamber in the prince's tower in which he would receive men from his druzhina). Boyars were those older men with whom the prince held council over all affairs in war, whether foreign or domestic; we had also seen that Saint Vladimir held council with the boyars when he was considering his conversion to Christianity. The princes would send boyars to the peasants in the city as ambassadors to foreign states and appoint them as commanders of militias from the countryside, who would come with their leaders, men at arms, and appointees.

While assembling ranks for war, the druzhina was ordinarily placed on both flanks of the large rank, or the front, which consisted of soldiers from the country.[100] By this method, the large rank would ordinarily lead the battle, and the druzhina on the flanks would secure the victory. The druzhina's most valuable item was its prince, and the prince's was the druzhina. Indeed, we have also seen how loyal to their princes the druzhinas always

---

[100] Translator's note: In Russian, this lexical language is meant to indicate that the soldiers who weren't in the druzhina had less training, experience, and prestige, and would probably have been recently conscripted.

were and how the princes loved their druzhinas. Upon returning from the campaign in Constantinople, Oleg didn't shirk from making sails for his druzhina's boats from the most expensive fabrics they had plundered. Svyatoslav didn't want to be baptized to not be laughed at by his men; his druzhina was always prepared to lay down their bones beside their prince. Saint Vladimir, upon hearing his drunken druzhina complain about their wooden spoons, immediately ordered silver ones to be forged for them. Lastly, Mstislav the Bold has been remembered for a long time for his boundless love for his druzhina.

All the men of the druzhina were completely free and always able to depart the service of one prince and enter into that of another; in reality, however, this was a very rare occurrence in these times.

In addition to the princes, the princesses also had their druzhinas, especially those who truly loved to take part in the affairs of the Russian Land.

The druzhina's upkeep was the responsibility of the princes and was generally quite costly, which is why they weren't very large; eight hundred people was already considered a very large druzhina. But if the druzhina wasn't so large, its membership selection could be made especially carefully. This selection was always made by the prince himself, and members would enter into his ranks from an early age. We have seen the young boy Svyatoslav, just four years of age, leading the druzhina into battle. Generally speaking, the life of the princes would begin early in those days: they would often marry at age eleven or twelve to a bride about eight or nine years old and would begin to take part in affairs of governance and bear all the burdens of military life. By the age of twenty, they would have developed into a true, mentally mature man schooled in the business of the country and would not only be an outstanding fighter, but could also skillfully take command of an army himself.

The prince's comrades with whom he would grow up would also be as young as he was, warrior children; the remainder of the population, following the prince's example, strove to distinguish themselves with great bravery and accomplishments. Just recall the outstanding lad who made his way through the Pecheneg camp, with a horse's bridle in his hands, all the way to General Pretich during the siege of the Pechenegs against Kiev during the princehood of Svyatoslav. And ever since then, when war occurs amid the Russian nation, great youths are always found, sometimes no older than thirteen or fourteen, who not only perform feats of bravery, but also, following the example of this young Kievan hero, stand out for their outstanding composure and judgment in the face of great danger. As for those youth of today, who constitute the bulk of the modern Russian army, it is well known to everyone that as they are outstanding heroes on par with the older soldiers, they always hold the line in the face of the enemy.

People of all nations and tribes, as well as all sizes and builds, would be taken into the prince's druzhina. Their only requirement was that they should be good, brave, and intelligent men. Even the man of the simplest background could count on being accepted into the druzhina's most honored positions exclusively according to his personal valor.

We have seen that Svyatoslav's first man after himself was the giant Ikmor, taken out of the ordinary rank due solely to his extraordinary exploits in war; we have also seen during the battles of Saint Vladimir against the Pechenegs that he made the simple peasant Jan Usmar a boyar, along with his father, for his glorious victory over the Pecheneg strongman.

By this fraternity and equality between the military men and their sovereigns, regardless of where they came from, the army of the Rus' always stood out. Moreover, we have remained this way up until modern times.

The Bogatyrs

What the princes valued especially highly was when exalted bogatyrs,[101] glorified for their valorous deeds, would serve in their ranks.

In our ancient ballads, we find that a prince would greet unknown bogatyrs who were coming to him with the following words:

> Hey, you fine fellow!
> Speak now, by what given name thou art called;
> And by that name thou can provide the means,
> Whereby we may greet you by your patronymic.[102]

This greeting of the princes to the heroes is more clearly illustrated in one of the epics about Ilya Muromets (or Ilya of Murom):

---

[101] Translator's note: The only possible translations for this word are misleading and would make the reading of this text appear trite, since Nechvolodov comments extensively on the nature of bogatyrs. "Knight," "hero," and "champion," are the best possible translations, but carry different connotations that don't quite capture the intended meaning and would add extra meaning that doesn't apply.

[102] It's unclear which ballads Nechvolodov specifically cites in this section, so all quotations here are from the present translator.

Ilya Muromets came to Kiev city,
And shouted out with his loud voice:
"Thou, O father, Prince Vladimir!
"Hast thou need of us, art thou taking
"Strong heroes, and mighty men,
"Unto thee, father, and thy venerable capital,
"Of praise and honor, to aid its defense?"

And Prince Vladimir answered:

And how could I needst thou not?
In all places do I seek and ask after thee!

In the old times, good men, famous for their courage, immense strength, and Christian souls, who were always ready to help their weaker brothers in distress, and defend them from wrongdoing, were nicknamed bogatyrs. And there was wrongdoing to be suffered then. Filthy idolaters, as the nation of the Pechenegs and other predatorial tribes were called, prowled the steppes; in the forests, hostile men were lying in wait—Nightingale Robbers—who could skillfully switch between various animal voices and birdsongs when they gave each other information about travelers as they approached on the paths. There was also the Accursed Jew from the Khazar region, and a few other evil enemies, called Zmeya Gorynych, Tugarin Zmeyevich,[103] and other aliases. All these enemies of the Russian Land would suddenly attack single persons or entire villages, lying in wait in forests and ravine pathways; they would rob, murder, burn, and take captive any or all defenseless people—elderly, women, and children. The prince's druzhina was not very big, and moreover was almost always busy with war. Moreover, Kievan Rus' was so vast, and there were so few roads within it, that a great deal of time was required for the druzhina to get to the place where a robbery or a raid had happened; therefore, obviously, thieves and robbers could always escape in time. We have seen that it could even be impossible to catch up to a large Pecheneg force and get to the steppes; Prince Boris, sent by Saint Vladimir with the druzhina against the Pechenegs, returned later, not having caught up to them when he reached the Alta River and learned of his father's death.

Here is how our great bogatyrs would conduct themselves in ancient

---

[103] Translator's note: Dragons, but in Slavic lore, are shapeshifters who have anthropomorphic forms and engage in dalliance and deception with humans.

Kievan Rus': as defenders of the poor people in their regions and loyal servants to the princes. They would either be sent to the princes themselves or
enlisted by local residents to defend against invading enemies; here, they
would perform their sometimes immensely difficult feats and, of course,
become national favorites and heroes.

Common in the ranks of the bogatyrs at that time was the *polienitsy*.

Virtuous women in the country were nicknamed polienitsy, ordinarily
daughters or sisters of the bogatyrs who, possessing all the best properties
of the female soul, were also strong and daring enough that they could put
a man down; they also, just as their fathers and brothers did, would serve
the holy cause of the defense of the nation and take part in decisive battles
against raiders and other invading peoples. The polienitsy would wear ordinary female dress but rode horses and were armed with spears, shields,
and sabers.

The daring polienitsy, being fearless and terrible warriors, were nevertheless women and, upon getting married, would become wives and house-
masters.

This is how the folk legends depict them.

The chronicles almost don't speak of the bogatyr's deeds at all, and they
don't because they were drawn up to bring to mind the legacy of important
state affairs that had significance for all of Kievan Rus'; for this reason, they
were only depicted briefly, without very many words. The valorous exploits
of the bogatyrs and polienitsy were ordinarily related to specific events or
regions and not to the entirety of the Russian Land; thus, they were not in-
corporated into the chronicles. From the information of the chronicles we
know only that the bogatyr could be found in Kievan Rus' until the Tatar
invasion, in the first battle of which they all laid down their bones for the
Russian Land.

To become acquainted with the bogatyrs and the polienitsy in detail
can be done in the folkish bardsongs.

The *byliny*[104]—these legends about the bogatyr's deeds were composed
out of folkish admiration for them; they would come to places in the story
and astound their admirers with their absurd strength and unbelievable
feats. However, just as the ancient Greek myths about centaurs and amazons contained much truth, so can many actual facts be found within our
byliny about the bogatyrs.

---

[104] Translator's note: This word could be translated as "epic," "bardic song," "tale," etc., as a
specific literary genre with its own cultural context.

Reading the byliny, we come to be acquainted not only with the names of our esteemed bogatyrs and their fantastic deeds but also how we conducted ourselves in the times when they lived. These byliny thus consist of living truth; the morals of every bogatyr are also shown in them, as well as their opinions of each other and their taunts, which they would occasionally heap on one another. Reading the byliny, it is as though you are present at the bogatyr's feasts; you see their clothes and weapons and the fine horses upon which they would ride.

The tales of the Kievan byliny are connected in that they are all continuous.

The bogatyrs in them are arranged into two generations—the elder and the younger.

Of the older bogatyrs, two are especially well known: Svyatogor-Bogatyr, a giant of such heft that "he was a mighty even to strongmen," and even stronger than him—the plowman-bogatyr Mikula Selyaninovich. According to the tales of the byliny, Mikula Selyaninovich pushed such a heavy plow that the entire druzhina of the skinny bogatyr Bolga Vseslavevich was unable to move it. Still, he, Mikula, grabbed it with one hand and pulled it like a tree from its roots.

The story of Mikula Selyaninovich's strength is obviously fantastical, but the byliny about him are profoundly instructive and show us the distinction and value with which our ancient ancestors viewed the tillage of the land, since they heralded a deft and virtuous plowman to be their very own magnificent and exalted bogatyr. The profound wisdom of our forefathers is here indicated, for the Russian nation can only be truly glorious when her breadwinners—her farmers—are virtuous, strong, and skilled masters of their own affairs.

Here is how the valiant Mikula Selyaninovich is depicted in the byliny:

Roaring through the fields, the plow prods on,
The roaring rack creaks,
Its blades scratched by pebbles;
Roaring through the fields, the plow prods on,
From edge to edge of the groove it sweeps;
To the edge it goes, and no other is seen;
Pulling oaks from the earth, drilling out wells,
As huge stones are cast out into the furrow;
Only the curls of the plow touch down,
Scattering pearls cast over the shoulder.
Of oak the implement is made,

Its blades of pure silver,
And tipped with beautiful gold.

While pushing his plow, Mikula ran into Bolga Vseslavevich, an elder bogatyr and a famed hunter of giant beasts. A conversation takes place between them, after which Mikula suggests that the druzhina try to drag his plow over the land. When they cannot do this, he easily pushes it through the bushes; amazed at his strength, Bolga asks:

Thou plowman's plowman, hark!
Prithee, tell what name thou art given,
And what thou bearest as a patronym?

And Mikula answered:

Just as I shall reap the rye, so shall I stack it in piles,
In piles shall I stack it, so from the field I shall I haul it,
From the field I shall haul it, so at home I shall grind it,
And so shall I mash it and ferment it to beer,
The beer I ferment shall I then serve to guests,
My guests shall then drink, and also shall eat,
And then shall be happy and sing out my praises,
"Cheers to you, Mikula Selyaninovich!"

Such was the greatest of the bogatyr—the peasant-plowman Mikula Selyaninovich.

Mikula Selyaninovich had three daughters, all renowned polienitsy. The eldest of them, Vasilisa Mikulichna, apart from her strength, was distinguished by her extraordinary wit and married the rich Chernigovian merchant Stavros Godinovich. In one bylina, it is said that she saved her husband from a disaster with her intelligence. It happened in this way: Stavros Godinovich had gone to Kiev to Prince Vladimir and, during a feast, took his wife aside and said:

Should it fall to me to brag of my young wife,
Vasilisa, daughter of Mikulichna?
How bright the moon on her forehead,
By her braids thick with stars,
Her eyebrows darker than black sable,
Eyes brighter than a falcon,

Shall all you boyars and Prince Vladimir as well,
Be willingly bought and thereafter exchanged.

At these words, all those at the feast went silent, and by them, Vladimir was quite displeased, and spoke these words in reply:

You, my servants, my faithful servants!
You shall seize Stavros Godinovich,
By his hands so white,
By his finger rings and for this outrage,
For his insolent words,
Take him away to a cold cell,
And send him water and gruel,
Though not too much nor too little, for an even six years,
May Stavros there then reflect,
And let's see how his young wife,
Shall help her husband in his cell,
To see that you, the prince's boyars,
And myself, Vladimir,
Are willingly sold and thereafter exchanged.

When Vasilisa Mikulichna learned of the mishap that had befallen her husband, she immediately understood that it wouldn't be possible to help him with force, but only by her feminine intuition. Following this line, she dressed in male clothing and rich armor, took forty companions, and went straight to Kiev, impersonating an emissary from an emperor by the name of Kalin, to claim tribute from Vladimir, who had been required to pay this cruel Kalin for twenty whole years.

Appearing before Vladimir, she menacingly demanded a large payment, having identified herself as Vasily Mikulich, emissary of Tsar Kalin. After this, Vasily Mikulich began to stare at Vladimir's young niece Zabava Putyatichna, and asked the prince for her hand in marriage.

What happened next was:

Vladimir, the handsome Kievan said:
"Hey you, young Vasilyushka, son of Mikulich!
"I shall take my niece away and deliberate on it."
He pulled his niece away from her dancing,
And asked her, pryingly,
"Hey you, my kind niece!
"Wouldst thou take this awful emissary,

"This unfledged Vasily Mikulich?"
The niece then ever-so-softly said:
"Hey you, my beloved uncle!
"What are you considering?
"What do you have in mind?
"Don't give this girl away to marry,
"Don't become the laughing stock of Holy Rus'!"
Vladimir the handsome Kievan said:
"How can I not give in to the terrible messenger,
"The horrid emissary, this dog of Tsar Kalin?"
"A horrid emissary he is not, but a woman,
"I know all the markers of womanhood:
"To walk like a duck floats;
"And dance the Gorenka quite often,
"As knees sit together on a bench,
"As mulling eyes do look about.
"He squeaks when he talks like a woman,
"He has thick hips like a woman,
"And fingers thin like a woman,
"Even his temples have not all come out of his headpiece.
"Two for two, let's at least be free of doubt!"

Then Vladimir, in order to test the emissary, proposed that he wrestle with the younger princes, thinking that if he was in fact a woman, she would refuse. But Vasily Mikulich, as a former woodswoman, was prepared for this. She quickly bested all the young princes and easily put them down to the ground.

Prince Vladimir spat and went away,
"Stupid Zabava, how senseless!
"A great voice you have, a little wit:
"A woman called a bogatyr:
"Now here, an ambassadress, how unprecedented!"
Zabava argued against her uncle-prince:
"Hey you, my lordly, saintly uncle!
"Not your awful emissary, but a woman,
"Who bears in himself all markers of womanhood."

Then, in order to test the emissary again, Vladimir proposed that he shoot from a taut bow with his sons. The emissary not only agreed but also even ordered his own bow to be brought, which was so heavy that ten men could barely carry it; afterward, with one arrow, he broke a huge oak tree into splinters. Vladimir was finally convinced that this was a real man and an emissary of Tsar Kalin; he then asked him to play a game of Chinese checkers and suggested, moreover, that he would bet his glorious city of Kiev if the emissary would bet the unpaid twenty-year tribute. They agreed and started to play. After three rounds, Vladimir had lost all the games, and the emissary said to him:

"Hey you, Prince Vladimir, you handsome Kievan,
"You've lost your exalted city of Kiev to me."
Vladimir the prince said to him:
"You've cheated me, emissary, and taken the guise of a woman."
The emissary answered this:
"It wouldn't be necessary for you to give up your princehood,
"Nor indeed to leave your Kiev to me;
"Lest you give your niece to me in marriage,
"The young Zabavushka Putyatichna."
With great joy, Prince Vladimir,
Gave Zabava with no more questions,
And put his favorite niece up to be taught,
That she could be given to the awful emissary Vasily Mikulich.

When the day of the wedding came, the young ambassador became dejected and sent for fools to be brought in order to make merry with their play. Vladimir had the jesters brought, yet they could not raise the spirits of the ambassador, who would then ask for all prisoners who could play the harp to be released. They were released, but they played uninspiringly.

Then, at last, the ambassador asked if there happened to be a guest from Chernigov, Stavros Godinovich, who could play the harp rather well. Hesitant, Vladimir said to himself, "If I free Stavros, I shall have to see him, yet if I don't free him, I will anger the ambassador." Stavros was finally released and began to play the harp. When the ambassador asked, "Will he recognize me?" then Stavros answered, "There is nowhere I could recognize you from."

Then the ambassador warmed up to Vladimir and asked him, "I don't need your tribute, of all your fellows, I'd rather you give me Stavros Godinovich."

Vladimir became hesitant again but then decided once again to fulfill the desire of the ambassador and gave him Stavros. Then the ambassador suggested Stavros come with him into a field to see his brave druzhina of forty merry men.

Seated on fine horses, they set out,
And came to the druzhina brave.
Into a white pavilion went legate Vasily,
And changed into feminine dress,
"Greetings, Stavros Godinovich,
"How is it now, do you know who I am?"
Stavros Godinovich answered thus:
"Hello, my beloved wife,
"Tender Vasilisa, daughter of Mikulichna!"
"Yet why exactly, Stavros Godinovich,
"Were you placed in a cold cell by the prince?"
"I boasted of you, dear wife,
"That all the prince's boyars and indeed himself,
"Would by you be willingly bought and thereafter exchanged."
"Then let us soon be seated on our fine horses,
"And away to our lands, of Chernigov town,"
Vasilisa, daughter of Mikulichna said,
"Yet neither honor nor praise is there at all,
"For us to part from Kiev as thieves,
"So, let's go finish the wedding play,
"The bought-and-sold boyars and sun-prince to see there."

When they returned to Kiev, Vasilisa said to Vladimir:

"I, the awful emissary, Stavros' dear wife,
"Vasilisa, daughter of Mikulichna,
"Have returned to finish the wedding play.
"Would you still be willing to give me your niece?"
And Zabava, Putyatichna's daughter did say:
"Hey you, my uncle, Prince Vladimir!
"You've nearly been made the joke of all Rus',
"You've almost given your niece in marriage to a woman!"
Vladimir, sun-prince of capital Kiev,
Assuredly then said the following words:
"Stavros, Godinov's son, you are truly blessed,
"You were right to brag of your dear wife,
"For everyone here she has bought and exchanged,
"Even myself, Vladimir, and moreover, willingly.
"For your boasting most great,
"Let you trade in Kiev for a century,
"And let your trade for a century be duty-free."

Thus was the nature of the great Vasilisa Mikulichna, the eldest daughter of the elder and minor bogatyr Mikula Selyaninovich.

Of the younger bogatyrs, those who are especially well known are: Dobrynya Nikitich, of noble birth; Alyosha Popovich, the son of a priest; and Ilya Muromets, a simple peasant's son. Of these three bogatyrs, in the byliny epics, the first place again goes directly to the son of the land—the exalted Ilya Muromets.

Ilya Muromets, according to this tale, was a straightforward and incorruptible man, a loyal and faithful servant of Prince Vladimir. As a peasant's son, his speech was a little rough, and he was somewhat intemperate with respect to feasting; plus, he had no tact with his jokes and would fight when drunk. However, he always upheld righteousness, even in a fit of anger. He was stronger than all the Kievan bogatyrs and older than them in years; he had obtained his great might from three boons of the elders, who had prophesied that "for him, death in battle is not written." And Ilya fearlessly fought against the enemies of the Russian Land until the end of his days, sparing neither sweat nor blood.

Dobrynya Nikitich, the son of a boyar of the druzhina, in addition to his courage and mettle, was known for being especially vengeful, as opposed to Ilya Muromets, and could speak beautifully and reasonably and sang most wonderfully the byliny of the elder bogatyrs with a harp in his hands. Moreover, he possessed an extraordinarily pious and profoundly Christian heart, as we shall see when he speaks of his wife.

The third great bogatyr, Alyosha Popovich, was, once again, a different person altogether. He was very courageous, sharp, quick-witted, and eloquent, yet boastful, envious, and not firm in his word. "He took not to strength, for he took to craftiness," as the old Ilya Muromets would say of him.

Of the three bogatyrs, Dobrynya and Alyosha were much younger than Ilya Muromets. Still, they had begun their heroic service before him because Ilya Muromets was bedridden with the effects of a disease from the young age of thirty where he could not move his hands and feet. Since he would have remained in that helpless state, Ilya prayed fervently to God and asked him to be healed so he could kill Solovya the Bandit, who was notorious in the woods and wanted in Kiev for having committed a great evil against a carriage traveling through the country. By this prayer, some elder travelers once came into his father's yard; they healed him of his sickness in addition to bestowing great might upon him and prophesied that he would never die in battle.

The delighted Ilya immediately climbed onto his horse and went after Solovya the Bandit, whom he took prisoner and tied to his saddle after many fantastic adventures. With the arrest of Solovya, Ilya went straight to the capital city of Kiev, where, having heard Divine Liturgy, he appeared before the very eyes of Prince Vladimir the Splendid Sun, in the guardsman's hall where at this time, as always on Sundays during the daytime, there was a mountainous feast. Vladimir, as was his custom, greeted the arriving knight warmly and asked him from whence he came and what his business was. Ilya Muromets answered that he had ridden straight to Kiev and made it to Divine Liturgy. In response to this, Alyosha Popovich said to Vladimir:

> Lo, warm sun, Prince Vladimir!
> In his eyes I see he lies like a child,
> In his eyes I see he would insult us!
> Really, a redneck driver he seems,
> Ridden straight direct to Kiev?
> Stomping the mud in Bryansk Forest....
> Thieves would sit on oaks in threes, on the same boughs,
> And as Solovya the Bandit, son of Rachmanovich,
> Would whistle like a nightingale,
> Another bandit would hiss like a snake,
> A dog would growl like a beast,
> All the ants would devour the grass,
> All the azure flowers would go dormant,
> All the land's dark forests would bow down,
> And all the people there would lie dead.

But the gallant Ilya Muromets said:

> Hey you, Vladimir-sun, the supreme Kievan!
> Solovya the Bandit is in your yard,
> I knocked out the villain's right eye,
> And chained him to a damask stepladder.

After this, the prince and queen and all the bogatyrs went to the yard to see Solovya the Bandit, who had just startled so many to death with his awful whistle that Ilya Muromets struck him down to the ground and killed him with an arrow. Then Ilya returned afterward to the guardsman's hall, where Vladimir spoke these words to him:

"You are greatly thanked, valiant Ilya Muromets,
"For having spared us from dying in vain!
"I shall bestow a new title upon you:
"You shall be the chief bogatyr in Kiev,
"Old Ilya Muromets, indeed the son of Ivan,
"Live with us here in Kiev the capital,
"And may you live from now until forever!"
And then they went off to the royal dinner.
Vladimir the supreme Kievan said:
"Hey you, our chief Kievan bogatyr!
"Old Ilya Muromets, indeed the son of Ivan,
"I shall offer you three places to sit:
"The first—alongside me,
"The next—alongside the queen,
"The third—wheresoever you wish."
Then Ilya walked from the window,
Passed all the lesser princes and boyars by,
The bogatyrs too, so mighty and brave,
Finally reaching Vladimir himself,
Alyosha the Bold, who had fallen from favor,
Took up a damask knife from the table,
And threw at Ilya Muromets;
Ilya caught the knife right out of the air,
And stuck it in the oaken table.
Then Dobrynya Nikitich the Young said to Ilya,
"Hey you, our chief Kievan bogatyr,
"Old Ilya Muromets, son of Ivan!
"We've all got our hopes up about you,
"Please take me, Dobrynya, with you,
"And with me my younger brother,
"Alyosha Popovich the Bold,
"And brothers of the cross we shall be,
"With you, Ilya, as our elder brother,
"I, Dobrynya, as the middle brother,
"And Alyosha as the younger brother."
Then Alyosha Popovich the Young said to him:
"Are you in your right mind, Dobrynyushka?
"Indeed, is my brother in his right mind?
"You, Dobrynya are from a boyar family,
"While I, Aleshenka, am from the old Popovski tribe,
"And nobody knows the elder clan,
"From whence he comes, for he brought no word of it,
"He's called a peasant's son from around Murom,

"Indeed, it's strange to us, and unwanted in Kiev."
Then the great bogatyr Samson Samoilovich said to Ilya:
"Hey you, our beloved nephew!
"Our chief bogatyr Ilya Muromets,
"Don't get angry or be hurt by Alyosha,
"He's a Popov of the Zachlyshchi clan,
"And whether he's sober or drunk,
"Will bicker and scold like no other!"
Aleshenka Popovich the Younger then said:
"Oh you, Uncle Samson Samoilovich!
"Nor shall it be said of you in anger:
"You've been a chief bogatyr till now,
"And now who is granted the status of nephew,
"And appointed your superior?
"A country bumpkin, a hillbilly!"
Then Samson Samoilovich said:
"Here now, Dobrynya Nikitich the Young:
"You ring the goosebells quite well,
"Sing then of the olden times,
"Recant a tale of a well-sung hero to Alyosha,
"About that bogatyr-peasant, Mikula Selyaninovich."

Dobrynya took up his harp after this and lectured arrogant Alyosha in song with a bylina about great Mikula Selyaninovich and his meeting with Volga Vseslavevich, already heard by us when all of Volga's druzhina were unable to move Mikulina's plow.

As soon as young Dobrynya was quiet,
Vladimir, the supreme Kievan spoke out:
"Hey you, our beloved harpist Dobrynyushka!
"You've sung us all a healthy draught,
"And now sing something fun,
"Firstly, to make us merry,
"Secondly, to bring to shame,
"The daring Alyosha Popovich;
"Who sits on yon bench, not curled in a ball,
"But fixing his jealous gaze on the oaken table."

After Vladimir spoke, Dobrynya drank an entire glass of white wine when one of the bogatyrs, Bermyata Vasilievich, began to reproach him, for in his song about Mikula Selyaninovich, he forgot to say anything of his three marvelous daughters:

The young polienitsy all were daring,
As strong and brave as their parents;
The eldest—Vasilisa, Mikulichna's daughter,
The middle—Maria, Mikulichna's daughter,
And the youngest—Anastasia, Mikulichna's daughter.

Then Alyosha Popovich joined Bermyata Vasilievich and addressed Dobrynya:

Hey you, our glorious harpist, Dobrynyushka!
You've just forgotten the daring polienitsy!
Go on, send a prayer up to God,
For your Mikula has already passed on,
Since for your wonderful memory,
Reward you with his very own hands he would,
By way of pennies from the wayside,
Attached by string to his cat-o'-nine-tails.
Though Mikulin's daughters live yet,
Yes, there's the older, smarter one,
Vasilisa, Mikulichna's daughter,
Has married Stavros Godinovich,
In Chernigov she lives with her husband,
Eating bread by the stove;
Having managed to convince everyone,
Prince Vladimir as well to be bought and sold willingly,
And you couldn't mention her in acknowledgment.
Then there's her sister, still single,
Both valiant polienitsy all the same,
Bounding through the open field in search of adventure,
Now saddle up some fine horses fast,
You, Dobrynya, with your older brother,
The chief bogatyr Ilya Muromets,
And go off into the wild yonder,
Bound through the field in search of adventure,
Perhaps to call on the valiant polienitsy,
There, you could beat them in combat as honorable fellows,
Not too great a feat the former;
And whoever bests a polienitsa in a fight,
Shall, for that act, become her husband.
Straight to the crown of gold in God's church,
And from the crown straight to the wedding feast!
Simply do as Stavros Godinovich,
They will put you in white hands,

Don't withdraw, don't be angered!

Ilya Muromets refused to go fight the polienitsy, saying that "to marry old is not the conduct of gentlemen." But Alyosha wouldn't be stopped and insisted that Ilya and Dobrynya should go do battle with the daughters of Mikulka Selyaninovich. Then Dobrynya said the following to him:

> Oh, how you are bold, Alyosha Popovich the young!
> It is good for a great and might bogatyr
> To take the field in search of daring deeds,
> And stake his claim to heroic repute,
> His strength against his foes to measure,
> And against those who blaspheme Holy Rus'
> And to place their rowdy, unruly head,
> Upon the gatepost to stay for at least a century
> For the orphans, the widows, and the poor unfortunates.
> Yet do not honor, nor praise bogatyrs,
> Merely for the fun of it,
> For to spill the blood of those innocents,
> Would mean to deprive a bogatyr's family,
> Of a fair wife and Mikula's young children.
> The man Mikula Selyaninovich,
> Strives not for fame nor glory:
> He takes the field behind his plow,
> From side to side he tills the Mother Earth,
> The breadstuffs of all Holy Rus' to gain,
> And for us and you, oh mighty bogatyr;
> The weight of the world he carries with a sweaty brow,
> He, the one who makes our bread,
> Does carry on his peasant-shoulders,
> The weight of the entire world,
> That not even the strongest hero could do.

After this, seeing Alyosha's grin, Dobrynya took up his harp and began singing a bylina of when the two old bogatyrs—Svyatogor and Mikula—met, and at this meeting, the strongman Svyatogor was unable to lift Mikula's small bag, in which he carried the weight of the world. After this, Dobrynya finished his bylina: Svyatogor, struggling to lift the sack, sank down into the ground where it was lying and gave up his soul to God. Bermyata, again like Vasilievich, corrected Dobrynya and said that Svyatogor yet lived in the sacred mountains.

Then the unappeasable Alyosha Popovich suggested to Prince Vladimir to send Ilya Muromets to the holy mountains in order to find out who was true in what they said—Dobrynya or Bermyata. To this preposition, Ilya immediately agreed, saying that "a might bogatyr suffers not to merely stay at home, feeding his belly." Prince Vladimir let him go and sent his comrade Dobrynya Nikitich, with whom Ilya would bond on the path and exchange gilded crosses. On this journey, Ilya would go to the holy mountains, find Svyatogor, bury him, and receive Svyatogor's great sword and his strength in thanks. Dobrynya then split with Ilya on the path, for they met with a daring polienitsa, the young daughter of Mikula Selyaninovich, Nastasya Mikulichna. Dobrynya started a fight with her and struck her with his mace twice, but she didn't raise an eyebrow. But when he struck her a third time, she spoke:

> I thought I was being bit by a mosquito,
> With those taps from a Russian bogatyr!
> And tired of Dobrynyushka's yellow curls,
> She knocked him off his horse,
> And put him deep into her leather bag.

But Nastasya's fine horse refused to carry two bogatyrs—her and Dobrynya—and then she took him out of the bag and said:

> "If it's an old bogatyr, I'll cut off his head,
> "If a younger bogatyr, I'll take it all.
> "If I should fall in love, I'll marry him,
> "If I don't, I'll crush him with my bare hands,
> "And make this bogatyr into an obscure bylina."
> As soon as she looked at the fair Dobrynyushka,
> She fell in love with him and said:
> "Hello, my darling, Sir Dobrynyushka!"
> Dobrynya replied to this, asking:
> "Hey, polienitsa, you daring girl!
> "How do you know the fair Dobrynyushka?"
> "I've been to the capital, Kiev,
> "It was there that I saw the fair Dobrynyushka....
> "Should you take me, Dobrynya, in marriage,
> "Shall you then make a great vow to me,
> "I'll then release you, Dobrynya, alive;
> "Though should you take me not, I'll crush you with my bare hands,
> "And make of you an obscure bylina!"

Dobrynya, of course, immediately agreed to be wed to the great polienitsa and set out for Kiev with her after seeking a blessing from his mother, the pious Afim Aleksandrovna. He took Nastasya by the golden crown, after which a great feast was prepared for all the bogatyrs, though not calling upon the younger brother—the mocking Alyosha Popovich.

Then the young couple began to live in great piety and harmony.

At Prince Vladimir's feast, all his bogatyrs had drank heavily and began to boast among each other:

"A clever man would boast of his father and mother,
"A silly man of golden treasures,
"And Dobrynya of his fair wife."
At this time, Uncle Vladimir the prince rose up and said to them:
"All you, fine sirs, have boasted;
"But I, your prince should boast of what?
"How it is that in far-off open fields,
"The dark shadow of the enemy's power there does fly,
"And writes out threats to me,
"The call to arms goes out,
"To steel yourself against the adversary.
"Already would someone of his ranks invite me to fight,
"To clear the main roads,
"And fortify the outposts."

To this, Ilya Muromets stood up from his chair and said that he had recently come from the main roads and the outpost where he had stayed for twelve years without even an eye of the enemy coming. Now he had threats against him, and Dobrynya Nikitich sent to it.

Dobrynya, drinking a glass of white wine, immediately went home, took leave of his mother and wife, and said to Nastasya Mikulichna the following words:

Expect Dobrynya to return in three years,
Three years you must wait, and another three,
If these six years should pass,
And your Dobrynya should not return,
Consider then that Dobrynyushka has died,
And you, free-willed Nastasya,
May live here as a widow or take another husband,
Or go to the prince as a warrior,
As a bogatyr, or as a merchant,

Or live simply as a peasant,
Though go not alone,
To endure a woman's ridicule,
From Alyosha Popovich:
He, that dog, who is called my brother,
Indeed the one called brother is worse than a true one.

After this, Dobrynya left, and no news was heard of him for six years; all this time, his wife and mother remained at home and eagerly awaited his return. When the six years had passed, Alyosha Popovich brought them some unpleasant news that Dobrynya had been killed and lay unburied in an open field.

Nastasya Mikulichna was sorely grieved for her husband, as was her mother-in-law, but then Prince Vladimir and the queen decided to give her a husband, a marriage for which the crafty Alyosha Popovich arranged to have himself made the prospective groom.

But Nastasya Mikulichna wouldn't submit to these arrangements and announced that she would await her husband for another six years. When these six years passed once more and Alyosha had convinced her that Dobrynya's bones had already been scattered in the forest, then Nastasya Mikulichna, persuaded by Vladimir and his wife, finally decided to marry Alyosha Popovich.

The wedding day was set to be in the evening after a great feast held by Prince Vladimir.

Dobrynya returned just at that very time. Learning that his wife was set to marry Alyosha Popovich, he told nobody of his return and, dressed as a jester, took up his *gusli* in his hands and went to the prince's tower room where the wedding feast was happening.[105] When he went in, nobody recognized him, and Vladimir ordered him to sit by the stove in the jester's section. Dobrynya did so and, holding his gusli, began to sing. He sang so well that Nastasya Mikulichna realized that only her husband could play so well, and Vladimir invited him away from the stove to his table and allowed him to choose whichever place he wished. Then Dobrynya sat down opposite his wife and asked the prince's leave to have a glass of the wine that Dobrynya himself would have. Vladimir let him. Filling the glass and putting his wedding ring in it, Dobrynya brought it to the couple and proposed

---

[105] Translator's note: A gusli is a Slavic stringed instrument.

a toast. As soon as Nastasya saw this wedding ring, she immediately fell at her husband's feet and begged his forgiveness:

> Forgive me in my deviousness,
> In my intoxication, in my female folly,
> That I did not obey your instructions,
> And married Alyosha Popovich.
> They put up to it dishonorably,
> They took me against my will."
> Fair Dobrynyushka Nikitich said:
> "I do not wonder at the female mind,
> A woman's hair is long, but her mind is short,
> I wonder at my so-called brother,
> Who takes a wife from a man yet living;
> I wonder also at the sun-prince,
> With his queen's ineptitude:
> Since I fought for them against the enemy,
> Just now returning from driving the enemy away,
> For twelve long years, I held the fort,
> And they play matchmaker with my legal wife.

Then Prince Vladimir and the queen were ashamed, and the architect of this scandal, Alyosha Popovich, fell at Dobrynya's feet and begged his forgiveness.

To this, Dobrynya said that he was unable to forgive him, not because he wanted to be wed to Nastasya, but because the false news of his death had caused such sore grief for Dobrynya's mother; then picking up the lecherous Alyosha by his hair with one hand, Dobrynya thrashed him from behind with his gusli.

Then old Ilya Muromets stood up and soon reconciled the two bogatyrs. Dobrynya forgave his wife, kissed her, and went to bring his mother the good news of his return from their long separation.

This is how the tales of the byliny recount the lives of the younger Kievan bogatyrs.

From these tales, we see that the byliny are of fundamental importance to the analysis of the lives of our glorious ancestors. It is possible that the brave Dobrynya Nikitich never argued with the envious Alyosha Popovich; maybe the both of them never even lived in the world at all and were other bogatyrs with different names. Without a doubt, the underlying tales of the bogatyr, in contrast to mere fairy stories, draw an image of what the lives and attitudes of our ancestors truly were and why.

The life of a Rus' bogatyr, as portrayed in the byliny, was quite remarkable. There were also many bogatyrs in Western Europe and Poland at that time; they were called knights and also performed acts of valor as ours did in Russia.[106] They even took part in the so-called Crusades in the Holy Land to retake the Holy Sepulcher from the Arabs, which was kept in Jerusalem.

However, there was a great difference between these knights and our Russian bogatyrs. In the West, a knight could only be a person of the upper class who was considered noble; even other members of the upper class would seem so low and insignificant to these lordly knights that they didn't consider them people. Polish knights especially stood out for their pride, especially those who were influenced by the Germans and began to imitate their customs; regardless of the fact that the Polish king Zemovit was of humble birth, the Polish knights profoundly despised peasants and plowmen.

Our bogatyrs on the other hand could be people of all classes, but they were obliged to serve this vocation with the utmost prowess; thus, the peasant-plowman Mikula Selyaninovich was famously considered to be the greatest of the bogatyrs.

When he came to the prince's feast, the unknown peasant's son Ilya Muromets, all the other bogatyrs, with their prince Vladimir at the head, called him the number one person of all those in attendance. They were convinced of this as soon as he showed up with the terrible Solovya the Bandit. Only the covetous Alyosha Popovich would make a mockery of Ilya, but he was immediately humbled by Dobrynya and the old bogatyr Samson Samoilovich and then by Prince Vladimir, Kievan-in-chief.

Although the knights went to liberate the Holy Sepulcher, and a few of them were greatly pious men, most of them were chiefly concerned, above all things, with fortifying themselves in impregnable stone castles on high rocks, only going out of these castles outfitted in iron from head to toe to commit predatory raids on the local population to rob and pillage them. Through their raiding, these knights gradually increased their power and resources to the point that they began to be defiant and flippant even toward their own sovereigns.

Yet without exception, our bogatyrs put all their strength and effort toward the affectation of a great Christian undertaking—the defense of their

---

[106] Translator's note: рыцар (rytsar) as "knight," though with cultural difference, as bogatyr is also often translated as "knight."

country, orphans, widows, and the elderly against enemies from the steppe and marauding peoples; because of this, they were always the prime emissaries of their princes and would selflessly remain in borderland outposts as servants for many years in very remote places. If it ever so happened that one of them should think to attack the peaceful citizens in order to rob them, then he would obviously immediately be stripped of the exalted title of bogatyr and immediately become an ordinary thief and brigand.

Out of vanity, the knights in the West would constantly test each other's strength and, to this end, would engage in deadly duels in front of the people, the kings, and other knights, only to prove their strength and primarily to win the favor of *damsels,* who were women often present at these duels with the very same husbands who these famous knights would often treat very coldly, and, as it happened, slap them on their cheeks with iron gauntlets.

This is not how our bogatyrs were: they considered it a great sin to draw one's weapon with the mere aim of testing their strength against good people of the same allegiance as themselves, since they believed they should sacrifice their lives only against the enemies of the Faith and the State, and against enemies and bandits who robbed innocent people.

Furthermore, to cast eyes upon another's woman was considered a most shameful affair by us and for which one would be punished as Alyosha Popovich was. Our bogatyrs loved their wives very strongly and gently. If it happened in the West that some knight had committed mischief with a woman as Alyosha had done with Dobrynya's wife, then without a doubt the western knight would have killed Alyosha as well as his wife, or in the best-case scenario for her, would have her thrown into the dark dungeons of his castle and then forced her to be sheared and enter into a convent.

Our Dobrynya viewed the actions of his wife as a true Christian and, moreover, as a reasonable person and loving husband. He understood that his twelve-year absence could have convinced Nastasya Mikulichna of his death and influenced her to marry Alyosha Popovich, which is why he immediately forgave his wife of everything, embraced her, only spoke out against the prince and queen for their matchmaking, and gave Alyosha Popovich a minor thrashing.

It was especially forbidden in the West for the widows of knights to remarry anyone, even if they were of noble birth, who did not belong to the knight's clan. Then we have Dobrynya, leaving to fight against the barbarians, to be separated from his wife for a long time, telling her that she could marry:

A prince, a boyar,
A bogatyr, a visiting merchant,
Or a simple man of the peasantry.

In this way, the byliny clearly demonstrate just how immeasurably better life in Russia was at that time than in Western Europe. The upper classes there looked at everyone else with untold disdain. To us, however, all were considered equal brothers, and each class valued the other, being well reminded that everyone in society can't be involved in the same occupations and thus can't belong to the same class. Such mutual respect between Russians, regardless of the difference in occupation, happened for a very important reason: that all of our ancestors, since the most distant times, were always nobles by birth, and thus valued their relationships with one another in a noble and honorable spirit. As a result of this noble spirit, the mutual respect for other people's occupations was never broken between them, no matter how humble a man should be.

Lastly, because of this common nobility and equality of origin, a simple attitude toward each other was instilled between our ancestors. The princes, the boyars, the druzhinas, the simple peasants—all would speak to each other politely and simply, as though they were relatives; those who were advanced in years were called grandfather or grandmother, the younger folk were called brothers, and the even younger ones were called as sons, daughters, nieces, and nephews. This exclusively Russian spirit of simple kinship, a marvel to all foreigners, has been preserved in Russia to this day. Every peasant, whether he happens to be speaking to his Sovereign Emperor, speaks to him simply as "you, papa tsar,"[107] or in their roles as leaders as well, all commanders of the Russian military would address their soldiers as fellows, as brothers. This has never been the case in any other country or at any time. Still to this day, and since ancient times, this remains our way, as we have written here.

Christ's teachings, brought to our Fatherland by Prince Vladimir, and further established by all the best people of historical Russia, instruct us to treat our neighbors with brotherly conduct and strive with all our might and will to serve the common good of our country.

---

[107] Translator's note: Like most languages that are not English, Russian has multiple forms of the second person (you), such as one that is singular and used for informal circumstances (ты) and another that is plural but also used for formal circumstances (вы), i.e., with people who are unknown to you or people considered higher in social rank such as the military. Nechvolodov has written the informal form of "you" (ты) here.

Truly, it was a marvelous time back then in Russia. Wise princes, valiant fighting men, great bogatyrs, brave and intelligent merchants, mighty plowmen and peasants—all lived life to the fullest amid many trepidations, perils, and dangerous adventures, but also did many great and praiseworthy deeds in the service of their fatherland, deeds highlighted by their recent adoption of the Faith of the Holy Savior.

Indeed, paganism was still strong in the ethics and customs of the time; even wise Yaroslav had to recognize the laws and customs of the local people, so strongly embedded in the blood of the new Christian converts. While still believing in Christ and the Holy Trinity, our nation would maintain its pagan superstitions for a long time and, in times of need, would often seek the advice not of priests but of witches and wizards. But regardless of this residual paganism, the teachings of Christ brought its light further and further into the hearts and minds of the Russian nation.

The Clergymen

Due to the measures taken by Vladimir and Yaroslav toward the spread of Orthodoxy and the promulgation of literary education among the children, we would soon have many Russian priests and bishops.

Management of the Church was based on the rules set down by the patriarchs of Constantinople and assembled in the so-called *Kórmchaia Book* (also known as the *Books of the Pilot*), as well as the ecclesiastical statutes of Saint Vladimir and Yaroslav. In addition to the metropolitan established in Kiev, there were also bishops in Novgorod, Rostov, Chernigov, Belgorod, Vladimir-Volynsky, and a few other cities.

The metropolitan and bishops' upkeep came from funds raised by the tithe churches, given by the princes, court fees, and income generated by real estate donated by the faithful. These funds would not be used exclusively by the metropolitan and the bishops, but also for the maintenance of the cathedral church and its clergy, feeding the poor, the sick, the elderly, the orphans and widows, allowances for victims of fire and crop failure, as well as the restoration of churches and monasteries. The house of the bishops served as a care home for all those living in poverty. In addition, parish churches would sometimes be provided as donations by their builders. Thus, Yaroslav, having built churches in the towns and villages, always appointed a certain salary to the priests, and most of all, as there are now, there were well-meaning offerings for the priests from parishioners.

To the great fortune of the Rus', there were many men among their first metropolitans and bishops who possessed remarkable intelligence and Christian fervor. They had great influence over the princes, and no important state-related decision would be made without them because they constantly took part in the prince's council, along with the boyars and town elders.

Michael, the first metropolitan, sent by the patriarch of Constantinople following the baptism of Kievan Rus' under Saint Vladimir, became well known during his life for his zealous promulgation of Christianity and after his death for the incorruptibility of his remains, which were placed in the Kiev Monastery of the Caves.

Another set of incorruptible remains belonging to the blessed Hilarion, the first metropolitan of Rus' heritage, were beatified resting in the Theodosian Caves, having been placed there by the assembly of Rus' bishops when Yaroslav, after the war with the Byzantines, wanted to demonstrate the complete independence of his state from theirs in every way possible. Hilarion was the closest and most active collaborator to the grand prince in strengthening the faith and disseminating the gospel.

Beyond the holiness of their lives, many of our bishops were also fantastic preachers; they needed not only to strengthen their newly converted flock in the Christian faith but also defend Orthodoxy from Catholic and Jewish propaganda, which were already quite strong in those times, so distant from us. From these teachings and sermons, three have made it to us from Metropolitan Hilarion,[108] one teaching from the Novgorodian bishop Luka Zhidyata, and a whole range of teachings from unknown saints who, out of humility, didn't wish for their names to be preserved in posterity.

These teachings preached the need to hold fast to Orthodoxy, as well as the love for one's neighbor, the excellence of eternal life above the fleetingness of the mundane, and the goodness of Christian humility. The most penetrating teaching was that of Christian humility. It would resonate in the hearts of everyone. This showed that the Rus' people thoroughly understood the truth of Christian doctrine, gave themselves heartily to it, and only in humility could find the strength to soften their pagan hearts.

"Be not intemperate or proud; remember that perhaps you shall be stinking pus and worms tomorrow. Be humble and meek; the devil resides in a proud heart, and the Word of God shall not take rest within it," Bishop Luka Zhidyata preached to his congregation.

In teachings of the unknown saints, we find this parable:

---

[108] *Sermon on Law and Grace*, *Confession of Faith*, and *Sermon on Spiritual Benefit to All Christians*.

There were two horsemen: a publican and a pharisee. The pharisee saddled two horses for himself: one horse was virtue, and the other was pride. Pride overpowered virtue, and the chariot crashed, killing the rider. The publican saddled two horses: one was an evil deed and the other was humility; and he found no despair, but absolution, saying only, "Lord God, purify me of my sin!"

By this divine wellspring, from which rays of the Christian faith, the truth of the Gospel, ardent brotherly love, and glorious examples of holy, selfless life emanated over all of Russia at that time, the monastic abode of the caves (Pechersk Lavra) was founded in Kiev.

Of the founding of this abode, the *Primary Chronicle* says the following: "Many monasteries have indeed been founded by emperors and nobles and magnates, but they are not such as those founded by tears, fasting, prayer, and vigil." (*RPC*, 141)

The blessed metropolitan Hilarion determined the grounds of the Kiev Monastery of the Caves when he was still a simple priest in the grand ducal village of Berestove, which became especially well known under Prince Vladimir for its cheerful and bustling liveliness.

Hilarion went into the dense forest that spread around a hill overlooking the Dnieper near Kiev to retire from this bustling life for a few hours. Here, he dug himself a small cave about fourteen feet wide and secretly became an ascetic within it, dwelling in psalmody and prayer.

At that same time, there lived another famous Rus' ascetic by the name of Antipas. Antipas was born in Liubech, near Chernigov, and from his childhood possessed the fear of God and aspirations of monastic achievement. Still quite young, he retreated into the Liubech Caves, existing until that time on prayer and fasting diligently. Here, the Lord instilled in his head the idea to go to the country of the Byzantine Greeks, to Holy Mount Athos.

Mount Athos is one of the holiest sites for the Orthodox peoples because, in the very first days of Christianity, it was, according to legend, chosen by the Theotokos herself by lot and has served as a place of retreat as well as the abode of many great deeds of Orthodox saints and icons.

This mountain is located on a narrow peninsula, bathed by the waves of the sea on three sides, and is about eighty versts (fifty-three miles) in length and about twenty versts (thirteen miles) across in some places. Its heights approach about two versts (1.3 miles) above sea level. Vegetation is scarce on the mountain, there are very few birds and animals, and everyone on it is disposed toward retreat and contemplation. In pagan times, there was an important temple on Mount Athos to the Greek god Apollo. But the Holy Gospel would soon shine the light of the Resurrected Lord upon her.

Here is how Saint Demetrius of Rostov told of this in his *Cheti-Minei* (Lives of the Saints). When the Holy Apostles in Jerusalem, along with the Theotokos, were casting lots to see who would carry the evangelizing mission to which land, the Theotokos got the Land of Iverskaya, also known as Georgia in the Caucasus; but an Angel of God just then told her that this land would be evangelized at a different time, "and you," the angel said, "are expected to administer to another Land, into which God Himself shall lead you." Meanwhile, Lazarus, a friend of the Lord, whom Jesus Christ had resurrected after four days being dead, was at that time a bishop on the island of Cyprus and diligently awaited the sight of the Theotokos; however, he feared returning to Jerusalem because of a great persecution of Christians by Jews there, and thus, by her permission, Lazarus sent a boat for her on which she could come to Cyprus.

During this journey, a strong wind blew the boat away from Cyprus and into the pier of Mount Athos. At this time, many nations would come to worship the idols erected in honor of the god Apollo. Suddenly, while the Theotokos' boat was approaching, cries from the side of the idols sounded out: "All you people seduced by Apollo, go down to the pier and accept Mary, Mother of the Great God Jesus." Hearing these unusual cries, the astonished people rushed to the pier. Upon seeing the recently arrived boat, all who had come received the Theotokos with great reverence and asked her how she gave birth to God and what his name was. Mary then announced Jesus Christ; at this, all fell to the ground and worshipped him and showed her every honor; then, having accepted the faith, they were baptized.

The Theotokos performed many wonders at Athos in those days. After the baptism of the newly enlightened converts, she made one of the men among them into a teacher and with a rejoicing spirit, said, "Let this place be dedicated to me by lot, given by my Son and God." She then continued speaking to the faithful people, "May the grace of God be in this place and those who come here with faith and reverence, keeping the commandments of my Son and God; may the blessings necessary for life on Earth be plentiful to them with little effort, and may everlasting life in heaven await them, and may the mercy of my Son not fail from now until the end of time; I shall ever be patroness to this place and loving petitioner for it before God."

After saying this, she blessed the people a second time and left for the island of Cyprus for her meeting with Lazarus.

From that point on until today, regardless of the various terrible disasters befalling Greece, including multiple declines of their country, great and pious Orthodox Christian monks, who are virtually the only ones who populate it, are not moved from Athos; it is there that many patriarchs and other famous fathers of the Church have been sent to live out their lives in solemn deeds.

About eight hundred years after her first visit to Athos, the Theotokos appeared in a dream to one of the Athonites, Saint Peter, and again called the holy mountain hers by lot and reaffirmed her everlasting mercy toward it.

At this time, on the holy mountain, the great deeds of Saint Athanasius the Athonite were especially revered, and there also arrived to the island the young Antipas; here he began to zealously practice asceticism under the guidance of the hegumen Theoktist,[109] in the then and now existing caves under the Greek Esphigmenou Monastery, in which he then took the monastic habit with the name Anthony.

After that, as Theoktist noticed Anthony was firmly strengthened in monastic life, he told him, "Anthony, go to Rus'; there you will be revered as a holy mountain, for many monks shall come to you in Kievan Rus'." Anthony obeyed and, upon arriving in Kiev, settled on the almost inaccessible riverbank cave carved out by Varangians who had been raiding along the Dnieper. This was in 1013. Prince Vladimir Equal-to-the-Apostles would soon pass away, and bloody turmoil initiated by Svyatopolk the Accursed came to Kievan Rus'. The grieved and distressed Anthony returned to holy Athos. He passed many years in deep asceticism and was finally ordered again by the hegumen to return to Rus', which he did.

His second excursion was in 1028, at a time when total peace had come to Russia. Anthony decided to remain a hermit and selected for himself the cave that had been dug by pious Hilarion on the forest hill near the Dnieper, where he had also settled. He began praying the following words to God with tears in his eyes: "Lord! Let me remain in this place, and yay, upon it there shall be the blessed holy mountain of my spiritual father who tonsured me."[110] Having begun to live there, Anthony fed exclusively on dry bread and spent all his time in poverty, prayer, and labor. To his comfort,

---

[109] A hegumen in the head of a monastery, called an abbot in the West.
[110] To tonsure is to initiate someone into religious life, often with a ceremonial hair cutting.

the cave was far from any populated area because Berestove Hill was surrounded by dense forest. However, word of his extraordinary monastic
feats had spread around Kiev and far beyond, and soon he became known
under the name Anthony the Great,[111] by which more and more would begin
to address him with reverence.

Along with this, Anthony began gathering other people who, like him,
sought to live in seclusion and aspire to feats of great asceticism. The first
to express interest in living with him and sharing his labor was the Venerable Nikon,[112] who was already a hieromonk; he assumed the duty of hegumen in the nascent cave dwelling for a long time because Anthony, out of
extreme humility, refused not only hegumenhood, but priesthood as well.

In 1032, a young man came to Anthony, fell to his feet, and asked for a
tonsure. His name was Theodosius.

Theodosius led a remarkable life from the very days of his youth. He
was born near Kiev, in the town of Vasylkiv, but in his childhood he went
to live with his parents in Kursk. From his early years, he was found to possess a devotional soul. He had no fondness for children's games or antics
and went to church every day, listening to the readings from the priestly
books with great attentiveness. He then beseeched his parents to give him
to a teacher of some sort to be trained in literacy. He learned quickly and
stood out for his extraordinary meekness: "He not only listened to his
teacher, but to all those who studied with him." Possessing remarkable ability, Theodosius came to comprehend all the sciences which were taught to
him quickly so that all marveled at the astounding meekness and intelligence of this child. At thirteen years of age, he lost his father. From that
point, Theodosius understood the bitterness of life. His soul would aspire
totally toward the Lord and toward deeds undertaken in his name, but his
mother did not agree. She loved her son dearly but expected him to lead a
vain and secular life and deeply resented his inclinations. Given her short
temper and the harshness of her nature, she was often cruel and unfair toward her son. He, the heir to a significant property, wore only the simplest
and thinnest clothes and, more than anything, loved helping the household
servants in their tasks. Seeing this, his mother rained beatings upon him

---

[111] Not to be confused with the desert father Saint Anthony the Great of Egypt (252–356). The
Saint Anthony referred to here is also known as Anthony of Kiev and Anthony of the Caves
(983–1073).
[112] Venerable Saint Nikon the Dry, of the Kiev Caves (d. 1101), not to be confused with Patriarch
Nikon of Moscow (1605–1681) nor with the *Nikon Chronicle*, written in the mid-sixteenth
century under the court of Ivan the Terrible.

and constantly reprimanded him that he was betraying his birth by not living how the people of his class ought to live.

Considering such difficult circumstances, Theodosius became increasingly convinced that to save his soul, he would have to leave his home. One time, some pilgrims came to him on their way to Palestine to worship at the Tomb of the Savior. He asked them to take him with them and secretly left home. His mother caught him, however, and unloaded the full extent of her anger on him. She thoroughly beat him with an intense fury and then locked him in a room and forbade him from eating for two days; next she fed him but kept his feet bound so that he couldn't leave. Switching from anger to affection, she begged her son with all her heart not to leave her. Theodosius obeyed but continued to attend church diligently.

Noticing that Divine Liturgy was rarely held due to a lack of prosphora,[113] he began to bake it himself. His mother didn't like this undertaking of her son's, and she kindly asked him to stop baking the prosphora. "You are inflicting," she said, "a great dishonor on your family; I cannot bear to hear how people mock you for this activity." The kind and clever son politely explained to his mother the great meaning of prosphora, and she was satiated for some time. But seeing how blackened Theodosius had become in the following year from the fire of baking, she again impeded him from baking prosphora with threats and sometimes with beatings. With nothing to do, Theodosius again decided to secretly leave home and went to the neighboring town to the one priest, where he continued his baking of the prosphora. His mother soon found him and took him back home, strictly forbidding him from baking prosphora. A boyar stationed in Kursk finally heard of all this and invited Theodosius to him, probably to make him a lector in the local church.

Having grown fond of the meek and humble Theodosius, the boyar frequently presented him with nice clothing, but he gave them all away to beggars while he went in rags. Once, a kind governor was given a large banquet by the city's celebrities. To attend as a guest, Theodosius needed to appear in clean dress. When he was changing his linens, his mother saw blood on his shirt. This revealed that her son was wearing iron chains around his neck.[114] She again flew into a great rage, ripped the chains off him, and thoroughly beat him. But it was all in vain: Theodosius would always strive

---

[113] Prosphora (sing. prosphoron), the Greek word for offering, is the name for the leavened bread that becomes the Eucharist during the Divine Liturgy.

[114] As a mortification, a penance.

more and more to give himself wholly in service to the Lord.

Once while in Divine Liturgy, he heard the following words from the Gospel of Matthew 10:38–39:

> He who loves father or mother more than Me is not worthy of Me. And he who loves son or daughter more than Me is not worthy of Me. And he who does not take his cross and follow after Me is not worthy of Me.

Hearing these words at this time strongly affected Theodosius, and he decided to follow them. His mother soon left the city for some time, and he hastened away to Kiev, where, as he had heard, there were monasteries. Not knowing the way, he came across a convoy headed to the capital city, where it arrived with him three weeks later. He visited all the monasteries and asked if they would take him in. But seeing this youth by himself and unknown to anybody there, dressed in meager clothes, none of them wanted to take him in. Much to Theodosius' delight, however, during these wanderings around the Kievan monasteries, he heard of the great hermit Anthony; his spirits uplifted, he set out in search of him. Upon finding the old holy man, Theodosius fell to his feet and begged him to take him in with tears in his eyes. "My child," Anthony said, "you shall see, these caves are narrow and gloomy! You are young and shall have to endure much austerity."

To this, Theodosius answered, "You know, revered elder, that God Omniscient has sent me to your hermitage, that I should be saved by you. Thus, all that you command, I shall obey."

The blessed Anthony then said, "God be praised to have given you the strength for such a feat, my child!"

And then Nikon, under the order of the blessed elder, tonsured Theodosius. He was twenty-three years old at that time. Having received his long-desired initiation, Theodosius submitted himself wholeheartedly to asceticism, fasting, prayer, obedience, and humility, to the point that Anthony and Nikon marveled at him. Theodosius, however, still had a great challenge to face. In 1036, about four years after he left Kursk, his mother, after having searched for her missing son in vain, heard from some travelers from Kiev that he had been seen at one of the monasteries. She immediately made for Kiev and began to look for him at all the monasteries, but she could find her son nowhere. Then, finally, she was told of Anthony's cave monastery. Sending word to Anthony that she had come from far away after having heard of his great saintliness, Theodosius' mother deceptively suggested that they meet. Anthony, assuming nothing was afoot, went to her.

She immediately began interrogating him about her son, saying, "I have so strongly mourned him, not knowing if he was alive!"

Anthony, a simple and trusting soul, not suspecting any trickery, said, "Your son is here; mourn him not, for he is alive. If you want to see him, go home today, and I shall go to him and persuade him lest he should not wish to be seen by anyone."

But Anthony's persuasions were in vain, and the next day, he had to break the news to the mother that "I have beseeched him to go see you very strongly, but he doesn't want to."

Theodosius' mother then flew into a rage and shouted at him, "You have insulted me, old man! You have stolen my son, imprisoned him in your cave, and you don't want me to see him. Bring my son out to me, lest I die of grief. I shall bring myself to ruin before the very doors of your cave if you do not show him to me."

Deeply affected by this outburst, Anthony renewed his efforts to convince Theodosius to go see his mother and finally succeeded. Seeing her son in a state of deep asceticism, with his face transformed by mortifications and abstinence, she embraced him and wept bitterly; she then calmed down after a while and asked her son to return home, pleading, "The affairs of our home shall be under your will entirely, but please don't abandon me."

To this, Theodosius firmly replied, "Mother, if you want to see me every day, then go be tonsured in one of the Kievan convents. Then move into one, and you will see me each day. Should you not do this, then never shall you see my face again."

For a time, his mother would not assent but finally decided to devote herself to God at the Church of Saint Nicholas, founded on Askold's grave. Theodosius also praised the Lord for his mother's happy acceptance of his monastic undertaking.

Life in the cave monastery was generally quite strict.

The monks sustained themselves solely on rye bread; on Saturdays and Sundays, they ate sochivo (boiled peas or beans). To keep this subsistence, they did simple needlework, which earned them enough money to purchase the rye, and after sorting it they would grind it by hand with stones. By late morning, they would till the soil in their kitchen gardens, and in the afternoon they would perform their monastic austerities in their underground cells. Theodosius was even more austere than both of the elders.

Spry in body, he would always take a part of their work on himself: carrying their water, chopping wood, grinding the rye. Sometimes, on a hot night, baring his chest and shoulders, he would give his body as food to the gnats and flies; the blood would seep out all over him, and he would quietly take a bath and recite the psalms. In the small chapel they had set up in the cave, he would always show up before the others and, standing in his place, would not move until the end of the service.

According to the *Primary Chronicle*, there were three luminaries living in the cave: Anthony, Nikon, and Theodosius.

Soon, another holy man would join them, the venerable Saint Moses the Hungarian, brother by family to Saint George, the courageous servant of blessed Prince Gleb, murdered alongside him at Alta when he went to cover his master's body with his own, and brother by family also to Saint Ephraim of Novotorzh. Moses also served Prince Boris and was with him at Alta; of all the prince's servants, he alone survived and fled with the prince's sister, Predslava. After this, during Boleslaw's takeover of Kiev, he was captured by the Poles and spent five years in chains. He was unwittingly noticed for his handsome and regal face by a single Polish noblewoman who was rich and well known and who came to feel a strong attraction to him. Buying his freedom, she announced her feelings to him and began attempting to seduce him in every possible way, saying that she wanted to marry him. But Moses, already irrevocably decided to devote himself to God, refused her.

The Polish woman shifted her mood from affection to cruelty: she locked him in a dungeon and began starving him. She then complained about him to King Boleslaw, but this did nothing to help. Moses remained steadfast in the dungeon and would soon be granted the opportunity to make his vow to God, for a monk from Mount Athos soon came to tonsure him.

Learning that her prisoner had already become a monk, the outraged Polish woman cruelly ordered Moses to be mutilated in revenge for this slight against her beauty, to the point that the unfortunate holy man barely survived. In her indignation toward the monk from Mount Athos, Moses' initiator, she petitioned Boleslaw, over whom she exercised considerable influence, to banish all the monks from Poland. However, the Lord's justice would not escape them: Boleslaw suddenly died, and a rebellion began in Poland, as a result of which the wicked and cruel Polish woman, a mutilator of the righteous, was killed. This was in about 1027. A few years later, after gradually regaining his strength, the long-suffering Moses set out for the caves of the venerable Anthony. Here he would live on for ten years in fasting and prayer, though persistently weakened from his experiences to the point that he could only walk with the aid of a staff. The venerable Moses had been given the miraculous gift of being able to heal certain ailments and had also foreseen his own blessed end. It is believed that he passed away on July 26th, 1043; his remains are resting in the Antonian Caves.

In 1054, Grand Prince Yaroslav died.

Soon after his passing, and having taken up the grand prince's throne as his paternal birthright, Izyaslav, along with his druzhina, went to Anthony and asked him for blessings and prayer. After that, a youth came to Anthony, the son of the great warlord Yan Vyshatich and grandson of the great general Vyshata, who, for his choice to remain with the defeated Rus' warriors after their unsuccessful sea battle with the Byzantines, was captured and blinded by the Byzantines. This youth heartily beseeched Anthony to be taken among the ranks of the cave monks. Seeing his extraordinary conviction, Anthony consented and ordered Nikon to perform the right of tonsure and to give the boy the initiate name of Varlaam (or Barlaam).

After Varlaam was initiated, the most loyal and favorite servant of Izyaslav then came to Anthony and was also, by his own request, initiated under the name Ephraim.

These two initiations would, of course, later cause great displeasure for Anthony.

The boyar Yan Vyshatich came to him with numerous footmen, scattered all the monks, and forcefully pulled out his son. He then stripped him of his black monastic clothes, dressed him in the bright robes of a boyar, and took him home.

Grand Prince Izyaslav was also very angry with Anthony, having learned of the tonsuring of his favorite servant. He ordered the blessed Nikon, who had performed the tonsuring, to be brought before him, and threatened to send him, Anthony, and the remaining monks into prison and to destroy the caves. "Do as you please," answered the venerable Nikon, "for I cannot deprive the Lord of Heaven of warriors." Seeing the great anger of the prince, Anthony decided to leave the caves and take all the monks to another place. However, learning of the holy man's intentions, Izyaslav's wife, Polish by birth, petitioned the prince not to banish the monks in anger and told him of the ruin that befell Poland when Boleslaw did just that. She quelled Izyaslav's wrath, and he sent a message asking Anthony to return to his former place. The prince's emissaries found Anthony after thirty days of searching and begged him in great Izyaslav's name to return. The holy man consented and set out for his cave, praying incessantly. He then gathered the whole of his dispersed herd. Young Varlaam also returned, after hiding in a house without food or water for three days, finally convincing his father, who took pity on him, allowing him to return to Anthony. In addition, Yan Vyshatich, touched to the very depths of his soul by his son's ascetic vocation, became a zealous visitor to the cloisters and came to have an especially deep admiration for Theodosius.

Little by little, the monks increased their numbers to twelve; they dug out more caves, set up churches, and dug out more cells for themselves. A few more monks then came, and of the older ones, a few departed the caves to establish monasteries elsewhere. Thus, the venerable Nikon departed, setting out for Tmutarakan, where he founded the Holy Mother Monastery. With Nikon gone, Theodosius was appointed priest and oversaw the Divine Liturgy in the cave church.[115]

The number of monks in the monastery had reached fifteen when the venerable Anthony announced in front of everyone that "God has gathered you all here, my brothers, and the blessing of Holy Mount Athos is with you, handed down to me by my hegumen who tonsured me and given by me to you now. I shall now appoint a new hegumen to you, and I shall retreat to live in solitude as I did before." He then named Varlaam as hegumen and went to dig himself out another cave, which until now has been called the Antonian Near Cave, at a distance of six hundred feet from the former.

Having settled in this cave, Anthony lived in it for forty years with strict asceticism. Devoting himself in this way, however, in the highest level of monastic undertaking, his heart always remained near to the affairs of the cave cloisters he founded, for the inhabitants of the cloister kept constant communication with him and would always seek his council and blessings. His love for true monasticism extended so far that he would take food each day to the monk Isaac who guarded the gate, and this went on for eight years.

As more and more monks came to the caves, they gathered before Anthony to seek his blessing to start the construction of a monastery on the mountain. Anthony not only approved this endeavor but also sent a message to the grand prince with the following request: "My prince! God has

---

[115] These monks were not ordained priests but were rather a lower-order monastic, unless called upon to become a priest for the good of the monastery, as there must be at least one to say the Divine Liturgy.

increased our brotherhood here, and we have only a small space; might it be fitting for you to give us the mountain that stands above the cave?" Izyaslav willingly assented to Anthony's request, and a small wooden church dedicated to the Dormition of the Theotokos was built on the mountain,[116] but the monks remained living in the caves. This was in 1057. Then Izyaslav founded and dedicated the new monastery in honor of his patron Saint Demetrius and installed Varlaam as hegumen.

After Varlaam, the cave brotherhood elected Theodosius as their hegumen. Saint Anthony confirmed the election, and Theodosius began his great undertaking.

Accepting hegumenship over the monastery didn't affect his humility or way of life: he would always show up first for work and Divine Liturgy.

His first act was the completion of the construction of the Kiev Monastery of the Caves and the church dedicated to the Dormition of the Theotokos. After establishing the monastery, which had significantly grown in size, Theodosius began establishing the code of communal conduct, taking an example from Saint Theodore the Studite of the Stoudios Monastery in Constantinople. This code of Theodosius was adopted from the Kiev Monastery of the Caves by all other Russian monasteries.

The monastic brotherhood was divided into four degrees: some were still not initiated and wore earthly garments (novice); others remained uninitiated but dressed in monastic garments (Rasophore); the third section was initiated and wore capes (Stavrophore or Little Schema); and finally, the fourth wore the Great Schema.

Everything in the monastery was done only with the hegumen's blessing and sanctified with a prayer. In their lodgings, it was not permitted to hold property, neither food nor clothing. Theodosius himself strictly enforced all of his rules and softly confronted those guilty of breaking the rules, then forgave those who repented and assigned penances to others.

He often gave sermons with tears in his eyes, but most of all, he affected his brothers with his example.

In brotherly meals, he only consumed dry bread and boiled greens with

---

[116] The Holy Dormition Cathedral was built shortly after this. It's unclear whether the name of this small wooden church was the same or not. The Dormition is the three-day period during which the Theotokos is said to have died, in order to experience death like her Son, though she was sinless, after which her body was joined with her soul in heaven, which is why there is no burial place or relics of the body of the Theotokos. The Western Churches refer to this same event with emphasis on the rejoining of her soul and body in heaven, termed the Assumption.

no butter and didn't drink anything but water; he wore old and thin clothing with a rough gown under it. To sleep, he never laid down, but after evening prayers he would sleep while sitting. Often he spent nights without
sleep, praying for himself and for the monastery, which was often noticed
by those awake at night, who heard him crying and bowing when they
would come for their morning blessings. During the Great Lent, he'd go to
a cave, known to this day as the Theodosian Caves or the Far Caves, and
sometimes would venture into another cave closer to the monastery, returning to it in the wake of Lazarus Saturday.[117]

Theodosius would labor daily with the brotherhood. "He'd often go to
the bakery among the other bakers and, happy in his spirits, would squeeze
dough and bake bread."

Once, before a holy day, a cellarer told him that there was nobody to
carry water.

Theodosius hastily got up and began carrying water from the well. In
another incident, there was nobody to chop wood. "I'm free, and I'll go,"
said the hegumen; others were instructed to go for their meal since it was
around dinner time, and he began chopping firewood himself.

His life outside the monastery walls was also no less ascetic. He would
visit anyone in need of help or advice and would teach Orthodoxy and defend against various false teachings.

At night, when the monks were asleep, Theodosius would go to the city
gates and argue passionately with the Jews, proving the superiority of the
Christian faith.

His humility was awe-inspiring. Once, Grand Prince Izyaslav, who
heartily loved and respected Theodosius and had him as a guest, ordered
his servant to drive him to his monastery in a carriage due to the late hour.
The servant who was assigned to this task, upon seeing a monk in poor garments, spoke to him: "You, monk, spend all day doing nothing while I work
and labor all day. You can sit on the horse while I lay down on your spot and
rest." Theodosius, without uttering a word, acquiesced to him and changed
seats. As the dawn came, the boyars they encountered would dismount and
bow to Theodosius. Seeing this, the servant got scared, but Theodosius
simply offered him the horse again. Before the monastery gates, the monks
greeted their hegumen with appropriate honors, and the poor servant was
entirely confused. Theodosius, however, ordered them to feed him as best

---

[117] The day before Palm Sunday, the Sunday before Pascha/Easter, celebrating the day Jesus
raised his friend Lazarus from the dead.

as they could. Saintly Theodosius' charity was also no less impressive. He was a true defender of the oppressed and the wronged. Most of all, he loved the poor: he built a special place for people who were maimed, blind, and lame and gave them a tenth of the monastery's finances. Every Saturday, he would send out carts full of bread to prisons. Once, they brought to him thieves caught in the monastery's village; seeing them tied up, Theodosius cried, ordered them to be freed and fed, then, upon giving orders not to harm them and providing them with necessities, he released them peacefully.

Theodosius' power of faith was shown in many cases. Having gathered a multitude of monks, he didn't care about acquiring more supplies for the monastery but cared about helping the poor more than anything and relied on faith in God in all things. When there was not enough bread and other supplies for the brotherly meals and to offer to the poor, or wine or oils for Divine Liturgy, the monks would report it to Theodosius, and he would always tell them not to be alarmed, as God's intention would not abandon them. And indeed, every time, upon Theodosius' prayer, everything appeared in due time. It would either be a rich boyar, who by God's intention would send carts with bread, fish, juices, wheat, and honey, or the grand prince's custodian would send carts with wine and oils. Finally, there was an occasion where Theodosius was presented with an unknown philanthropist at the time when there were no funds in the monastery to buy bread and nowhere to expect help from; the philanthropist, a young statured warrior, upon entering Theodosius' cell, bowed to him silently, placed a golden grivna in front of him, and silently left with another bow.

Blessed Theodosius called in his custodian and, giving him the golden grivna, said, "Brother Anastasiy! Now you can't say we have nothing to buy bread with, so go buy it." Upon telling the custodian how this grivna had appeared, Theodosius added, "Never despair, be strong in your faith; lay your burdens to God. He cares about us. So prepare a feast for our brothers."

Needless to say that all Kievan princes, boyars, druzhinniks, and city dwellers loved the pious and gentle monks who lived in the monastery, especially since they not only partook in fasting, prayer, and helping the poor, but they also diligently spread literacy, read sermons, and gathered ancestral tales about the feats of the past days. To hear these luminaries of enlightenment, they would often visit the Kiev Monastery of the Caves and, in their own regard, considered monks their most esteemed guests when they went to visit them.

The monks of the Kiev Monastery of the Caves also loved the people of Kiev like they were their own children. In the name of love and truth, they would intervene in their domestic and civil affairs. They especially loved the family of the warlord Yan Vyshatich, Varlaam's father. Yan lived with passionate love and harmony with his wife, and they both were noted for their extraordinary piety and charity. Once, while visiting them, Theodosius gave them a very detailed description of what would happen to them in the afterlife and the significance of church rites performed over the dead.

Listening to him, Yan's wife thoughtfully asked, "Does anyone know where I'll be buried?"

Hearing her wish, the saint answered, "Truly, wheresoever I am lain to rest, so there shall you be lain as well."

And so it happened eighteen years later. In the year 1091, when Saint Theodosius' relics were solemnly transported to the Holy Dormition Cathedral at the Kiev Monastery of the Caves and placed at the corner on the right side, two days later, Yan Vyshatich's newly deceased wife was buried there.

In his communications with princes and nobles, Theodosius showed the same humility, simplicity, and love for truth without any sycophantry, just like he did with simpler folk. Grand Prince Izyaslav often visited him and never entered the monastery on horseback or brought an extensive retinue with him. Once Izyaslav came to the monastery during the brother's after-dinner leisure time when Theodosius forbade the entrance of anyone so as not to disturb the rest of the monks; the gatekeeper, even though he recognized the prince, didn't dare to let him enter without reporting to Theodosius first. Izyaslav waited for the monastery's hegumen and not only wasn't offended by the strictness of the monastery but started to like Theodosius even more.

Theodosius had a custom of inviting worldly people who would come for midday prayer to join them afterwards for brotherly dinner.

Once, during such a dinner, Grand Prince Izyaslav asked him, "Tell me, holy father, what does it mean? That my house is full of various worldly riches, but never have they made food there as tasty as here?"

"Because," answered Theodosius, "here, the brotherhood prepares food with prayer and blessings, and your servants have arguments, curse each other, and get beatings from their superiors when they make your meals."

Despite being humble and patient, Theodosius also could be tough when prescribed so by his consciousness. When feuds began among Yaroslav's sons contrary to the wishes in his will, and Svyatoslav, allying with

Vsevolod, banished Izyaslav and took his place for himself, Theodosius refused to communicate with Svyatoslav for a long while, and in his prayers he would only mention Izyaslav. He also didn't stop accusing Svyatoslav and sent him a letter in which he compared him to Cain, who murdered his brother Abel.

Svyatoslav was furious and wanted to imprison Theodosius.

"I'd be very happy," answered Theodosius, "since it would be the greatest thing in my life. What do I have to be afraid of? To lose property and riches? Would I lose children or villages? Naked, I came to this world; naked, I'll leave it." Upon hearing such a retort, Svyatoslav lost his spirit and put all of his efforts into seeking peace with him.

As a result of the spirited requests of the brotherhood and in the name of the rightful prince, Theodosius finally agreed to mention Svyatoslav during his prayers due to his great love for the Church. Svyatoslav meanwhile went to the monastery and, after patiently listening to reprimands from the holy sage, begged him to visit the prince's palace to provide him with guidance. Theodosius agreed and, while visiting Svyatoslav at some point, witnessed a joyous feast: songs were being sung, and music was being played. Theodosius sat away, lowered his gaze, then looked at the prince and said, "Will it be like this in the afterlife?" Svyatoslav teared up and ordered the music to stop being played.

Afterward, the music would always cease in the prince's palace whenever Theodosius visited. "If my father were to return from the dead," Svyatoslav would say to Theodosius, "I wouldn't be as happy as I am made by your visits."

Anthony, who secluded himself in his cave, was also famous for his directness with princes. Upon the banishment of Izyaslav, he immediately began talking to Prince Vseslav Bryachislavich of Polotsk, who had been imprisoned by Izyaslav, which was unjust in Anthony's view. When Izyaslav returned to Kiev after several months and sat again on his throne, he was furious at Anthony for his interactions with Vseslav. The righteous Anthony then moved away to Yelets Monastery, in the town of Chernigov, and then to the nearby Boldin Mountain, covered in dense forests, where he dug himself a new cave and where monks would travel to see him. However, Anthony soon had to return to Kiev, to his cave, since Izyaslav admitted his fault with the holy sage and begged him to return.

In addition to the propagation of the light of Christ's teachings, the love for one's neighbor, and literary enlightenment, the Kiev Monastery of the Caves also has the glory of an extremely important undertaking: the first chronicles that have come down to us of the events that transpired in the Russian Land and how it was established. The one who created this chronicle (the *Primary Chronicle*) is generally considered to be the venerable Nestor, as we have said, who came as a seventeen-year-old youth in the time of Theodosius to the Caves where his incorrupt body now rests in the Near, or Antonian Caves.[118]

As is known, along with spreading the Christian faith, the first Russian Christians also brought us Slavic literacy, first developed by Saint Cyril Equal-to-the-Apostles. It was them who established the base of our *Primary Chronicle*. First, they were short notes made in church books for one or another event that was deemed important enough to be remembered in the future, such as the blessed passing of a pious man, the building of a new church, and the most important matters in the lives of Christian citizens. Mentioned in these notes were the deeds and deaths of the Kievan warriors Askold and Dir. Finally, the days of celebrations of Holy Pascha (Easter) and passing holy days were also entered into these notes. Thus, the first chronicled notes and short lists were created.

Since they were all created by faithful Christians and were recorded in church books, they represented the one and holy truth, especially since, in ancient times, the very word "book" could only mean Holy Scripture.

With the growth of the Russian State and the baptism of Kievan Rus', of course, the quantity of significant events in everyday Russia's life also grew. Finally, there came a desire to have one combined chronicle of these separated notes, to have a full description of all the exploits of the Russian Land from the beginning of time.

This, of course, could be accomplished excellently in the Kiev Monastery of the Caves, where there lived intelligent, educated monks and where all Kievans would go to share their joys and sorrows, telling them of their affairs.

Thus the first chronicle was created, the *Primary Chronicle* (*Tale of Bygone Years*). There is no doubt that it gathered not only all the separate handwritten notes in the chronicler's inventory but also the tales of civil and state

---

[118] Nechvolodov's note: In contemporary times, the belief is held that the oldest extant records we have are not Nestorian, but belonged to the hegumen Silvester; Nestor wrote *The Life of Saint Theodosius*, and probably a few parts of the *Primary Chronicle* that have gone into the archive. To review the question of the *Primary Chronicle*'s origins completely, the reader should consult the extensive work of the academic Aleksey Aleksandrovich Shakhmatov: *Research on the Eldest Russian Chronicle Compilations*, published by the Saint Petersburg Archaeographic Commission in 1908.

matters from the best men of Kiev, matters in which they partook or knew about from those who were close to them.

Also, without a doubt, the son of glorious Vyshata, the warlord Yan Vyshatich, who lived to ninety years of age, gave many accounts to the chronicler of those events which he witnessed himself or was told of by his father.

This is why our *Primary Chronicle*, along with church events, also vividly covers all the civil and stately matters that took place in Kievan Rus'.

So was laid the beginning of written chronicles among us. Since then, in many monasteries, well-read monks would continue the work of the initial historians and, rewriting the chronicle, would add mentions and additions about the events they knew of themselves.

Each one of them would finish his work with such words: "Gentlemen, fathers, and brothers, if I made a mistake somewhere, wrote too much, or didn't write enough, please read and correct it in the name of our Lord, and don't curse me, for books do age, while my mind is young and hasn't fully matured."

One of such rewriters and editors of the original chronicle, a simple villager from the Rostov area, ends his list with this touchingly humble address to his readers:

> I beg you, brothers, who will read and listen to these books: if someone finds many things here unfinished or unsaid, do not be too critical of me, for I'm neither from Kiev nor Novgorod, nor from Vladimir, but am a villager from the Rostov lands. I wrote what I found. How can I fill what is not in my power and what I do not see? I don't have a rich memory, and I never learned the master's trade of how to compose or embellish tales with wise words....

Our scribes approached the works of the tales of deeds of the Russian Land in this open-hearted way. Our princes helped them and, without anger, ordered them to include everything, both good and foul. Thus our chronicles abound with their truthfulness and simplicity, which the Western learned men can see are lacking in their accounts of their history.

One has to note that such a high and pure view on books and book writing, to our joy, remained for a long time in the Russian Land, and this view was dominant in all of Russia's written works up until recent times.

Aside from the writing of chronicles, the building of the great stone church of the Kiev Monastery of the Caves that exists to this day took place during the blessed lives of Anthony and Theodosius.

It happened thusly, according to the tale:

One of the descendants of the Varangian King Afrikan, named Sigmundr (Simon), having been banished by his people from his homeland, moved to Kievan Rus' during the days of Yaroslav I the Wise, who greeted him with honors and moved him in with his favorite son Vsevolod; Vsevolod, at the same time, also quite liked Sigmundr. During Izyaslav's rule, in the southern Rus' steppe, the Pechenegs were replaced with another predatory people, the Polovtsy,[119] who began assaulting our borderlands.[120] A campaign against them was launched by three princes: Izyaslav, Svyatoslav, and Vsevolod, along with Sigmundr.

While preparing for the campaign, Sigmundr visited holy Anthony for a blessing. The sage openly foretold their deaths to them. Sigmundr then prostrated himself at his feet and begged him to save him. To this, holy Anthony replied, "My son, many of you will fall to the sword or upon retreating will be trampled, maimed, drowned in water; you however will be saved, and a church dedicated to you will be built here."

Then the Rus' came to the river Alta; at night, they were attacked by the Polovtsy and, after a furious battle, were defeated; many warlords, as per Anthony's prophecy, were killed among the multitude of their warriors. Sigmundr, however, lay in the field wounded. Upon gazing at the sky, he suddenly saw a giant church and exclaimed, "Lord, spare me from sorrowful death with prayers of your Virgin Mother and of saintly Anthony and Theodosius of the Caves." And his prayer was heard. Soon he gathered enough might to leave the battlefield unnoticed, healed his wounds, and safely returned to Kiev. Upon visiting saintly Anthony and telling him what transpired, he added, "My father Afrikan made a cross the size of ten feet with a vision of the crucified Savior, and, as a sign of reverence for this relic, he placed over the thigh of the Crucified One a belt with fifty grivnas of gold and on his head a golden wreath. When I, banished by my relatives from my home, left for Rus', I took that belt from that cross and the wreath. I heard the voice, 'Do not place this wreath on my head, but bring it to the allotted place, where the righteous are founding a church to my Mother. Place it in their hands so it can be hung above my altar.' I fell to the ground

[119] Also known as the Cumans or Kumans, they were a Turkic nomadic people from Central Asia similar to the Pecheneg.
[120] Nechvolodov's note: a more detailed account of this shall appear in the second volume of *The Story of the Russian Land*.

in awe and lay there as if dead. Later, during my sea voyage, a storm of such
fury began that we were prepared to die. Then, remembering the belt which
the mysterious voice didn't mention, I exclaimed, 'Lord, forgive me, I'm
perishing because of a belt that I took from your holy image on the cross.'
Suddenly, I saw a church high up in the sky. After wondering which church
it was, I heard a voice from above: 'The one which is built in the name of the
Theotokos, and the one whose size is measured by that golden belt—twenty
belts wide, thirty in length, and fifty in height—there shall you lay.' Then
the sea came down." Upon telling this, Sigmundr added, "Until now, I didn't
know where such a church has even been built, but you told me it will be
this one, the one which is being built right now." After that, Sigmundr gave
Anthony the belt, saying, "This is the measure of the church's foundations,"
and then gave the wreath, saying, "May the wreath hang above the altar."

Anthony praised God and said, "My son, may you be now known not as
Sigmundr, but Simon." After calling for Theodosius, he told him of what
happened and passed him the belt and the wreath. This was in the year
1068.

After warming up to Theodosius, Simon visited him frequently and
once told him, "Father, give me your word that your soul shall bless me not
just in this life, but even after our deaths."

"This is above my power," answered Theodosius, "but if in my absence
from this world this new church will persist, if scriptures and my rules will
remain respected there, it will be a sign for you that I have God's favor."

Then Simon bowed down to the ground before him and said, "Father! I
won't leave you; give me your blessing in writing."

Then Theodosius gave him a prayer, the same one that is laid into the
arms of dead men in today's time. Thus began the tradition of placing pa-
pers with prayers written on them, read over the dead during funeral rites.

After receiving the prayer, Simon, preparing to build the church, asked
Theodosius to forgive his parent's sins.

Theodosius raised his arms and said, "The Lord bless you out of Zion,
and may you see the good of Jerusalem all the days of your life. Yes, may
you see your children's children."[121]

Following that blessing, Simon left Catholicism, his prior religion, and
became Orthodox.

Five years after Simon gave Saint Anthony the belt and wreath, in 1073,
four very richly dressed church master architects came to Kiev from

---

[121] Psalm 128:5–6.

Constantinople. Visiting Saint Anthony and Theodosius, they asked them, "Where do you want to build the church?"

The saints replied, "Wheresoever God shall point the spot."

The masters pointed out, "Wonderful, you will soon die, but still haven't decided the place for your church after we've been given so much gold for our work." Then the saints, in front of the whole brotherhood, asked the Greeks to explain what their words meant. They said the following: "Once very early in the morning, before the dawn, each of our houses was visited by angels, who said: 'The Lady calls for you to come to Blachernae.' And we, gathering all our relatives and friends, came to Blachernae and upon questioning each other, found out that the same angels used the same words to call for each of us. Then we saw the Lady and many warriors around her and bowed to her. And she said, 'I want a church built for me in Russia, in Kiev. I order you to take three years' worth of gold and go and build it.' At the same time, she instructed us to go to holy Anthony and Theodosius, adding that Anthony, who would consecrate the beginning of the construction, will go into eternity, while Theodosius will come after them in the second year. After sending us away, the Lady gave us relics of the holy martyrs Artemius, Polyeuctus, Leontius, Akakios, Afra, Jacob, and Theodore, that we should lay them in the foundation. Regarding the size, the Lady pointed out, 'For measurement, I have sent my son's belt; by his will, you will find open ground and know the church's size.' Leaving the church, we saw a church in the air and, upon returning, bowed to the Lady and asked, 'Fair Lady, after whose name should the church be named?' She said, 'I want it to be named after me.' We didn't dare ask the Lady for her name and were dismayed, and she, noticing that, said plainly, 'The church will be of the Holy Theotokos.' At the same time, she gave us a holy icon, adding, 'May she be the guardian.' So sending us, the Lady promised to reward us for this deed and to give us what 'eye has not seen, nor ear heard, nor have entered into the heart of man.'"[122]

Upon hearing of this tale, the monks all praised God and the Holy Theotokos; at the same time, Anthony told the architects that "none of us ever visited you," to which the architects replied, "We received the Lady's gold with multiple witnesses, and within one month of receiving it we set forth, and it has been ten days since we left Constantinople." Upon finishing the tale, the architects asked, "Where shall we build the church?"

---

[122] I Corinthians 2:9

Anthony said, "Wait for three days." Then he addressed God with passionate prayer and asked for a miraculous sign to determine the place for the church. Following his prayer, one night, on a certain spot, the land was dry while the area surrounding it was covered in dew, and the following night only that place had dew, while what surrounded it was dry.

The consecration of the place for the Holy Dormition Cathedral, the main church of the Kiev Monastery of the Caves, was the last earthly deed of Anthony. In the ninetieth year of his labored life, on May 7th, 1072, he peacefully gave his soul to the Lord. The relics of Saint Anthony lay under the ground in the same caves where he took his vows. The great humility with which he carried his whole earthly life conceals him from human glory even beyond the grave; all previous attempts to reveal his relics have been miraculously defeated.

Following the death of Saint Anthony, there soon came the founding of the new church in the appointed place. This land belonged to Prince Svyatoslav II, who eagerly gifted it to the monastery and began digging the moat for the church's foundation himself.

According to the tale, the church's main icon was personally given by the Theotokos to the architects, a small icon showing her and the apostles gathered together during her Dormition. What's incredible is that, regardless of all the enemy attacks, with multiple lootings of the church, countless fires, and other perils, this icon was never taken from the church.

When Tsar Peter the Great was informed of a horrible fire in the Kiev Monastery of the Caves, which happened in his time, he asked, "Was the miraculous icon preserved?"

"Preserved, Sire!" said the mournful archimandrite John, who personally reported to the tsar about this calamity.

"If the icon was saved," said Peter, "then the monastery was saved too."

This icon hangs over the Holy Doors like the crown jewel of the monastery in silvery-gold luster.[123] It's etched in the style of ancient Greek art on a cypress wooden board. The Theotokos is depicted resting on her deathbed, in front of which stands the Gospel, covering the opening in the middle of the board, where the relics of the seven martyrs were laid by her when she passed the icon to the architects. By the Theotokos' head, six apostles are depicted, among whom Peter is shown holding the censer, and at her feet, five; the apostle Thomas isn't depicted, since he, under God's special

---

[123] The Holy Doors (also called the Beautiful Gate or Royal Doors) are the ornate central doors of the iconostasis, a barrier separating the nave of the church from the sanctuary or altar.

order, wasn't present during the Theotokos' Dormition, and arrived only on the third day after it.[124] In the middle of the icon, to the left, stands the Savior, who holds the Theotokos' soul in swaddling clothes, and above, near him, two angels are depicted with white *ubrus*.[125] The whole icon, except for faces and hands, is covered in golden inlays and embellished with precious stones.

The recanted tale of the miraculous involvement of the Theotokos in the building of the Holy Dormition Cathedral shows us that the Queen of Heaven was herself now spreading her grace and blessings on the Rus' people, enlightened by Christian faith from her Church of Saint Mary of Blachernae, from which she had aided the Byzantines twice against the Rus' pagans.

At the same time, the great saint and martyr of God, Nicholas the Wonderworker, also didn't spare the Russian Land his blessings.

Once, due to the upcoming feast day of holy Boris and Gleb, Orthodox Christians from all over the land were gathering in Vyshgorod. A rich Kievan had also traveled there by boat along the Dnieper with his wife and infant son; on the return trip from Vyshgorod, the mother fell asleep and dropped the infant into the river, where he instantly drowned.

The devastated parents began begging Saint Nicholas for help and reached their house in great sorrow. On the same night, right before the morning prayer, the custodians of the Saint Sophia Cathedral in Kiev heard a child crying and then found a wet infant who was lying in front of the icon of Saint Nicholas. They immediately told the metropolitan about it, and he instantly ordered it to be reported to the whole city. The infant's parents were soon found and recognized their drowned child, to everyone's great surprise. From that day forward, the icon in front of where the infant was found was called the icon of Nicholas the Wet and is especially revered by the Orthodox. Nowadays, that icon is kept in the Saint Sophia Cathedral in a newer wing built in the name of Saint Nicholas.

A few years after this, another miracle-creating icon revealed itself in Novgorod as well, from which Grand Prince Mstislav I Vladimirovich, son of Vladimir II Monomakh, received a miraculous cure. We shall acquaint

---

[124] According to Church tradition, Thomas was evangelizing in India and so only returned to Jerusalem on the third day after the Theotokos died (her Dormition). His return was providential in that he went to visit her tomb and found it empty. The bodily assumption of the Theotokos was confirmed by the message of an angel and by her appearance to the Apostles.

[125] Translator's note: A cloth head wrapping worn by women in medieval Eastern Europe.

the readers with him in the second volume of our work. In honor of this icon, a stone church was laid in Yaroslav's court.

The year after Saint Anthony's death, according to the Theotokos' prophecy, Saint Theodosius also reached the time of his own peaceful passing.

He ordered the whole brotherhood, which was doing its work in villages and other places, to be gathered. When all had gathered, he tearfully taught them of the salvation of one's soul and the God-fearing life, of fasting, dedication to the Church, brotherly love, and humility. Then it was noted that the graceful hegumen was lying in feverish fatigue: he was cold, then hot, and he couldn't even speak. After three days, they wondered if he had actually died. Then he stood up and said, "Brothers and fathers! I know that the time of my life is nearing its end, as God has revealed this to me during my fasting in the cave." Then, blessing the chosen brothers and leaving them in the care of Hegumen Stefan, he looked up to heaven and, with a happy face, loudly said, "God is great! If so, then I'm no longer afraid, and with happiness I depart from this world." He then gave his soul up to the Lord on May 3rd, 1074, sixty-five years after his birth. The relics of the venerable Theodosius were first interred in the cave, and eighteen years later, when the construction and consecration of the Holy Dormition Cathedral was complete, it was decided to move them there.

The venerable Nestor was commissioned to unearth the relics. They showed no decay, the joints were not broken, and only the hair had dried on the head. The next day the standing bishops of Kiev gathered men from all monasteries, and numerous nations came; the saintly relics were brought to the great cathedral and placed in the vestibule. This was August 14th, 1091. Venerable Theodosius was recognized as a saint in 1108. His relics remained open until the Tatar invasion; since then, they have been hidden in the basement of the cathedral, and in the vestibule where they had been exposed, a sepulcher was set up covered with gilded silver icons with an image of the venerable saint.

After his passing, a few miraculous healings and deliverances were noted as a result of diligent prayers to him, and he has sometimes appeared in dreams to those who have prayed to him.

Unfortunately, far from all of the teachings given by Theodosius have been passed down to us. But from those that have survived, one can clearly see the great spiritual fortitude of this holy man.

"The love of God can only be earned through acts, not words," says

Saint Theodosius in one of his teachings, and indeed, his entire life was focused on acts in praise of Christianity. "We should feed the poor and the homeless by our labors and remain not idle in our cells," he continues. And under Theodosius, everyone in the monastery would labor, and he most of all. We know that he never slept lying down; at night, when the brothers slept, he would often go to the city gates where he would debate the Jews until the morning, trying to convince them of the superiority of Christianity over Judaism.

He attacked drunkenness viciously in his teachings, which even in this time afflicted those of all classes, regardless of their having accepted Christianity. On this topic, he said:

> A demoniac suffers involuntarily and can merit eternal life; a drunkard suffers of his own free will, and eternal torment shall befall him; to the demoniac, a priest shall go to say prayers over him and drive away the demons, but over the drunkard, even if all the priests of the land should come and say a prayer, they shall not drive away the demons of his self-inflicted drunkenness.

Of all Theodosius' creative fruits, his *Testament*, written to the Grand Prince Izyaslav I Yaroslavich when the pope's sly preachers tried to convince him to become Catholic, is especially wonderful. Here are its contents:

> God bless you! I have some words for you, O God-loving prince! I, Theodosius, meager slave of the Holy Trinity of Father, Son, and Holy Spirit, born purely in the Orthodox faith and brought up in good teaching by an Orthodox father and mother. Beware, my child, the worshippers of blood, and all their talk, for our land is filled with them. If one would enrich his soul, he should live only within the Orthodox faith. For no other faith is superior to our pure and holy Orthodoxy. Living in this faith, you shall be saved not only from sin and eternal torment but also partake of eternal life and be endlessly joyous in holiness. Those who live in other faiths shall not know eternal life. It is inappropriate to praise any other faith. One who would praise another's faith does the same as blaspheming his own. If one would praise his as well as another's, then he is a dual believer and close to a heretic.
>
> And so child, beware of them and always be true to your faith. Don't fraternize with them, but flee from them and realize your

faith with good deeds. Give alms not only to those of the faith but also to others. If you should see someone naked or hungry, or in trouble—be he a Jew, a Turk, or a Latin—be charitable to all, save him from suffering inasmuch as you are able, and you shall not be deprived of earning reward, for in this epoch, God himself has shared his grace not only with Christians but with the unfaithful also. God cares about the pagans and those of other faiths in this time, but in the hereafter, the wondrous blessing of eternal life shall not be theirs. However, we who live in the Orthodox faith shall receive all the blessings from God, and in the hereafter our Lord Jesus Christ shall reward us.

Child! Even if you should need to die for your Holy Faith, then go to your death valiantly. Thus have the saints died for the faith and now live with Christ.

Should you see, child, gentiles arguing with an Orthodox faithful and using flattery to tear him away from the Orthodox Church, help him. In this way, you shall save the sheep from the mouth of the lion. Should you be silent and give no help, it would be as though you had stolen a redeemed soul from Christ and given him to Satan.

If one should tell you: "Your faith, as well as ours, is from God," then you, child, must answer thusly: "Oh, worshipper of blood! You consider God to be a dual believer! You listen not to what the Scripture says: 'One God of one faith, one baptism' (Eph. 4:5)."

That was the venerable Saint Theodosius.

The abode created by him and Saint Anthony, regardless of the terrible and difficult times that Kiev and the entire Russian Land had to endure more than once, thrives to this day. Many pilgrims flock to Kiev all year round to give reverence to the miraculous icon of the Dormition, personally given by the Theotokos to the architect-builders of the Church of Saint Mary of Blachernae, and the relics of Saints Anthony and Theodosius, and also to the other holy men who are buried in the Near Caves and Far Caves.

In the Near Caves (also called the Antonian Caves or the Caves of Saint Anthony), there are three churches: the Church of Saint Anthony, the Saint Varlaam Church, and the Church of the Entry of the Mother of God into the Temple. Right there, hidden under the floor, the relics of Saint Anthony himself, as well as those of forty-nine saints, are resting in open tombs; counted among these forty-nine corpses are the relics of Saint John, son of

Theodore the Varangian, killed by an angry mob along with his father under Prince Vladimir the Great prior to his baptism. Further along in the Antonian Caves, ten hermits are laid to rest in their cloisters along with thirty myrrh-streaming heads of the unnamed saints.[126] Twelve Byzantines who built the Holy Dormition Cathedral are resting openly without graves: four architects sent by the Theotokos from the Church of Saint Mary of Blachernae; and eight artists, also blessedly sent by the Theotokos in 1083 to see to the cathedral's finery when it had been completed in the rough. All these twelve Byzantines, upon the completion of their work, took tonsuring, and their relics remain open and incorrupt to this day.[127]

In the Far, or Theodosian Caves, where the foundations of the original monastery were laid, the cell of Saint Theodosius has remained safe until now, and the small church along with it. There is also the stone Blessed Virgin Mary Annunciation Church, built by the hands of the first of the cave-monks, the Church of the Nativity of Christ, and the relics of the blessed saints: thirty-three are resting in open graves, and thirteen in closed ones; moreover, there are thirty-one myrrh-streaming heads and one incorrupt body of the unknown saints.

Of the holy men resting in both caves, to our great misfortune, there remain sixty-one saints who are completely unknown, even in name, whose heads stream myrrh, and also one incorrupt saint.

It is also unfortunate that their remains are kept not far from the rest of the cave-dwelling saints whose names are known. As for those monks

---

[126] The bodies of some saints are known to have a sweet scent of myrrh, "the scent of holiness."
[127] Nechvolodov's note: Finally, in the Antonian Caves are resting, in an open shrine, the incorrupt relics of the Righteous Saint Juliana the Virgin. Her body was uncovered in the beginning of the seventeenth century completely by accident, near the Kiev Monastery of the Caves, when excavation was being done for the construction of a tomb for another deceased. A stone was found there with the royal insignia of the Olshansky princehood and beneath it a sanctum in which there lay, as though still alive, a deceased young girl dressed in fine silk and golden clothes, also looking as if it had just been made. On the dead girl's neck there were golden grivnas with many beads, on her hands were precious rings, on her head a golden maiden's crown, and on her ears rich earrings with precious stones of great value. In the sanctum there was a gilded silver tablet with writing: "Juliana, Olshansky princess, daughter of Prince Gregory Olshansky, died a virgin in the sixteenth year after her birth." Since no further information of the virgin Juliana existed in the Caves, a shrine was built to her in the Holy Dormition Cathedral, but nobody paid much attention. She would however soon turn up in a wondrous vision to the metropolitan of Kiev, Peter Mogil, and showed him that it was fitting for great reverence to be applied to her relics. The metropolitan then ordered her relics to be honored as saintly. Later on, after a fire in the Holy Dormition Cathedral, they were installed in the Antonian Caves.

whose hagiographies remain, however, the descriptions are so brief that they give almost no image of the blessed deeds of the holy men for whom they are written. Thankfully, on the other hand, more detailed saints' lives exist concerning some of them, and through them we can get a very clear picture of life in the cave abbey, their deeds, and the trials they were subjected to.

Here are some short excerpts of a few of the lives of the monks who lived in the Kiev Monastery of the Caves and whose relics are still kept there.

The venerable Saint Isaac the Recluse was a rich merchant from Toropetsky. He came to desire an ascetic life, so, as the Gospels instruct, he gave away all his property and went to Saint Anthony of the Caves to ask him for tonsuring; Anthony accepted him and tonsured him. Isaac placed very harsh austerities on himself: he put on sackcloth with goatskin that had dried over it, shut himself up in a tight, narrow cave, and prayed to God with teary eyes. He spent seven years this way; for food, he had the Eucharist every other day, and water he drank in moderation. Anthony, as we saw earlier, would go to him and to a few others to feed them through small windows, through which hands could barely fit. Over these seven years, Isaac never came out of his hatch and never lay on his side but would only sleep briefly while seated; from evening to midnight, he chanted psalms and performed prostrations.

Once, when he began to rest after a night of worship, he was suddenly met with a wondrous vision: the cave was illuminated by a bright light, and two radiant youths entered it. "Isaac," they said, "we are angels, and Christ is coming to you; bow to him!" The hermit was deceived, protecting himself not with the sign of the cross nor with the awareness of his unworthiness, and fell to the ground before the demonic influence as though it were Christ himself. The demons proclaimed, "You are ours, Isaac; dance with us!" They picked him up, began to dance, and left him half dead. The next morning, Anthony went to the window as usual and said a prayer; there was no answer. The great elder reasoned that the hermit had already passed away; he dug up the cave and carried him out as though he were dead but then noticed that he was still breathing. Accustomed to spiritual life, the elders recognized the work of demons. At the time of the illness, the venerable Anthony went to him first, brought him to the cell of Theodosius, and began to attend to him as a mother would attend to a small child. Isaac was in such a weak state that he couldn't even stand, sit, or turn from one side to the other. He lay there like that for two years, unable to speak or listen; day and night, Theodosius prayed for him. Finally, in the third year, he spoke, began to listen, and, like a baby, began learning to walk again. They brought him to church by force and then taught him how to walk to the meal hall. Little by little, Isaac returned to his old self after the terrible upheaval and began to lead an austere life once again. However, tempted in his imprisonment, he didn't want to go to the cave at first but put on sackcloth and began helping the cooks in the kitchen. Before he did anything, he would go to church and stand still. In the wintertime, he would walk on crushed worms so that his feet would freeze to the ground and remain standing in one place until the end of Divine Liturgy. Having fully regained his strength, he again shut himself in; here, he was again subject to temptations without end but successfully repelled them. After his second feat of self-seclusion spanning twenty years, he passed away around the year 1090.

The venerable Saint John the Long-Suffering lived in the caves for thirty years near the relics of Saint Moses the Hungarian. His most ardent wish was to attain the purity of soul and thought of the venerable Moses, but toward the completion of this end, John, tormented by the evil one, experienced the greatest of temptations. In order to overcome them, he went six days without food, wrapped himself in heavy chains, and buried himself in the earth almost up to his shoulders for the entirety of the Lenten season; thus did he struggle for the entirety of his thirty years of life in the caves. On the day of Christ's most Holy Resurrection at the end of Lent, he was struck by visions of a huge, fiery serpent with its head in its mouth; when John said a prayer, the diabolical vision was gone, but the beard and hair on his head were scorched. After this trial, John not only attained the complete pacification of his soul but even received a special gift, the ability to see in complete darkness so that he could commit his prayer rule to write in the cave without the help of a lamp. Before his passing, he again buried himself in the earth up to his chest and stood there still as a monument to the glorious victory over the enemies of human salvation.

The venerable Saint Pimen (or Poemen), given the epithet Much-Ailing, was born sick and raised in illness. He asked his parents many times to let him take the tonsure, but they didn't want to give their son up to the monastery, for he was their sole heir. Finally, seeing no hope for recovery, they decided to take him to the Kiev Monastery of the Caves so the monks' prayers might grant him healing. But these prayers were unsuccessful because he himself prayed diligently not for health but for his illness to worsen in order to remain in the monastery. He wished only for one thing: tonsuring.

Thus, one night, the monks came to him unseen, performed the rite of tonsure over him, and dressed the ailing one in monastic garb. Nobody heard how they had come in a locked church. Pimen's hairs, cut away at his tonsuring, were found on the shrine of Saint Theodosius. Only when the rite was complete were the sounds of the chanting heard by a few who came to Pimen and found him already tonsured, with a lit candle in his hands. Pimen lived in ailment for more than twenty years, to the point where his servants considered him a burden and would often leave him without food and drink, but he bore it all happily. Another sick man was taken to the cave, so the servants found it prudent to lodge them together and would often leave them unattended. "Brother," Pimen said to the sick man lying next to him, "the servants are neglecting us. If the Lord should heal you, could you perhaps put this situation right?" The sick man promised to dedicate his whole life to the service of the ailing. By the word of the blessed Pimen, he regained his health and attended him, but he got lazy and became sick again. "Ye of little faith," Pimen said to him, "do you not know that the sick man and the one who attends him receive the same reward? Here, sorrow is light, and there, joy is of the ages. God, who healed you, could also heal me, but I do not want him to. Let me rot in this life that I may be without ailment there; let a horrid stench surround me here that there I may forever delight in pleasant fragrance." Before his death, the voluntary sufferer cured all who passed by his cell and, taking leave of his brothers, indicated a place for himself to be buried and departed from his earthly life.

The venerable Saint Prokhor (or Prochorus), a native of Smolensk, stood out for his incredible abstinence. He would even deny himself rye bread and, in its place, would take orach, grind it, and eat it like that. For this, he was given the epithet Orach-Eater. Except for the Eucharist and the orach bread, he ate nothing, not vegetables nor wine; he was never sad and always cheerfully worked for the Lord. Once when there was a famine, he doubled his labors in the gathering of orach and distributed to the starving people this bread, which seemed remarkably sweet, as though it were baked with honey.

The venerable Saint Damian the Presbyter and Healer was distinguished by his extraordinary meekness and his ability to heal the sick. He was so austere that he ate nothing except bread and water until the very end of his life. If a child or any sick person was brought to the monastery with any ailment, the venerable Theodosius would entrust Damian to say a prayer over the sick; he would perform the prayer, anoint the sufferer with sacred oil, and they would be healed. When he got sick and was close to his end, an angel appeared to him in the night in the form of the venerable Theodosius and promised him the kingdom of heaven. The next morning, Theodosius came and sat next to him. When the dying Damian saw the hegumen, he said, "Do not forget what you promised me in the night." Great Theodosius answered him, "Brother Damian, you shall have what was promised by me." He then gave up his spirit to the Lord.

The venerable Saint Agapetus was a native Kievan and served as a cost-free doctor in the monastery upon being tonsured. Whenever any of his brothers fell ill, Agapetus, departing from his cell, would go to the brother who was ill and tend to him, giving him boiled grass in place of medicine. The sick man, by his prayer, would be healed. Many from the city would come to him, and he refused his gracious help to no one. Once, the then prince of Chernigov, Yaroslav's grandson Vladimir II Monomakh, fell ill. He received no assistance from his doctors, so he sent messengers to call on Agapetus. "Were I to go to the prince," the blessed Agapetus reasoned, "then I should have to go to all who seek my help. I shall not venture beyond the monastery gates for any human praise so as not to break my vows."

He did not go to the prince, but sent him the boiled grass, which he ate. The healed prince went to thank the miracle worker, but Agapetus disappeared. Monomakh then went to his cell and left a few gold coins in gratitude; upon returning, Agapetus then threw out the gold. The miraculous healing of the cost-free doctor aroused the envy of an Armenian, who was then highly valued in Kiev for his skill in medicine. Having ensured through various experiments that the medical workings of Agapetus were made possible by the power of heaven, the Armenian became a monk himself after the blessed passing of Agapetus and ended his life in good works.

The venerable Saint Dionysius, hieromonk and warden of the caves, nicknamed Schepa (Kindling), on the feast day of Christ's Resurrection, went into venerable Anthony's Cave which displayed bodies of holy saints; coming into that place, which was called the commune or the mess hall, Dionysius, shaking, said, "Holy fathers and brothers! Today is a great day: Christ is risen!" And immediately, the voice of all the corpses answered, booming like a thunderbolt, "Indeed, He is risen!" Deeply affected by this miracle, Dionysius expired at the gate, where he had stopped.

Venerable Saint Nicholas, the great-grandson of Grand Prince Yaroslav, the first of the Rus' grand princes, voluntarily took tonsure, although he had a wife and children. Leaving the princehood, he passed through the various monastic ranks in the Kiev Monastery of the Caves. For three years, he worked with the brothers in cookery, chopped his firewood, carried water over his shoulders, and prepared food for the brothers; for three more years, he stood guard over the monastery, going nowhere except to church. From here he was taken to serve at the table, and everyone came to love him for his zeal. After these tonsuring initiations were performed, the venerable Nicholas, at the behest of the hegumen and all the brothers, was obliged to make himself a cell and to care only for his own salvation. He obeyed, and nobody ever saw him idle. With his own hands, he set up a small garden in front of his cell and was always busying himself with some handiwork while saying a prayer. The venerable Nicholas never ate anything except for the food at the monastery table. He had no property, for he had given everything he had gotten from his relatives to the poor and toward the construction of churches. His blood brothers tried to get him to return to earthly life for a long time, especially by way of a certain doctor who had taken up residence in Kiev for the saint-prince. "Your pious brothers," said the doctor, "are enduring difficulties from your poverty. Who among the princes has behaved in this way? Who among the boyars desired to live a monastic life, except for Varlaam, who was a hegumen here?" The blessed prince answered, "I have thought much, and I wished not to favor my flesh, lest it should overcome me; lest it is allowed, oppressed by many labors, to endure. If no prince before me has ever done this, then let me be the first, and whoever should desire shall follow in my footsteps. By the grace of my God, he has freed me from the workings of the world and made me a servant to his slaves, the blessed, black-robed monks. Let my brothers be mindful of their salvation, and the advantage shall be mine, should I die for Christ."

Venerable Saint Martyrius the Deacon was honored during his life with the gift of miracles for his great deeds and purity of living, so many would come to him for help in prayer and various other needs, and all those for whom he prayed, standing on the pulpit, received what was requested: healing of wounds, deliverance from sorrow and temptation, as well as every other need. After his saintly end and until modern times, his relics also bestow the gift of miracles to all who come to him in faith and prayer.

Venerable Saint Alypius, having learned iconography from the Byzantine masters who painted the Holy Dormition Cathedral, took tonsure afterward, labored vigilantly, and made icons free of charge for the hegumen, the brothers, and the churches of Kiev. For his pure and virtuous life, he was given the honor of priesthood and was glorified by God with the gift of miracles: he would anoint wounds with his paints as if they were medicine, and the afflicted person would be healed. One of the icons, beautifully produced in his cell, is now kept in the Rostov Cathedral of the Assumption, where it has remained unscathed after three large fires at the fall of the first stone church and from invasions of the barbarian Tatars and Poles. Another wonderful icon was made in the last days of Alypius' life. He told his brothers, "The angel who made the icon stands in front of me and wants to take me." With these words, the first Russian iconographer gave up his soul to God.

Venerable Saints Spyridon and Nicodemus baked prosphora, laboring diligently over thirty years. Since he was illiterate, the former learned the entire Psalter by heart and would recite it daily as he worked.[128] The image of a tripartite sign of the cross, which suddenly appeared on blessed Spyridon at the moment of his passing, has since then remained etched on his hand and still draws many Orthodox dissident Old Believers who believe that one must make the sign of the cross on themselves with two fingers.

Venerable Saint Eustratius Postnik was taken captive by the Poles, who besieged the Kiev Monastery of the Caves in 1096. He was soon sold into slavery, along with twenty Kievan people and thirty monastics, by a Jew. The Jew began to starve his slaves to coerce them into rejecting Christ, but brave Eustratius convinced them not to give up and constantly sustained them with teachings from Holy Scripture. These holy captives, whose names are honored but unfortunately unknown to us, encouraged by Eustratius, decided it was better to die than to apostatize against the Christian faith, and sure enough, tortured by hunger and thirst, died gradually. Fourteen days later, the only one remaining alive was Eustratius, who was accustomed to fasting from his youth. The Jew, seeing that he lost all the money he spent on the Russian slaves thanks to Eustratius, decided to take cruel revenge on him on Pascha (Easter) by having him crucified in front of many other Jews. While nailed to the cross, the crucified sufferer thanked Lord Jesus Christ for allowing him to suffer as he himself had. "I believe," he said to the Jews, "that the Lord shall never say to you as he said to the thief, 'Today you shall be with me in heaven,' but justice shall be served to you for spilling Christian blood." The enraged Jew pierced the martyr's body with a spear and threw him into the sea. This was on March 28th, 1096. God's wrath would soon befall the murderer: he was hanged. Many of the Jews present at the crucifixion of Eustratius were baptized. The holy martyr's relics were found by the faithful and laid to rest in the Antonian Caves.

Venerable Saint Kuksha was beatified by the Vyatichi, wherein at the

---

128 The Psalter is a long prayer consisting of the Psalms and other devotional material related to the liturgical year.

time of Theodosius there were still many pagans. Inspired by holy zeal for the faith, Kuksha departed the Kiev Monastery of the Caves with his student to preach the truth of the Christian faith to the barbaric pagans; his sermon was followed by miracles that instilled the faith into the hearts of the people, but this of course greatly angered the pagan magi, who subjected him to a painful death along with his student.

On the same day and at the same hour in the Kiev Monastery of the Caves, the venerable Saint Pimen, Kuksha's friend, also died. He could heal the sick and had the gift of foresight, and for two years had predicted his departure to God. On the day of Kuksha's martyrdom, he stood up in the middle of the church and loudly announced, "Our brother Kuksha is now dead," and then immediately passed away.

Saint Leontius, a disciple of the venerable Saint Anthony, was beatified for evangelizing the Rostov area, inhabited by a barbaric Finnic tribe, the Meryans. He encountered obstinate and brutal idolaters among them and endured insults and beatings at their hands. But Saint Leontius resolved not to abandon the flock entrusted to him. Settling outside the city of Rostov, he built a wooden church in honor of Michael the Archangel and began to invite children there, feeding and taking care of them. The children, of course, willingly went to the saint, and he taught them the basics of the Holy Faith and then baptized them. The children and a few adults were baptized as well. But the old-fashioned pagans were outraged and gathered around the church one day with clubs and various weapons. Surrounding Leontius, he became scared, but the saint remained calm. Dressed in robes, he, along with the priests and deacons, also dressed in robes, went out to the wild tribesmen. His firm calm surprised the pagans. They fell before him in fear and were baptized. Saint Leontius ordained many priests and deacons but failed to bring all the lost Meryans to Christ, and his apostolic mission ended in his martyrdom around the year 1070, it is believed.

Thus were the first inhabitants of the Kiev Monastery of the Caves.

Among the faithful departed who are resting in the Antonian Cave, one open coffin containing relics that draws one's attention bears the words "Ilya of Murom." The life of this righteous Ilya is completely unknown. Still, upon seeing his fair relics, one is reminded of another Ilya from Murom, the glorious bogatyr of our byliny. One supposes unwittingly whether he ended his earthly journey here, having humbly taken tonsuring, and after his saintly passing was glorified for the incorruptibility of his relics.

At these thoughts, each Russian person unwittingly makes the sign of the cross on themselves, and their hearts involuntarily send out prayers to

God so that, in the current days, the faithful sons of our motherland, with the mighty spirit of the bogatyr, would not be displaced in the firmness of their Orthodox faith.

Far gone from us are those times when the wondrous monks inhabited the Kiev Monastery of the Caves; long even has it been since Kiev ceased to be the capital city of all of Russia, but the hallowed memory of the holy baptism of the Russian nation that happened there, and of the great princes who ruled there, of the great exploits of our bogatyrs and our military men, and also the deeds of its humble cave dwellers will live forever in Russian hearts.

Always each of us is brought together with a special feeling of tenderheartedness at the mother of Russian cities by the Kievan shrines.

This feeling that Russian people have of having their spirits uplifted upon the sight of Kiev is very well expressed by Aleksey Stepanovich Khomyakov in his poem "Kiev":

High above me
Old Kiev lies on the Dnieper;
The Dnieper glistens 'neath the mountain,
Iridescent as silver.
Hail, Kiev eternal,
The cradle of Russia's glory.
Hail, our flowing Dnieper,
The purifying font of Rus'.
A song resounded sweetly,
In heaven the evening's call. . . .
"From whence have come
"The pilgrims to worship?"
"From where the gentle Don does flow,
"The beautiful steppes I have come."
"My region—the gentle coast of the Euksina"[129]
"My region—the coast of those distant lands,
"Where the hard ice floe
"Does fetter the ocean."
"The wild and fearsome heights of the Altais,
"Where the gleam of snow forever shines,
"That is the land of my birth!"
"My fatherland is old Pskov."
"I hail from cold Ladoga."

---

[129] Nechvolodov's note: Euksina is the Greek name for the Black Sea

"I hail from the blue waves of the Neva."
"I hail from high-watered Kama."
"I hail from mama-Moscow."
Hail, O Dnieper, your silver waves!
Hail, O Kiev, city of dreams!
The silent darkness of your caves,
More beautiful than a royal palace,
We know that in past centuries,
On ancient nights in darkness deep,
Russia of the eternal eastern sun,
Glanced upon thee.
And now from far-off lands,
From steppes unknown,
From deep rivers of midnight,
A myriad of children in prayer,
Around your shrines,
We are assembled with love.

Figures for Chapter Five

193. (Left) Saints Boris and Gleb riding horses.
Ancient Icon of the Old Believer Rogozhskoye Cemetery in Moscow.
194. (Right) Return of Saint Boris with druzhina after chasing off Pechenegs.
This and next six illustrations from the *Sylvester Miscellany*.

195. (Left) Svyatopolk sends assassins against Saint Boris.
196. (Right) Saint Boris prays in his tent to the Holy Savior.

197. (Left) The murder of Saints Boris and Gleb.
198. (Right)Two Varangians pierce Boris' heart.

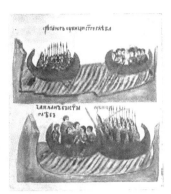

199. (Left) Saint Gleb rides a horse.　　200. (Right) Murder of Saint Gleb.

201. Yaroslav orders the death of the Novgorodians, for the Novgorodians have risen against the Varangians and beaten them. Yaroslav was angered and gave a speech to the Novgorodians: "These ones I won't ever resurrect." And he called for the best Varangian men, and they were killed. *Radziwiłł Chronicle.*

202. (Left) Coin of Svyatopolk the Accursed.
203. (Right) The Battle of Liubech: "Everything was frozen; Svyatopolk stood between two lakes, and he would have drank with his men all night were it not that a fierce battle broke out and the Pechenegs tried to help him by crossing the lake, but the ice fell out from under them."

204. (Left) Boleslaw the Brave. Guanini, *Exposition on the European Sarmatians*.
205. (Right) Golden gates of Kiev. Painting by a Flemish court artist of the Polish-Lithuanian Prince Janusz Radziwiłł, whose troops took Kiev in 1651.

206. (Left) Novgorodians are looking for the prince's boats. Yaroslav, upon arrival
in Novgorod, desired to flee to the sea, but Governor Constantine, son of
Dobrynya, upon meeting the Novgorodians searching for the boats
of Yaroslav, said "We still want to fight Boleslaw and Svyatopolk."
207. (Right) *Mstislav's fight with Rededya*. Illustration by K. O. Ryliev.

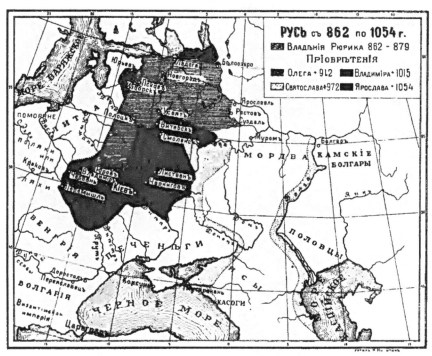

РУСЬ съ **862** по **1054 г.**

Владѣнія Рюрика 862 - 879

Пріобрѣтенія

Олега + 912   Владиміра + 1015

Святослава + 972   Ярослава + 1054

208. Kievan Rus' from 862 to 1054. See an English version of this map in the beginning of the book.

209. Drawing of Saint Sophia Cathedral in Kiev, ordered by the Polish-Lithuanian Prince Janusz Radziwiłł upon the capture of Kiev by his troops in 1651.

210. (Left) Immovable Wall, Saint Sophia Cathedral in Kiev, photo by G. Kulzhenko. 211. (Right) Ancient images of saints in Saint Sophia Cathedral in Kiev.

212. Illustration of a Skomoroh performance on the steps of Saint Sophia Cathedral in Kiev.

213. Depiction of a hunt on the steps of Saint Sophia Cathedral in Kiev.

214. Yaroslav the Wise with family, presenting the Saint Sophia Cathedral to Vladimir; to the right hand of Yaroslav, his four sons; to the left hand, his spouse Ingegerd and four daughters.

215. (Left) Cathedral of Saint Sophia in Novgorod.
216. (Right) Internal view of the Cathedral of Saint Sophia in Novgorod.

217. The Cathedral of the Transfiguration of Our Savior in Chernigov near the Church of Saints Boris and Gleb.

218. (Left) Image of Byzantine Emperor Constantine IX Monomachos, on Greek
manuscript from his era, kept in the library of the city of Modena.
219. (Right) "Emperor Constantine again sends his envoys to Vladimir
(Yaroslavich), and he again sends them back with dishonor." Skylitzes,
Synopsis of Byzantine History, along with the next four drawings.

220. Byzantine ships confront the Rus'.

221. A battle between Byzantine and Rus' fleets.

222. Retreating sailors burning a ship; the Rus' abandon their burning ships.

223. (Left) Blinding of a war prisoner.
224. (Right) Blind gusli players, illustration by V. M. Vasnetsov.

225. (Left) Golden coin of Byzantine Emperor Constantine IX Monomachos.
226. (Right) The departure of Anna Yaroslavna from Kiev
to France, illustration by Baron Klodt.

227. (Left) Capital letter of a Rheims Bible.
228. (Center) Yaroslav's grandson, the French King Philip I.
229. (Right) Signature of Queen Anna Yaroslavna: "Anna Ryna" (queen),
donated to a Soissons monastery, kept in the National Library of Paris.

230. (Left) Yaroslav's silver.
231. (Right) Yaroslav the Wise, carved into rock by Mark Antokolsky, kept in the Museum of Emperor Alexander III in Saint Petersburg.

232. (Left) Tomb of Yaroslav the Wise, hewn from white marble, in Saint Sophia Cathedral in Kiev.
233. (Right) Yaroslav the Wise, likeness according to the *Great State Book*.

234. The Bogatyrs Dobrynya Nikitich, Ilya Muromets, and Alesha Popovitch, painting by V. M. Vasnetsov.

235. (Left) Dobrynya at the feast of Prince Vladimir, illustration by A. Prohorov.
236. (Right) Yaroslav appointed Hilarion as Metropolitan,
gathering all bishops. *Radziwiłł Chronicle*.

237. (Left) Holy Mount Athos. 238. (Right) The Kiev Monastery of the Caves,
built by Saint Anthony the Athonite.

239. (Left) Saint Anthony the Athonite, sixteenth-century
mural in the Kiev Monastery of the Caves.
240. (Right) Tenth-century icon of Saint George the Victorious, carved
in stone, housed in the Vatopedi Monastery on Mount Athos.

241. (Left) Saint Anthony the Athonite's death, sixteenth-century mural in the Kiev Monastery of the Caves. 242. (Right) Chronicler and servant with a fan. Letterheads of a Holy Gospel copied from an ancient script in the middle of the twelfth century by order of the Serbian monarch, which may have been created in the first centuries of the Christian era. The Gospels were housed in the Hilandar Monastery at Mount Athos in 1896 when they were donated by Alexander I of Serbia.

243. (Left) Saint Theoktist being blessed by Saint Anthony to return to the Russian Land, mural in the Kiev Monastery of the Caves.   244. (Right) Anthony in Kiev.

245: (Left) A seal of Hegumen Studinsky from a monastery in Constantinople, tenth or eleventh century, housed in the Archeological Museum of the City of Athens.   246: (Right) Saint Nestor the Chronicler. *Radziwiłł Chronicle.*

247: (Left) Saint Nestor the Chronicler. *Kiev Caves Paterikon.* The saints of the Kiev Monastery of the Caves lived in very ancient times; the images however are of course no older than the seventeenth century.

248: (Right) Remains of Saint Nestor at the Antonian Caves.

249: The revelation to Simon (Sigmundr) the Varangian about the construction of the Holy Dormition Cathedral at the Kiev Monastery of the Caves. *Kiev Caves Paterikon.*

250: (Left) *The Delivery at Blachernae*, mural at the Kiev Monastery of the Caves.
251: (Right) *The Arrival of the Architects*, mural at the Kiev Monastery of the Caves.

252: (Left) The Great Kiev Monastery of the Caves Church, the Holy Dormition
Cathedral, Lubok painting, issued by the Lavra printing press.
253: (Right) The miraculous indication of the place for the building of the
Holy Dormition Cathedral, from the *Kiev Caves Paterikon*.

254: (Left) The Grand Prince Svyatoslav II begins digging a ditch for the
foundation of the Holy Dormition Cathedral, mural in the Cathedral of Christ the
Savior in Moscow. 255: (Right) Miraculous icon of the Dormition of the Theotokos
in the Holy Dormition Cathedral in the Kiev Monastery of the Caves.

256: (Left) Miraculous icon of Saint Nicholas the Wet in Saint Sophia Cathedral in Kiev, refurbished by A. V. Prachov. 257: (Top right) Saint Theodosius and the Cathedral of the Exalted Far Caves, mural at the Kiev Monastery of the Caves. 258. (Bottom right) Saint Anthony and the Cathedral of the Exalted Near Caves, mural at the Kiev Monastery of the Caves.

259. (Left) Feats of the Venerable Saint John the Long-Suffering. Nestor, *Kiev Caves Paterikon*. 260. (Right) The miracle with the Venerable Saint Dionysius on Pascha in the Cave of Saint Anthony. Nestor, *Kiev Caves Paterikon*.

261. (Left) The Venerable Alypius the Iconographer. Nestor, *Kiev Caves Paterikon*.
262. (Right) The Venerable Spyridon and Nicodemus baking prosphora.
Nestor, *Kiev Caves Paterikon*.

263. The Venerable Eustratius Postnik, crucified by a Korsunian Jew.
Nestor, *Kiev Caves Paterikon*.

264. View of Kiev and the Monastery of the Caves from the left bank of the Dnieper. Svinyin, *Paintings of Russia*.

265. In the caves of the Kiev Monastery of the Caves. Svinyin, *Paintings of Russia*.

266. From the Ostromir Gospel, 1056–57.

CONCLUSION

Observing this long and vital path we have described, which our ancestors have established over the millennia, traversed since the time of their migration from the Aryan Motherland to the creation of mighty Russia, we can say with pride that they were compelled to grow in strength and in glory exclusively by their principle quality of spirit—their nobility.

Clearly, it is only this that gave them the constant, selfless virility and fearlessness before death for which they are glorified for all time. Virility and fearlessness were necessary to avoid being killed in battle with enemies both terrible and numerous, always trying to stick their hands into the Russian Land. It is vital to remember firmly that every inch[130] of the Russian Land on which we happen to live is clearly our Motherland because each inch has been steeped in the blood of not only our forefathers but also in the blood of our valiant and daring foremothers, who constantly sacrificed their lives.

That is why this Land is so dear to us; we are bonded to it by blood, in a long line of our great ancestors. That is why each of us bears the sacred duty of always safeguarding it, and we must uphold it with all of our strength, both in body and soul, and in times of need we must undauntingly lay down our lives in its defense.

That same nobility of spirit, which always bestowed on our ancestors the virility and fearlessness to achieve victory over the numerous enemies

---

[130] Translator's note: Nechvolodov here uses "pyad" (пядь), translated as "span," an ancient unit of measurement from the thumb to the tip of the forefinger, which would sound awkward in English.

of the Russian Land, has also always guided their efforts in peacetime affairs, so vital to the security and consolidation of Land acquired by blood; it guided them in the great arts of cultivating the earth and venturing out to sea, and it guided them on difficult hunts after wild fur-bearing beasts and in matters of honest trade.

And in all of this, our ancestors also gained great fame by the grace of this basic quality of their spirit, which compelled each of them to treat whatever end they served honestly and heartfully. Since time immemorial, our bread has been considered of the highest quality and has been exported to many far-off countries; precious furs, artfully acquired by our brave beast hunters, have become famous in all countries and have been valued very highly. Boatfuls of our brave sailors have sailed many seas and traversed unknown rivers along the most remote frontiers. And finally, Russian merchants have become famous for their profitable business dealings, friendliness, and great honesty.

When it came to domestic life, the chief quality of our forefathers was loyalty to their loved ones, adopted brothers, and leaders, whom they would follow on great hunts to death. This incredible loyalty of the ancient inhabitants of the Russian Land that greatly impressed other nations was also a direct result of their elevated spirit.

Their attitude toward women was also based on this quality of spirit. We know that polygamy prevailed in pagan times. However, regardless of this, the position of women in the family was still quite high and honored at that time; girls were ordinarily free to choose the husband they wanted, which is why ancient Russian women, upon marrying, were passionately loyal to their husbands and stood firmly as their supporters in every undertaking. They would often fight alongside them and even sacrifice their lives, not wishing to endure widowhood.

The respect the gentry showed to the other classes, in which all labor was considered honorable, was again a consequence of an elevated feeling of morality.

Regardless of the great harshness of their temperament that prevailed in ancient times, however, we have seen that our ancestors never got to the level of such atrocities with their slaves as did the Greeks and Romans; on the contrary, they were ordinarily quite gentle with them and considered them a part of their household. All this demonstrates the great kindness of heart possessed by the ancient Russian people.

Finally, the Russian pride, never forgiving an insult inflicted on any one of their number, and for which our ancestors would always fervently seek vengeance, even rising to the occasion where it was necessary with the entire nation, should also be considered as one of their greatest characteristics; obviously, we as well, as their descendants, should follow their example in those circumstances and allow nobody to humiliate the Russian name or the Russian people.

As we know, the never-ending mutual quarreling of the Slavs has been a constant source of woe, and the enemies of the Slavs have *always* been *all* the nations that live around them. For a long time, this ardor for discord did not allow our ancestors to unite themselves into one strong state; on the contrary, this strife brought us under the shameful yoke of the Avars, and then the Khazars, and in the south of Europe, regardless of their courage, a few other Slavic tribes have been conquered and even outright exterminated.

But when the Ilmen Slavs realized that it was impossible to live in mutual discord any longer, they made the wise decision to establish a reciprocal unification of absolute power and also convinced the Rus' princes that the power and strength of our state would immediately begin to grow at a marvelous rate. Yet in the days of Askold, in the famous sermon of Patriarch Photios within the walls of the Hagia Sophia, he called us, as a result of our humiliating subjugation to Khazaria, "a nation of no account, a nation ranked among slaves," and less than two hundred years later all the powerful statesmen of Europe would come to consider it a great honor to take the hand of one of the great Rus' prince's daughters, or to take refuge in his court during tumultuous times. This change in Russia's standing was quite large, due only to the great spiritual fortitude of our honored ancestors.

Our ancestors, in accordance with their noble characteristics, decided rightly to establish an overarching power over themselves and to surrender themselves into the hands of the appointed princes wholeheartedly, with selfless devotion. This almost immediately led to their complete freedom from the Khazar yoke and to the rapid expansion of the state, all the more so in that our first princes had a few outstanding generals in their midst; having a brave and selflessly devoted army under their command, they were also able to accomplish all of their marvelous victories with the goal of the glory of the Russian Land.

However, regardless of all the daring and manliness displayed by our rulers during the quick, bold, and victorious campaigns of Askold, Oleg, and Svyatoslav, even worthier of the deepest respect was their conduct in times of failure, which our princes would often encounter: we have seen that Prince Igor was generally misfortunate in military matters, and Yaroslav was hit on the head more than once. Finally, the great Svyatoslav himself finished his life of great deeds with failure at Dorostopol and sadly met his end on the banks of the Dnieper.

Right here, at the time of these painful trials, the conduct of our ancestors deserves the utmost respect and consideration.

A nation that is not stable, a nation with a small soul, a nation foolish and quarrelsome, withdrawn from its own land, a nation that does not possess or is unaware of its own past—in short, an ignoble nation always turns its back on its leaders when misfortune befalls it. Such a nation will always start to blame them for their failures in war, in the field, or in state life. In such a nation there is displeasure and the fomenting of military uprisings as well as shameful rioting; by this means does it finally weaken itself and then become easy prey for external enemies.

But this was not the fate of our wise, grounded, and noble ancestors. All of them understood that military success is fleeting, that disaster can be the face of anyone, and that the only remedy for restoring this success and happiness and for correcting mistakes lies in loyalty and devotion to one's leaders, as well as in a willingness to sacrifice everything to the very end and to gather new forces until the enemy is defeated.

And what do we see here? Regardless of Igor's series of failures, Svyatoslav's woeful demise, Boleslaw's capture of Kiev, constant Pecheneg raids—Kievan Rus', regardless of all of this, thanks to the extraordinary resolve of its sons and the devotion of its princes in difficult times, grew and grew and soon became the largest and most powerful kingdom in all of Europe. All this came solely as a result of the great spirituality of our ancestors.

Their nobility, transformed into a true spiritual magnanimity, was especially shown in the relationship between Yaroslav and the valiant Novgorodian men. Twice he had fallen into misfortune with exceptionally difficult circumstances, and both times they supported him, sacrificing their lives for him and their state. The first time, he wrongfully killed the majority of his best men in vengeance, but as soon as he fell into misfortune the next morning he heard immediately from the remainder the following unforgettable response: "We can still fight for you, oh Prince, even though our brethren are slain." (*RPC*, 131)

The second time, unexpectedly crushed by Boleslaw the Brave to such an extent that he could barely escape the battlefield, Yaroslav, coming to

Novgorod, went to the Varangians to prepare to fight anew. Still, the honorable Novgorodians, strong in their hearts, did not disappoint him. These daring men, the better part of them consisting of carpenters and craftsmen, had fixed the prince's boats and prepared them to set sail to the sea, announcing, "We still want to fight Boleslaw and Svyatopolk." They immediately began to gather together money and men for the new war and voluntarily imposed a heavy tax on themselves, about four coonskins from each man, ten grivnas per elder, and eighteen grivnas per boyar.

All of our great-souled ancestors swore fealty to the Christian faith. We saw what manner of marvelous faithful men emerged in Kievan Rus' after her baptism. We have also seen how heartfelt the faith of the peasant laity felt toward the chief Christian virtue of humility.

Of course, such a profound and full adoption of Christian doctrine could only be taken by those who possess spiritually inclined souls because our holy Orthodox faith is not merely from reason nor from wisdom but is to be comprehended solely by a devout heart and soul, which we understand is instilled by the great acts of our Savior and his divine advent.

These were our forefathers who created Kievan Rus'.

Having created it, they left to us, their descendants, three great men, three great testaments, to defend and cherish their holy inheritance, the Russian Land.

Each of these testaments must always be carried in our hearts.

As great Svyatoslav instructed at the Battle of Dorostopol:

We inherited brave deeds from our fathers and grandfathers! Let's stand strong. Saving ourselves by flight is not our custom. We either live and be victorious or die with glory. The dead do not know shame, but if we flee the battle, then how would we look our people in the eyes?

Yaroslav the Wise, gathering his children before him prior to his death, said:

If ye abide in amity with one another, God will dwell among you, and will subject your enemies to you, and ye will live at peace. But if ye dwell in envy and dissension, quarreling with one another, then ye will perish yourselves and bring to ruin the land of your ancestors, which they won at the price of great effort. (*RPC*, 142–3)

Saint Theodosius left these words:

> There is no other faith greater than our pure and holy Orthodox faith.

> If you should ever need to die for this Holy Faith, then go to death with boldness. Thus have the saints perished and reside now with Christ.

> It is not fitting to revere any other faith. He who reveres another faith is equal to one who blasphemes. If one should revere this and another faith, he is a double-believer, near to a heretic.

> Beware the idolators of blood and all their talk, for our land is filled with them.

> Beware them and always hold true to your faith.

> Do not join with them, but flee them, and strive for good acts within your faith.

> Give alms not only to those of the faith but also to those of other faiths. If you see someone naked or hungry, or fallen into misfortune, whether he is a Jew, a Turk, or a Latin, be merciful to them, and deliver them from suffering, as you are able—you shall not be deprived of your reward in God.

Bibliography

Note that the names of the following sources, provided by Nechvolodov in the following languages, have been translated into English, though no English edition may exist for the work. English editions found by the editors for certain quotations are specified in the English section.

Russian

Alexandria. Moscow: State Historical Museum archive, 17th-century manuscript.
Antiquities of Cimmerian Bosporus.
Athos Paterikon, The.
Avenarius, Vasily Petrovich. *The Book of the Byliny.*
Bestuzhev-Ryumin, Konstantin. *Russian History.*
Bobrinsky, Aleksei Aleksandrovich. *Tauric Chersonesos* (Crimean Peninsula).
Buslaev, F. *The Era of the Russian Bogatyr.*
Complete Collection of Russian Chronicles, The.
Demetrius of Rostov. *Lives of the Saints.*
"Expository Manuscript of Paley." Moscow Patriarchate library archive, Novgorodian letter of 1477.
Farmakovsky, Boris Vladimirovich. *Excavations of Olbia 1902–1903.*
Farmakovsky, Boris Vladimirovich. *Golden Upholstery of the Greatest of the Ilinetsky and Chertomlyk Barrow.*
Fyodorov, Nikolai Fyodorovich. *Philosophy of the Common Task.*
Golitsyn, Prince N. S. *Russian Military History.*
Grabar, Igor Emmanuilovich. *History of Russian Art.*
Great State Book (also called the *Royal Titular Book* and the *Great Tsar's Book*). 1672.
Guide to Holy Mount Athos, A.
Ieger, A. *A Universal History.*
Illustrated Chronicle of Ivan the Terrible.
Ilovaysky, Dmitry. *History of Russia.*

Index in Eight Volumes of the Complete Collection of Russian Chronicles, An. § I and II.

Karamzin, Nikolay. *History of the Russian State.*

Nestor the Chronicler. *Kiev Caves Paterikon: Lives of the Saints of the Kiev Caves Monastery.*

Klyuchevsky, Vasily Osipovich. *Aristocratic Thought in Ancient Russia.*

Klyuchevsky, Vasily Osipovich. *A History of Russia.*

Kondakov, Nikodim Pavlovich. *Russian Treasures.*

Kostomarov, Nikolai Ivanovich. *Russian History in the Biographies of its Main Figures.*

Kutepov, Nikolai Ivanovich. *Great Prince's, Tsar's and Emperor's Hunting in Russia.*

Lavrov, Pyotr Lavrovich. *Lives of the Chersonese Saints in Greco-Slavic Writings.*

Likhachyov, Nikolay Petrovich. *Exterior Life of the Holy Russian Princes Boris and Gleb.* Society of Lovers of Ancient Literature, end of 15th-century manuscript edition.

Likhachyov, Nikolay Petrovich. *Extracts from Lectures on Diplomacy.*

Likhachyov, Nikolay Petrovich. *Materials for a History of Russian Icon Painting.*

Likhachyov, Nikolay Petrovich. *Paleographic Significance of Paper Watermarks.*

Lopukhin, Alexander Pavlovich. *Bible History in the Light of the Latest Research and Discoveries.*

Monuments of the Christian Chersonese.

Obolensky, Prince M. P. *On the Primary Chronicle.*

Philaret, Rev. *Lives of the Saints of the Venerable Orthodox Church.*

Pirogov, V. *Russian Military Strength.*

Platonov, Sergei Fedorovich. *Lectures on Russian History.*

Pobedonostsev, Konstantin Petrovich. *History of the Orthodox Church.*

Pogodin, Mikhail Petrovich. *Extracts from the History of Slavic Migrations.*

Pokrovsky, N. V. *Essays on Monuments of Christian Iconography and Art.*

Polevoy, Pyotr Nikolayevich. *History of Russian Literature.*

Presnyakov, A. E. *Rulership of the Knyaz in Ancient Rus.*

Presnyakov, A. E. *Moscow Historical Encyclopedia of the Sixteenth Century.* 1900.

Prevo, Andrei. *Russian History in Paintings, or the Pictorial Karamzin.*

Prokhorov, Vasily Alexandrovich. *Materials on the History of Russian Clothes and the Life of the People.*

Pypin, Alexander Nikolayevich. *Works of Empress Catherine II.*

Radziwiłł Chronicle. Library of the Russian Academy of Sciences archive, 15th-century manuscript.

Radziwiłł Chronicle. Society of Lovers of Ancient Literature edition, with academic articles by Nikodim Pavlovich Kondakov and Aleksey Aleksandrovich Shakhmatov.

Rezov, M. *Essays on Events in Russian History.* 1839 edition.

Rittikh, A. F., and A. L. Bubnov. *Russia and Her Seas.*

Rudanovsky, V. *Two Notes on Questions of Russian Linguistics.*

Semenov-Tyan-Shansky, Petr Petrovich. *Geographical and Statistical Dictionary of the Russian Empire.*

Sergeevich, V. I. *Antiquities of Russian Law.*

Shakhmatov, Aleksey Aleksandrovich. *The Legend of the Called-upon Varangians.*

Shakhmatov, Aleksey Aleksandrovich. *Research on the Eldest Russian Chronicle Compilations.* Saint Petersburg: Archaeographic Commission, 1908.

Shakhmatov, Aleksey Aleksandrovich. *On the Rostovsky Chronicle.*

Shcherbatov, Mikhail M. *Russian History from Ancient Times.* 1794 Edition.

Shletzer, A. L. *Nestor: The Russian Chronicle of the Ancient Slavic Language.*

Skala, R. F. *Hellenism from the time of Alexander the Great.*

Solovyov, Sergey. *History of Russia from Ancient Times.*

Southern Radiance. (An album of art).

Stasov, Vladimir Vasilievich. *Miniatures of Some Byzantine, Bulgarian, Russian, Chagatai and Persian Manuscripts.*

Strekalov, S. *Russian Historical Dress.*

Sukhomlinov, M. N. *Composition and Character of the Chronicles.*

Svinyin, Pavel Petrovich. *Paintings of Russia.* 1839 edition.

Sylvester Miscellany. "The Tale of the Holy Martyrs Boris and Gleb." 14th Century.

Tatishchev, Vasily. *History of Russia from the Most Early Times.* 1774 Edition.

Tolstoy, Ivan Ivanovich, and Nikodim Pavlovich Kondakov. *Russian Antiquities in the Monuments of Art.*

Tolstoy, Mikhail Vladimirovich. *Shrines and Antiquities of Pskov and Novgorod.*

Tolstoy, Mikhail Vladimirovich. *Stories from the History of the Russian Church.*

Tornay, Baron N. *Academic Atlas of Russian History.*

Veisser, L. *Cartographic Atlas of World History.*

Veselovsky, Nikolai Ivanovich. *The First Antiquities* (A History of Young Russia).

Vlislotsky, Heinrich. *The Danubian Peoples.*

Yarygina, Y. *The Chernigov Lands of Yore.*

Zabelin, Ivan Yegorovich. *The History of Russian Life from Ancient Times.*

Old Church Slavonic

Miroslav's Gospel. Twelfth century. Edition of the Serbian crown prince Alexander.

Polish

Compilation of Original Polish Illustrations. Collection of the Imperial Academy of Arts.

Lelewel, Joachim. *The History of Poland.*

Paprocki, Bartosz. *The Nest of Virtue* (Polish armorial). 1578.

Greek

Skylitzes, John. *A Synopsis of Byzantine History, 811–1057.* Mid-fourteenth century manuscript. Collection of the National Spanish Museum in Madrid.

Latin

Guanini, A. *An Exposition on the European Sarmatians*. 1581 edition.

French

Daremberg, Charles Victor, and Edmond Saglio, eds. Dictionary of Greek and
    Roman Antiquities. Hachette, Paris: 1873–1919.
Froner, N. *Trajan's Column*.
Golitsyn, A. *The Attestation of the Contemporaries of Saint Vladimir*.
Hamdi Bey, Osman, and Theodor Reinach. *Royal Tomb in Sidon*. 1892.
Lobanov-Rostovsky, Andrei. *A Compilation of Historical Documents concerning Queen
    Anne, Wife of Henry I, and other Daughters of Yaroslav the Wise*.
Luzhie, L. *The Roman Slavic Gospel*.
Schlumberger, Léon Gustave. *A Byzantine Emperor at the end of the Tenth Century*
    (Biography of Nikephoros II). Paris: 1890.
Schlumberger, Léon Gustave. *Byzantine Epic Poetry at the end of the Tenth Century*.
    Three volumes. Hachette, Paris: 1896–1905.
de Vogüé, Eugène-Melchior. *Anna of the Rus, Queen of France and Duchess of Valois in
    the Eleventh Century*.

German

Baumeister, Karl August. *Monuments of Classical Antiquity*. 1885–8.
Bernoulli, Johann Jakob. *Greek Iconography*. München: 1901.
Furtwängler, Adolf, and Karl Reichhold. *Greek Vase Painting*.
Kruse, Friedrich. "On the Relation of the Rus' Who Came to Spain in 844 and
    Plundered Seville, to Russia." *Journal Ministerstva Narednego Prosvescheniya*
    (Journal of the Ministry of Public Education) 21 (1839): 159–179.
Kunik, Ernst. *Of the Russian Excursion to the Coast of the Caspian Sea in 944*.
Münster, Sebastian. *Cosmographia*. 1550 and 1572 editions.
Preller, Ludwig. *Greek Mythology*. Weidmann, Berlin: 1854–5.
Schlosser, Friedrich Christoph. *World History*.

English

Herodotus. *The Histories*. Translated by Robin Waterfield. New York: Oxford
    University Press, 1998.
Ibn Fadlan, Ahmad. *Mission to the Volga*. Translated by James E. Montgomery. New
    York: NYU Press, 2017.
Leo the Deacon. *The History of Leo the Deacon: Byzantine Military Expansion in the Tenth
    Century*. Translated by Alice-Mary Talbot and Denis F. Sullivan. Washington,

D.C.: Dumbarton Oaks, 2005.

Photius. *The Homilies of Photius Patriarch of Constantinople*. Translated by Cyril Mango. Cambridge: Harvard University Press, 1958.

Priscus. *The Fragmentary History of Priscus: Attila, the Huns and the Roman Empire, AD 430–476*. Translated by John Given. Merchantville, New Jersey: Evolution, Arx Publishing, 2014.

Psellus, Michael. *The Chronographia of Michael Psellus: Byzantine History, 970s–1070s*. Translated by E. R. A. Sewter. New Haven, Connecticut: Yale University Press, 1953.

Russian Primary Chronicle, The: Laurentian Text. Translated and edited by Samuel Hazzard Cross and Olgerd P. Sherbowitz-Wetzor. Cambridge, Massachusetts: The Mediaeval Academy of America: 1953.

Printed in the USA
CPSIA information can be obtained
at www.ICGtesting.com
LVHW050853021223
765467LV00047B/755